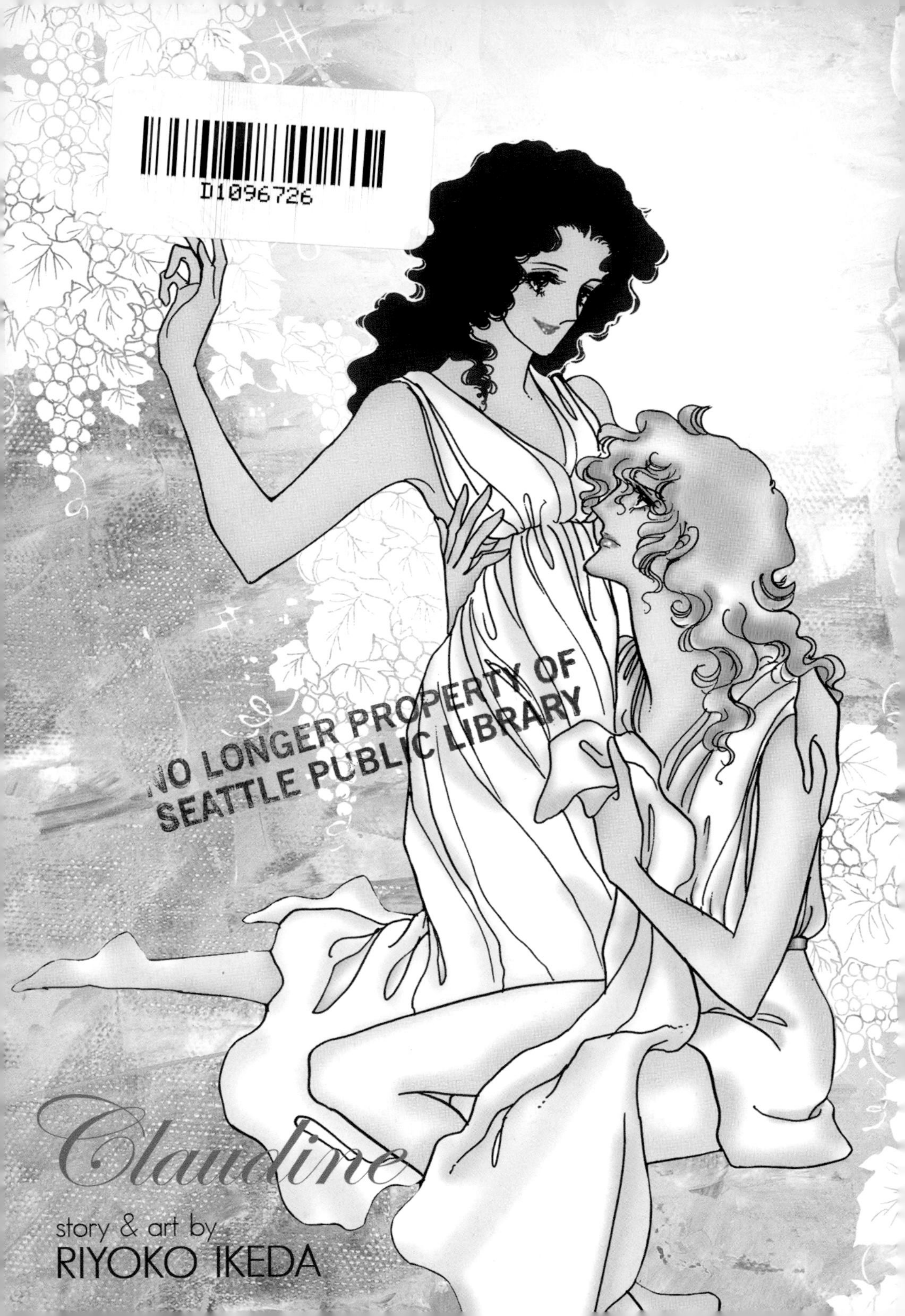

Claudine

story & art by
RIYOKO IKEDA

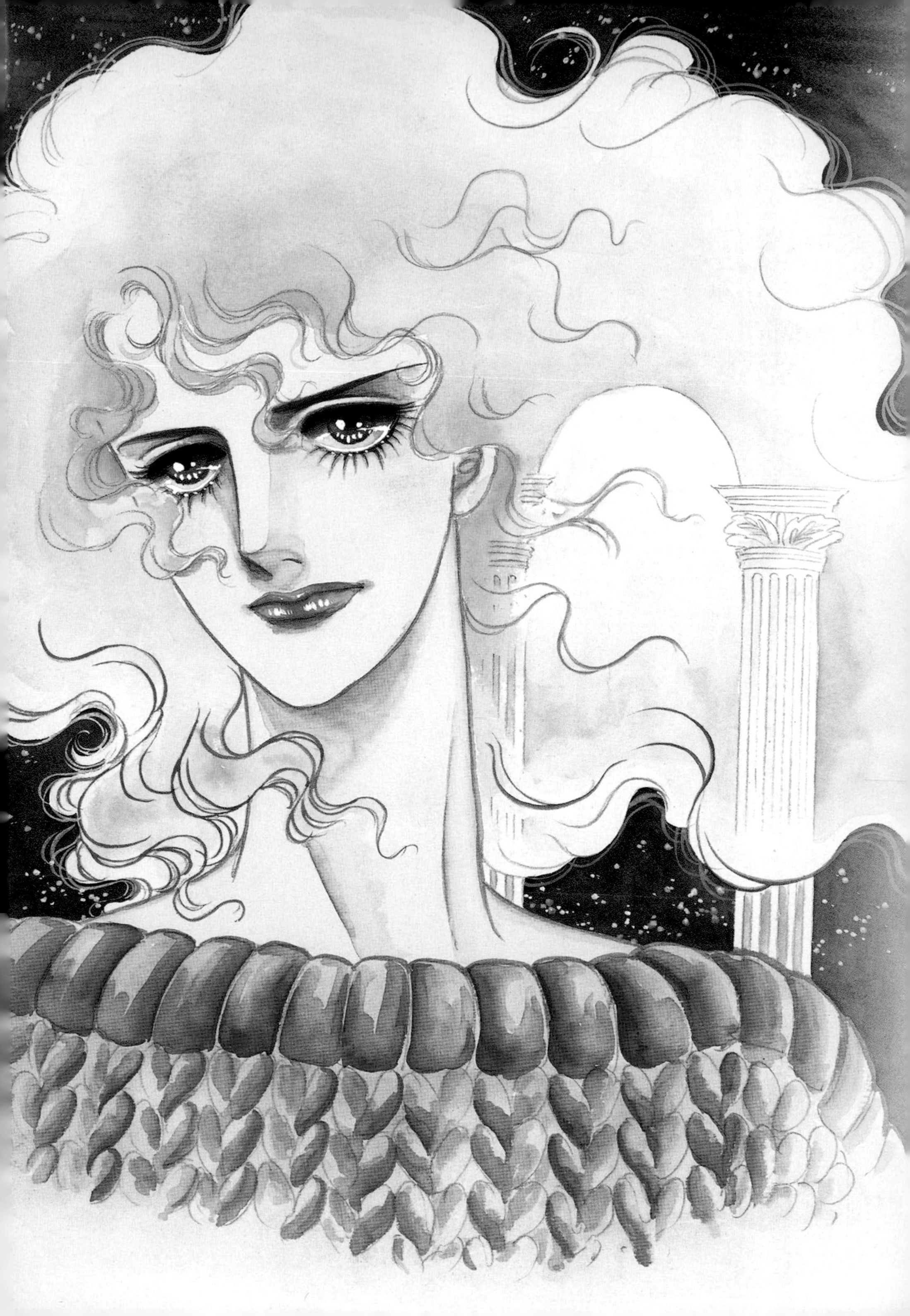

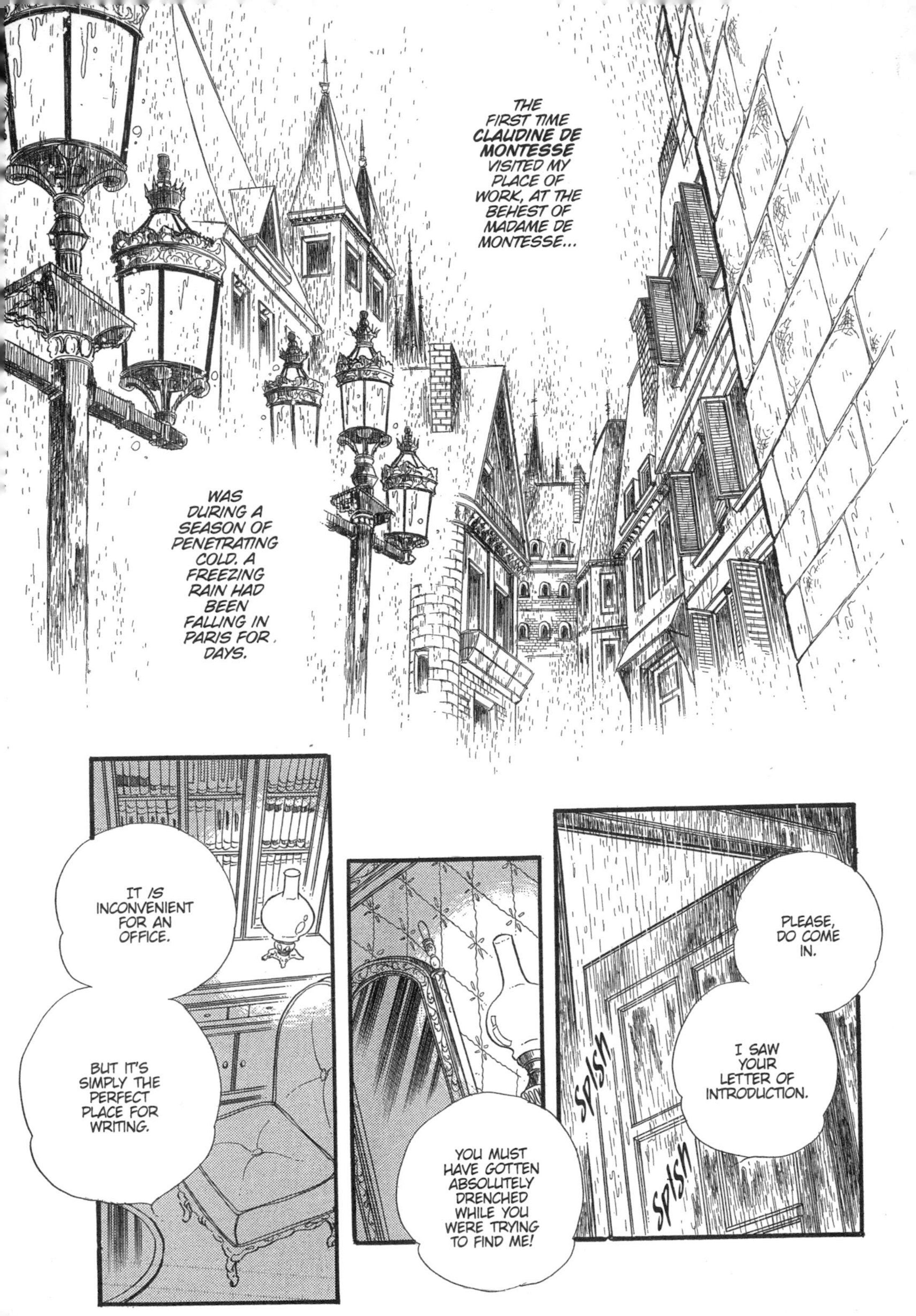
THE FIRST TIME CLAUDINE DE MONTESSE VISITED MY PLACE OF WORK, AT THE BEHEST OF MADAME DE MONTESSE...
WAS DURING A SEASON OF PENETRATING COLD. A FREEZING RAIN HAD BEEN FALLING IN PARIS FOR DAYS.
PLEASE, DO COME IN.
I SAW YOUR LETTER OF INTRODUCTION.
SPLSH
SPLSH
YOU MUST HAVE GOTTEN ABSOLUTELY DRENCHED WHILE YOU WERE TRYING TO FIND ME!
IT IS INCONVENIENT FOR AN OFFICE.
BUT IT'S SIMPLY THE PERFECT PLACE FOR WRITING.

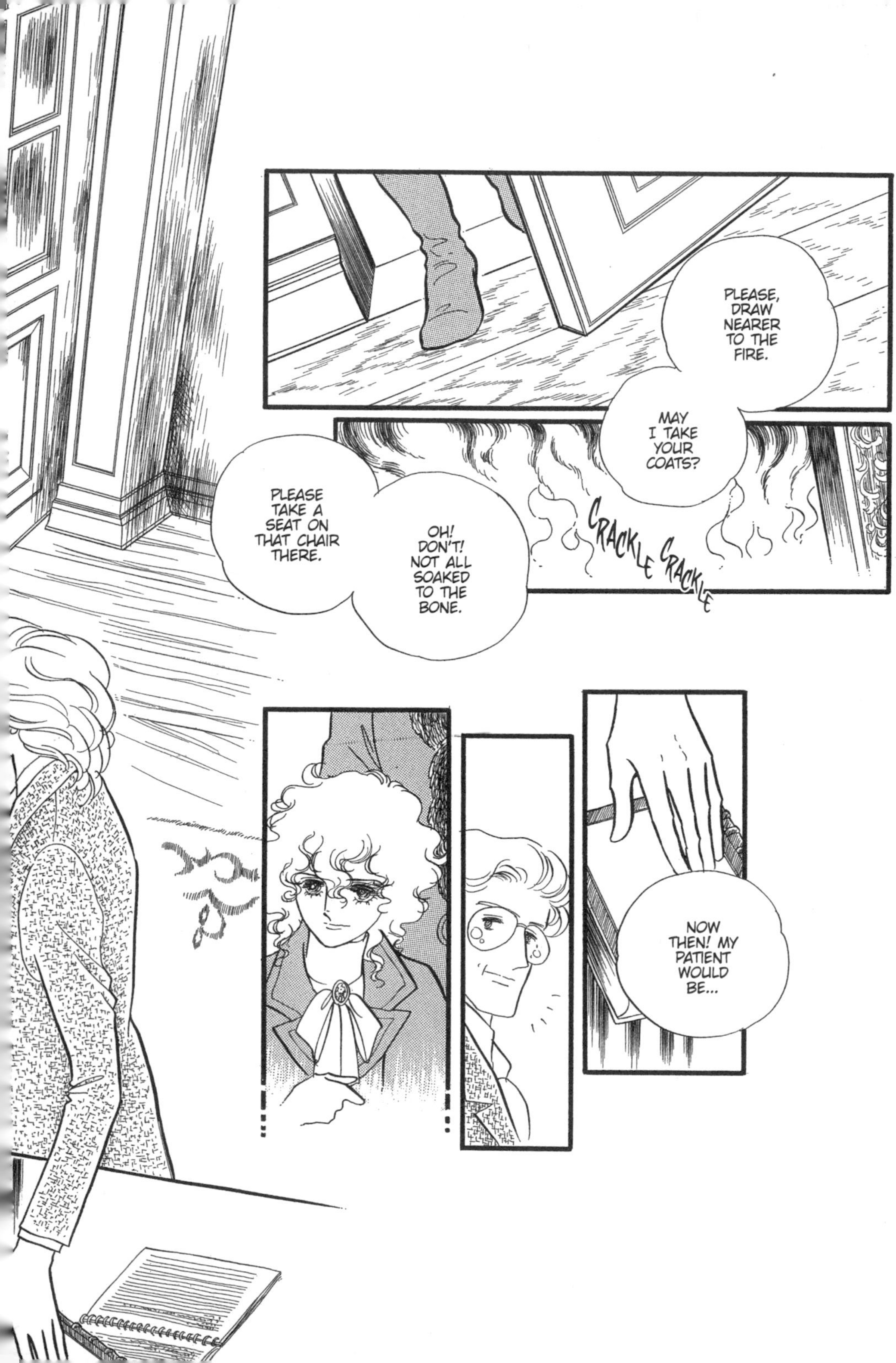
PLEASE, DRAW NEARER TO THE FIRE.
MAY I TAKE YOUR COATS?
CRACKLE CRACKLE
OH! DON'T! NOT ALL SOAKED TO THE BONE.
PLEASE TAKE A SEAT ON THAT CHAIR THERE.
NOW THEN! MY PATIENT WOULD BE...

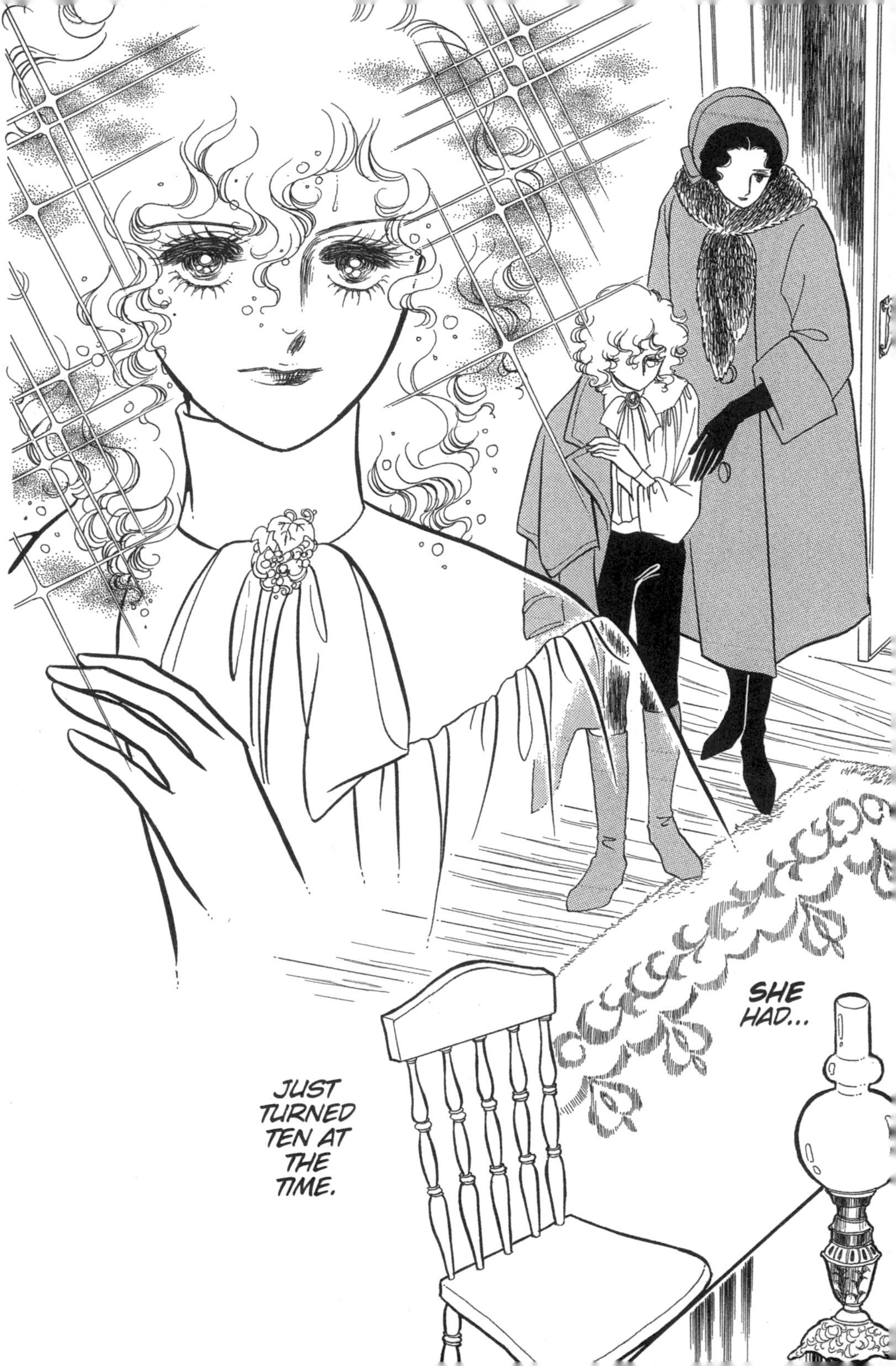
SHE HAD...
JUST TURNED TEN AT THE TIME.

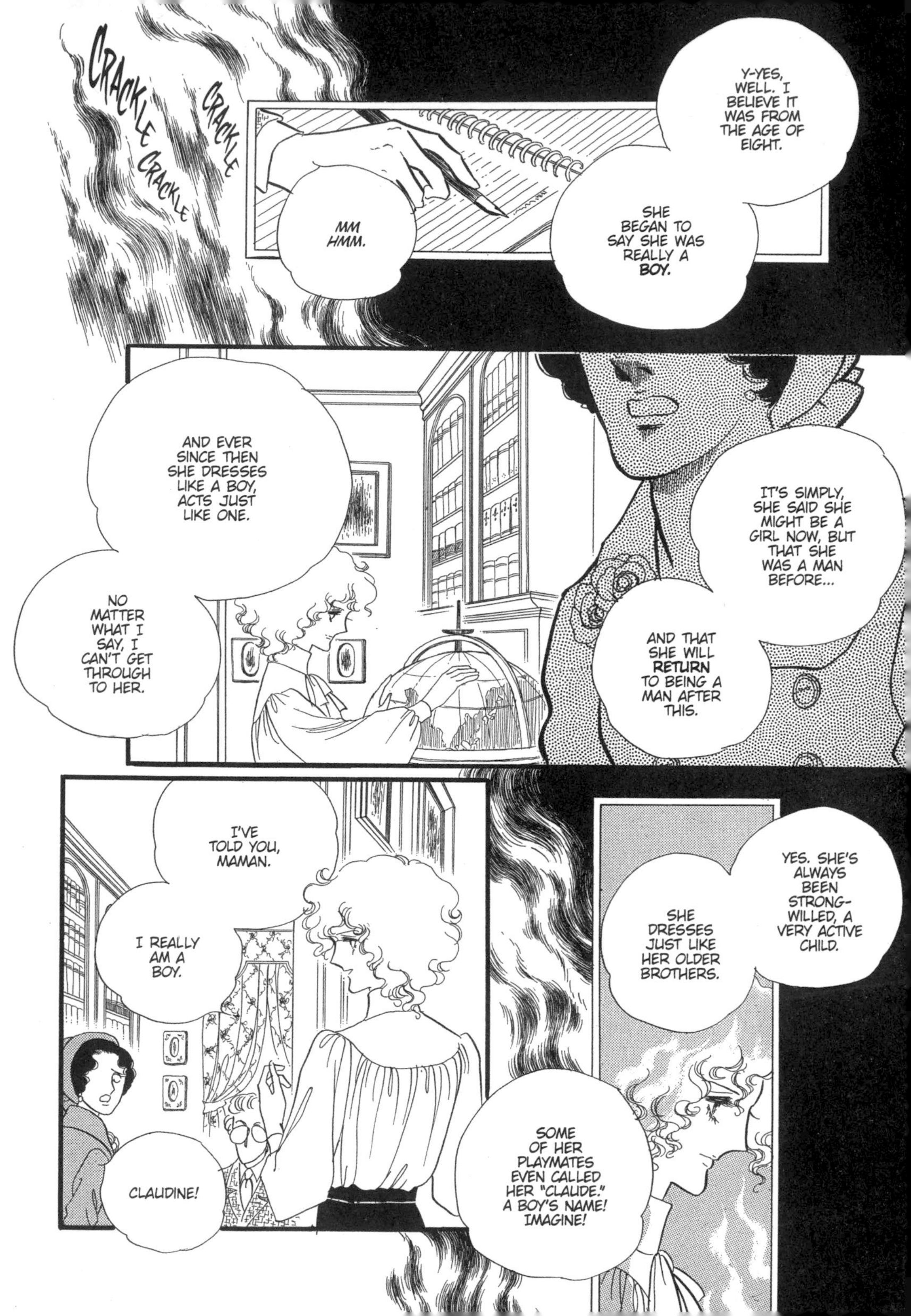
Y-YES, WELL. I BELIEVE IT WAS FROM THE AGE OF EIGHT.
SHE BEGAN TO SAY SHE WAS REALLY A **BOY.**
MM HMM.
CRACKLE
CRACKLE CRACKLE CRACKLE
IT'S SIMPLY, SHE SAID SHE MIGHT BE A GIRL NOW, BUT THAT SHE WAS A MAN BEFORE...
AND THAT SHE WILL **RETURN** TO BEING A MAN AFTER THIS.
AND EVER SINCE THEN SHE DRESSES LIKE A BOY, ACTS JUST LIKE ONE.
NO MATTER WHAT I SAY, I CAN'T GET THROUGH TO HER.
YES. SHE'S ALWAYS BEEN STRONG-WILLED, A VERY ACTIVE CHILD.
SHE DRESSES JUST LIKE HER OLDER BROTHERS.
SOME OF HER PLAYMATES EVEN CALLED HER "CLAUDE." A BOY'S NAME! IMAGINE!
I'VE TOLD YOU, MAMAN.
I REALLY AM A BOY.
CLAUDINE!

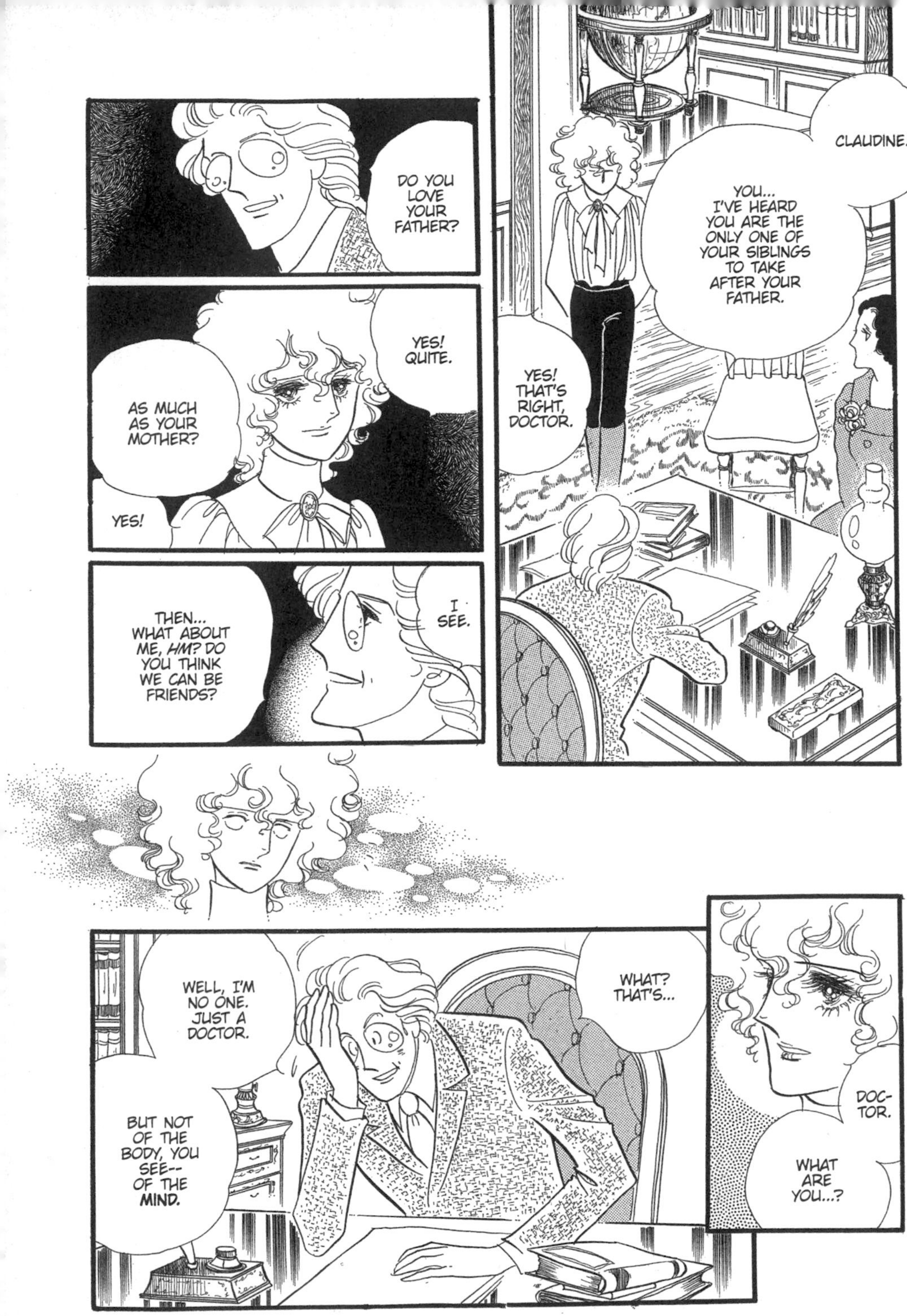
CLAUDINE.
YOU... I'VE HEARD YOU ARE THE ONLY ONE OF YOUR SIBLINGS TO TAKE AFTER YOUR FATHER.
YES! THAT'S RIGHT, DOCTOR.
DO YOU LOVE YOUR FATHER?
YES! QUITE.
AS MUCH AS YOUR MOTHER?
YES!
I SEE.
THEN... WHAT ABOUT ME, *HM*? DO YOU THINK WE CAN BE FRIENDS?
DOC-TOR.
WHAT ARE YOU...?
WHAT? THAT'S...
WELL, I'M NO ONE. JUST A DOCTOR.
BUT NOT OF THE BODY, YOU SEE-- OF THE **MIND.**

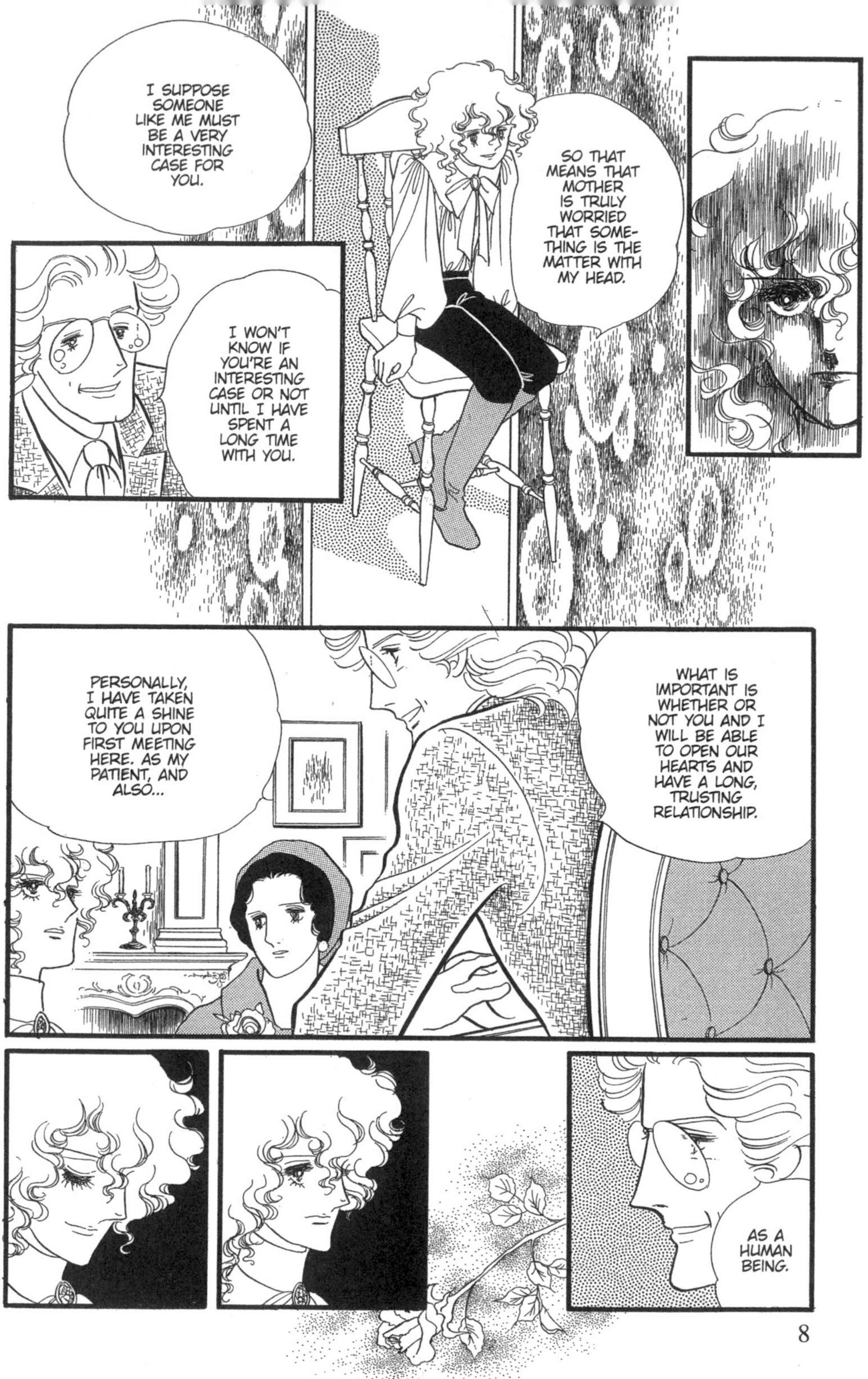
SO THAT MEANS THAT MOTHER IS TRULY WORRIED THAT SOME-THING IS THE MATTER WITH MY HEAD.
I SUPPOSE SOMEONE LIKE ME MUST BE A VERY INTERESTING CASE FOR YOU.
I WON'T KNOW IF YOU'RE AN INTERESTING CASE OR NOT UNTIL I HAVE SPENT A LONG TIME WITH YOU.
WHAT IS IMPORTANT IS WHETHER OR NOT YOU AND I WILL BE ABLE TO OPEN OUR HEARTS AND HAVE A LONG, TRUSTING RELATIONSHIP.
PERSONALLY, I HAVE TAKEN QUITE A SHINE TO YOU UPON FIRST MEETING HERE. AS MY PATIENT, AND ALSO...
AS A HUMAN BEING.

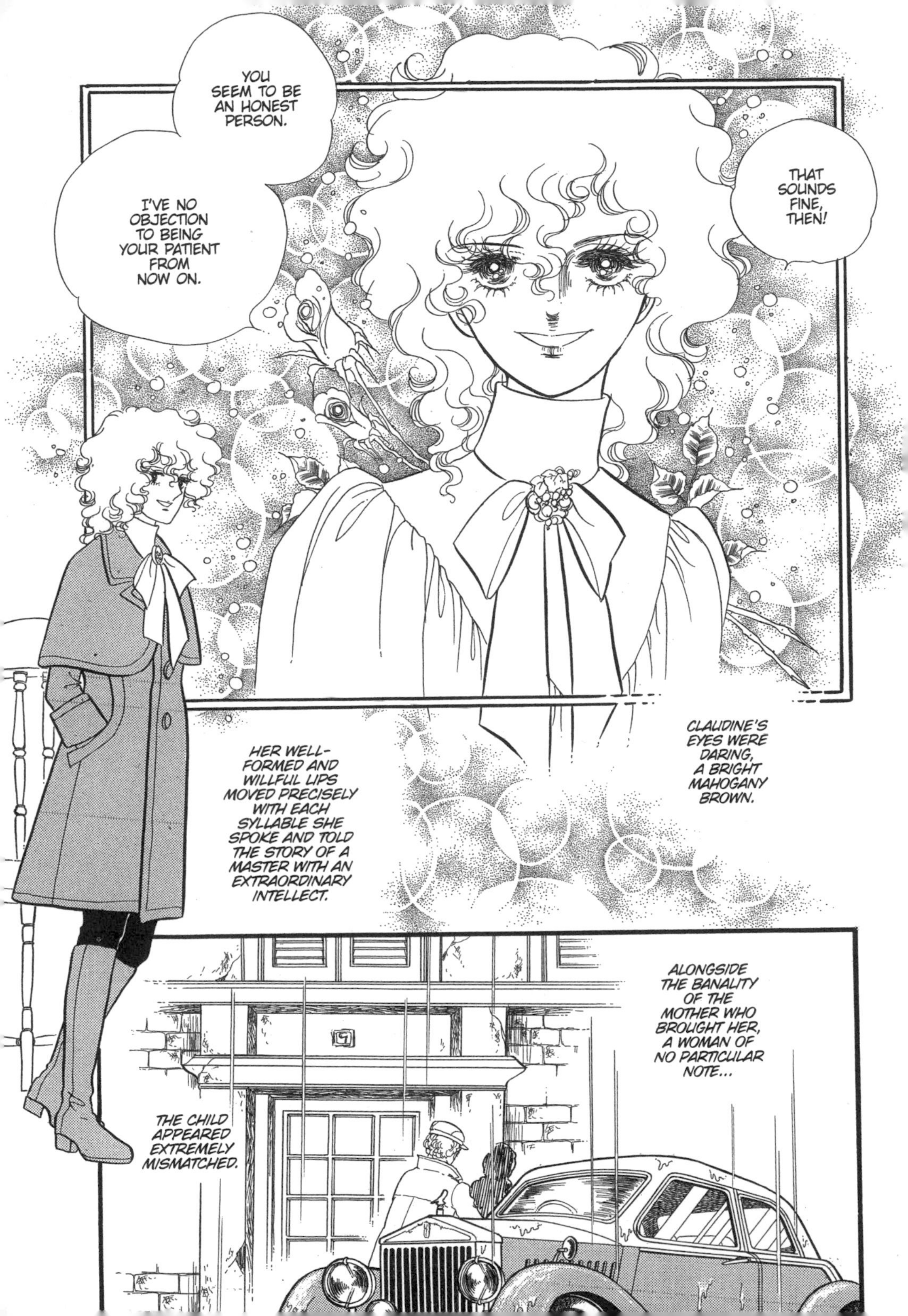
YOU SEEM TO BE AN HONEST PERSON.
I'VE NO OBJECTION TO BEING YOUR PATIENT FROM NOW ON.
THAT SOUNDS FINE, THEN!
CLAUDINE'S EYES WERE DARING, A BRIGHT MAHOGANY BROWN.
HER WELL-FORMED AND WILLFUL LIPS MOVED PRECISELY WITH EACH SYLLABLE SHE SPOKE AND TOLD THE STORY OF A MASTER WITH AN EXTRAORDINARY INTELLECT.
ALONGSIDE THE BANALITY OF THE MOTHER WHO BROUGHT HER, A WOMAN OF NO PARTICULAR NOTE...
THE CHILD APPEARED EXTREMELY MISMATCHED.

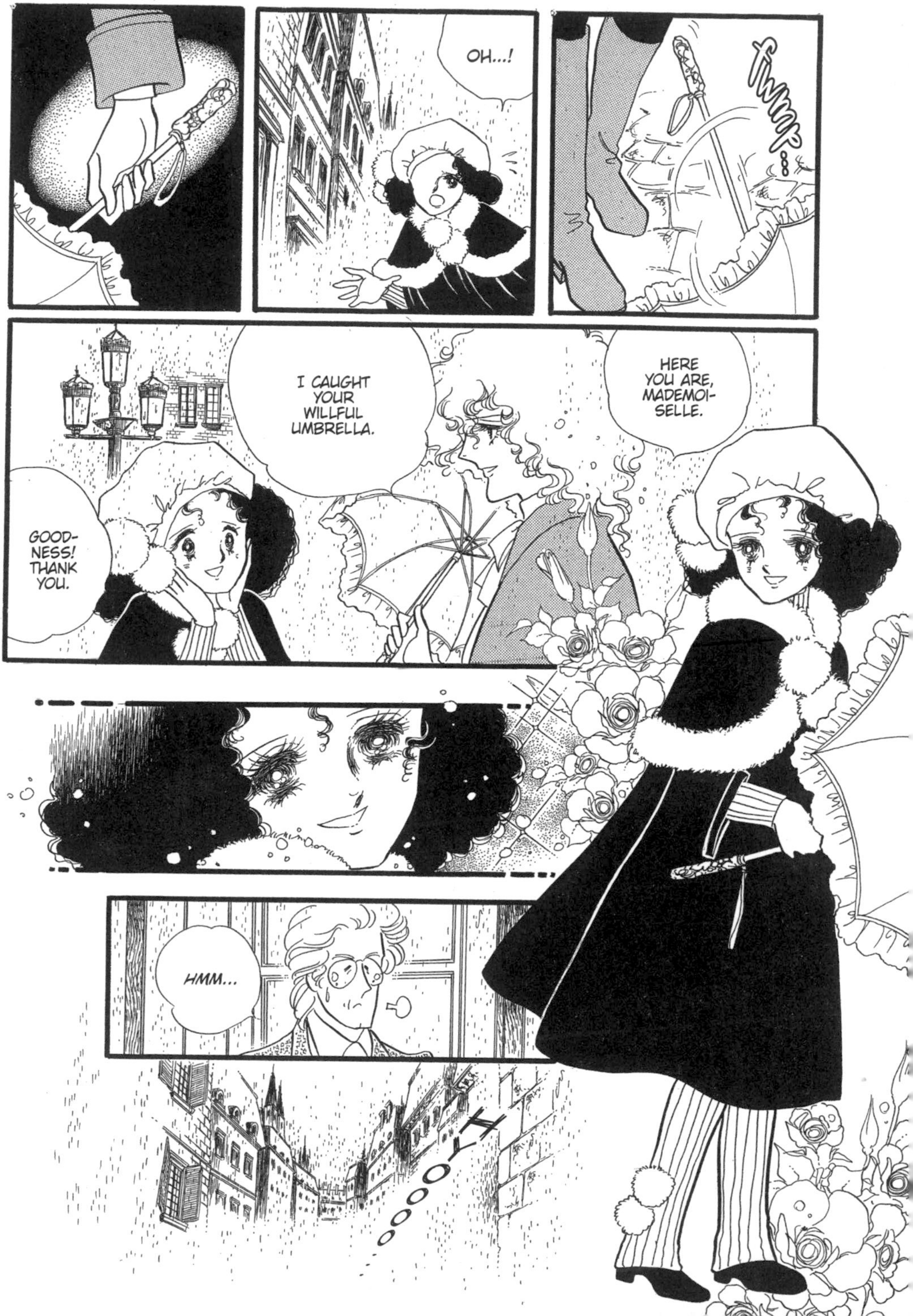
fwmp...
OH...!
HERE YOU ARE, MADEMOISELLE.
I CAUGHT YOUR WILLFUL UMBRELLA.
GOODNESS! THANK YOU.
HMM...
HYOOOOO...

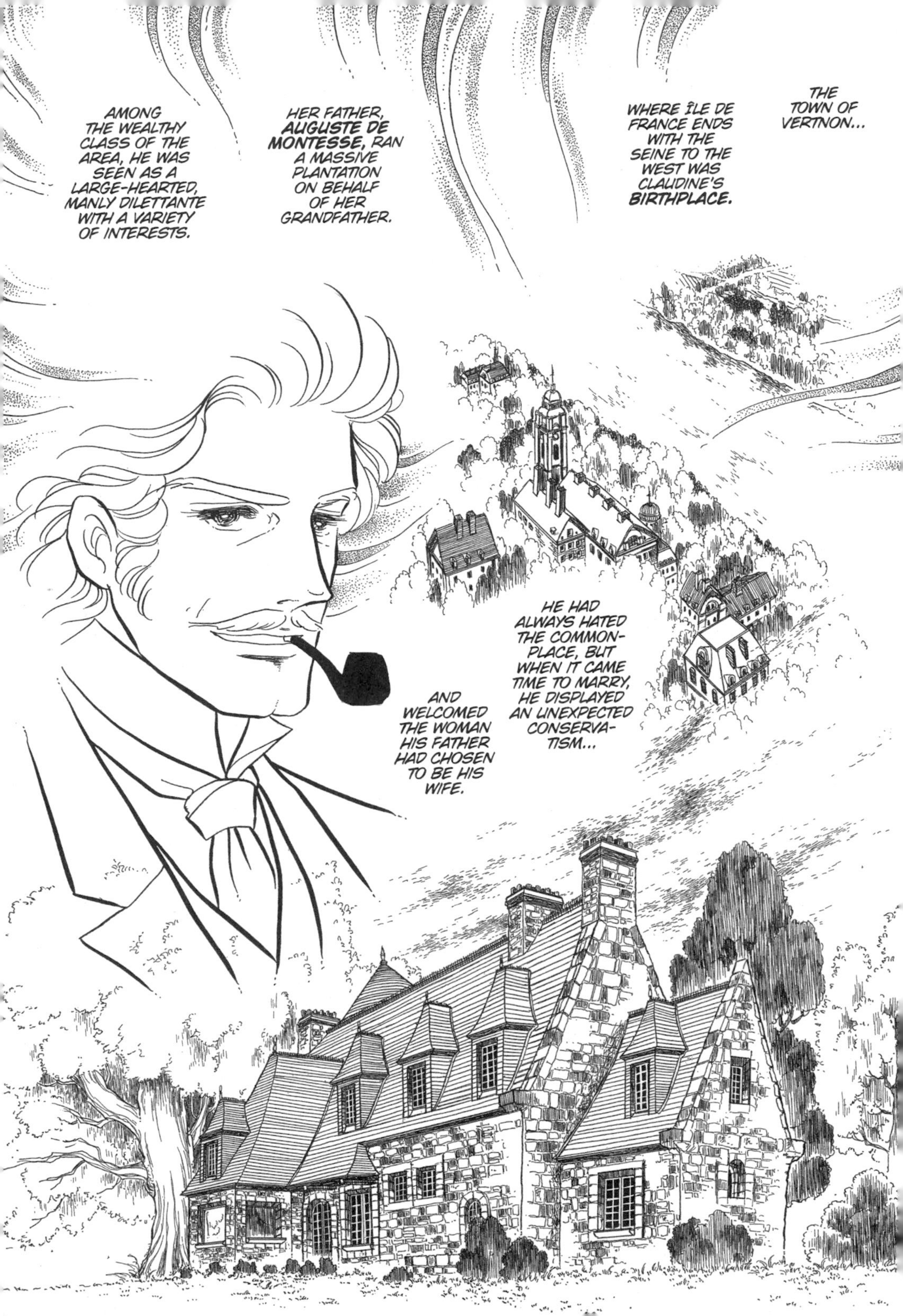
THE TOWN OF VERTNON...
WHERE ÎLE DE FRANCE ENDS WITH THE SEINE TO THE WEST WAS CLAUDINE'S **BIRTHPLACE.**
HER FATHER, **AUGUSTE DE MONTESSE,** RAN A MASSIVE PLANTATION ON BEHALF OF HER GRANDFATHER.
AMONG THE WEALTHY CLASS OF THE AREA, HE WAS SEEN AS A LARGE-HEARTED, MANLY DILETTANTE WITH A VARIETY OF INTERESTS.
HE HAD ALWAYS HATED THE COMMON-PLACE, BUT WHEN IT CAME TIME TO MARRY, HE DISPLAYED AN UNEXPECTED CONSERVA-TISM...
AND WELCOMED THE WOMAN HIS FATHER HAD CHOSEN TO BE HIS WIFE.

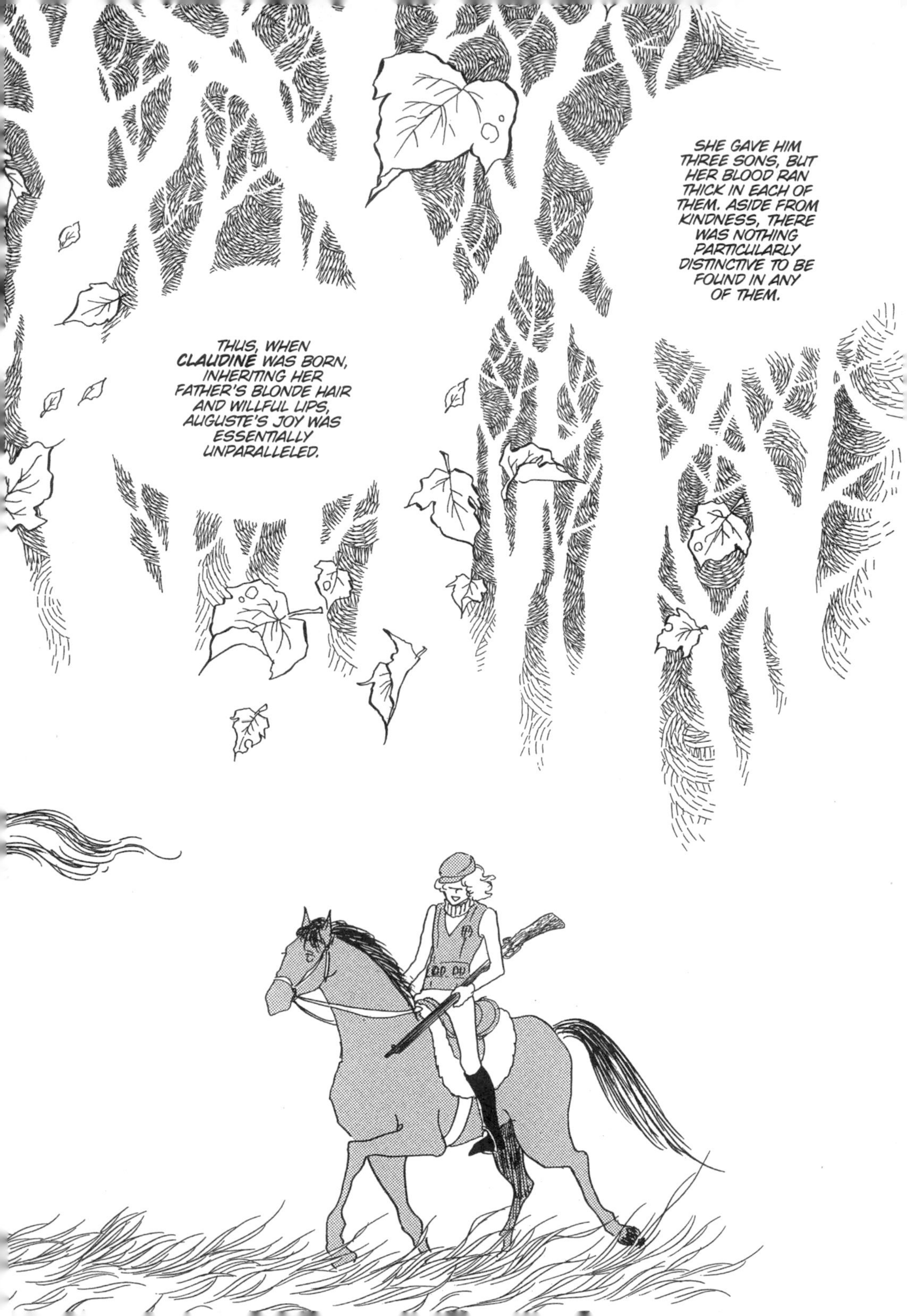
SHE GAVE HIM THREE SONS, BUT HER BLOOD RAN THICK IN EACH OF THEM. ASIDE FROM KINDNESS, THERE WAS NOTHING PARTICULARLY DISTINCTIVE TO BE FOUND IN ANY OF THEM.
THUS, WHEN CLAUDINE WAS BORN, INHERITING HER FATHER'S BLONDE HAIR AND WILLFUL LIPS, AUGUSTE'S JOY WAS ESSENTIALLY UNPARALLELED.

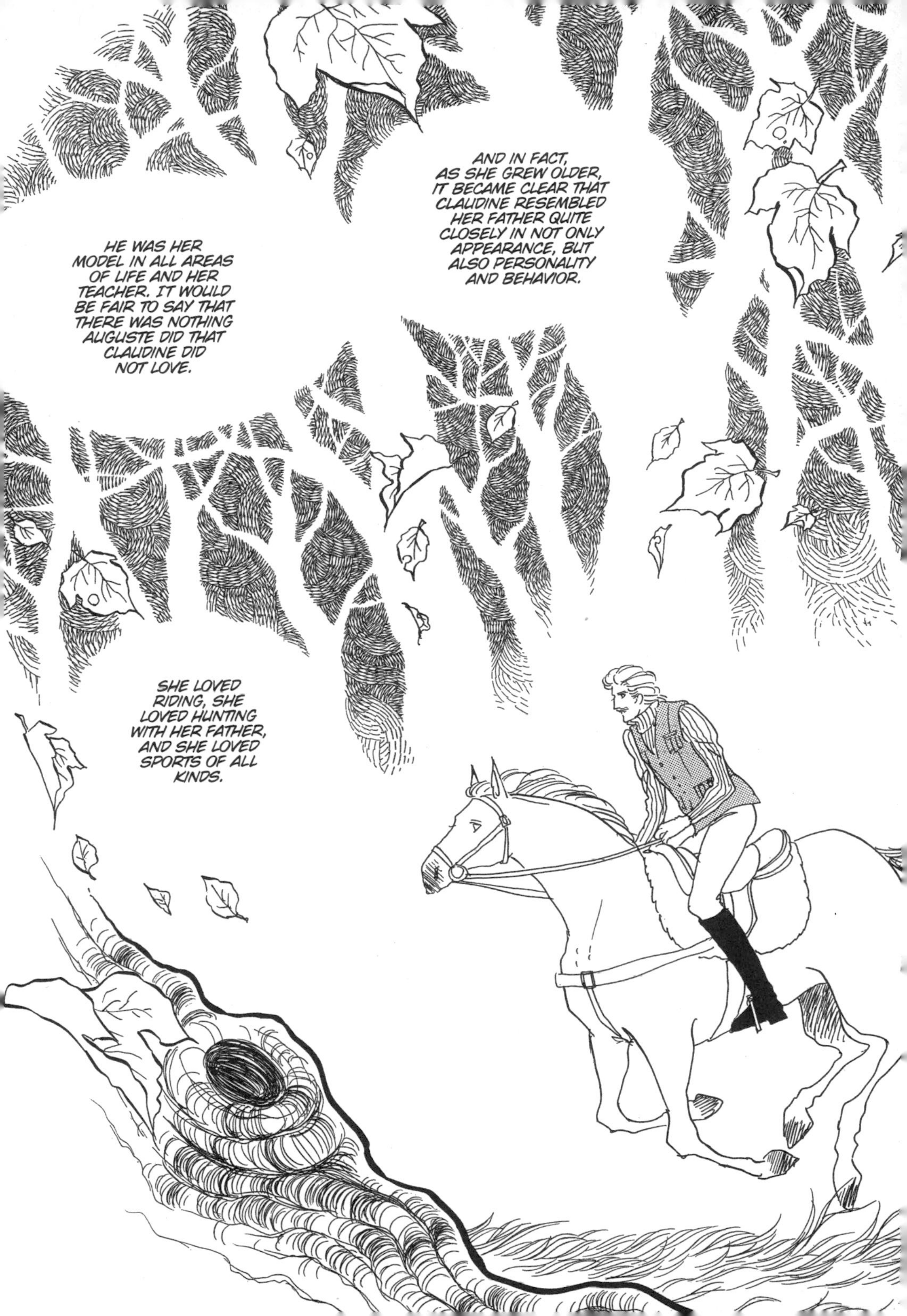
AND IN FACT, AS SHE GREW OLDER, IT BECAME CLEAR THAT CLAUDINE RESEMBLED HER FATHER QUITE CLOSELY IN NOT ONLY APPEARANCE, BUT ALSO PERSONALITY AND BEHAVIOR.
HE WAS HER MODEL IN ALL AREAS OF LIFE AND HER TEACHER. IT WOULD BE FAIR TO SAY THAT THERE WAS NOTHING AUGUSTE DID THAT CLAUDINE DID NOT LOVE.
SHE LOVED RIDING, SHE LOVED HUNTING WITH HER FATHER, AND SHE LOVED SPORTS OF ALL KINDS.

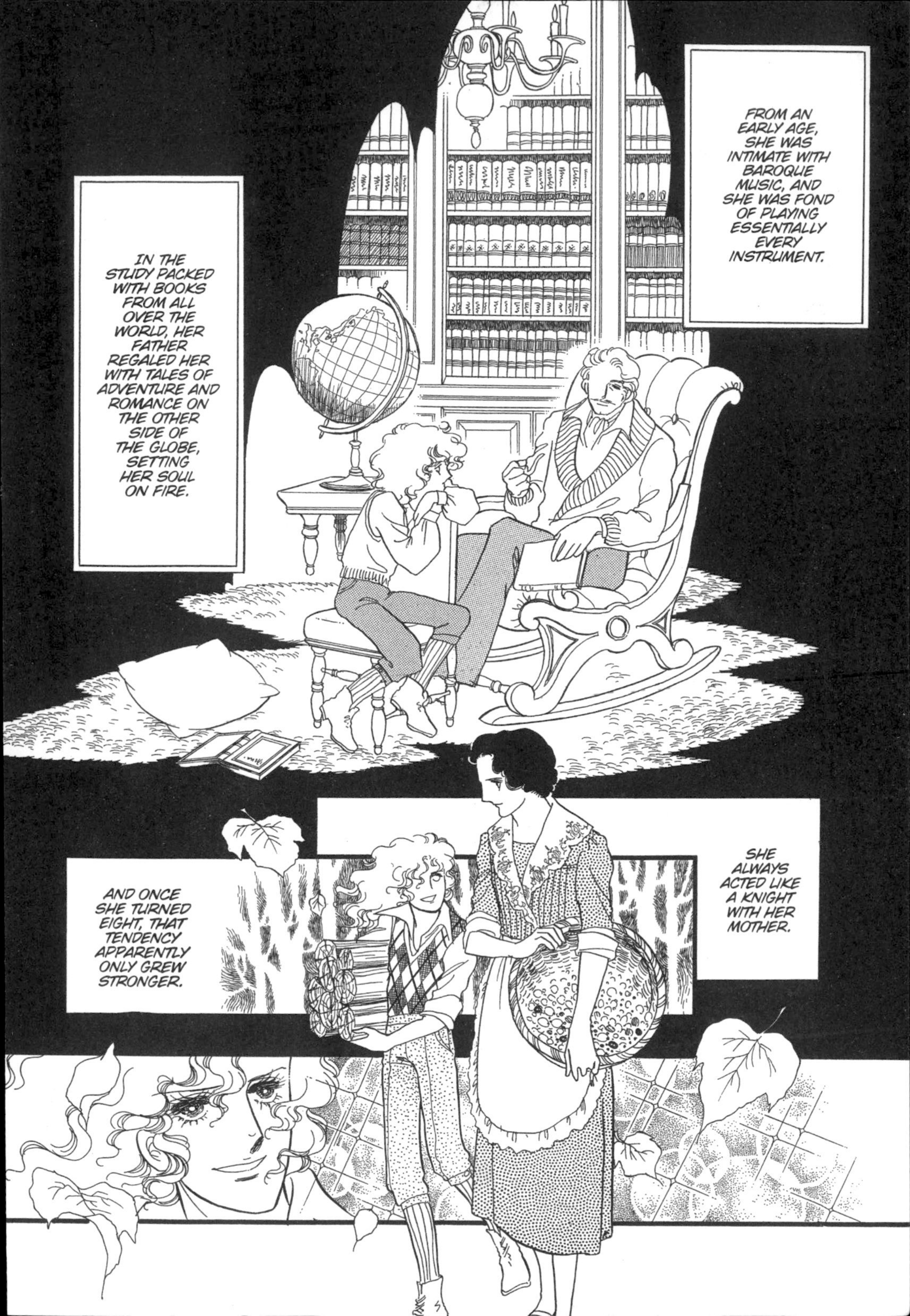
FROM AN EARLY AGE, SHE WAS INTIMATE WITH BAROQUE MUSIC, AND SHE WAS FOND OF PLAYING ESSENTIALLY EVERY INSTRUMENT.
IN THE STUDY PACKED WITH BOOKS FROM ALL OVER THE WORLD, HER FATHER REGALED HER WITH TALES OF ADVENTURE AND ROMANCE ON THE OTHER SIDE OF THE GLOBE, SETTING HER SOUL ON FIRE.
SHE ALWAYS ACTED LIKE A KNIGHT WITH HER MOTHER.
AND ONCE SHE TURNED EIGHT, THAT TENDENCY APPARENTLY ONLY GREW STRONGER.

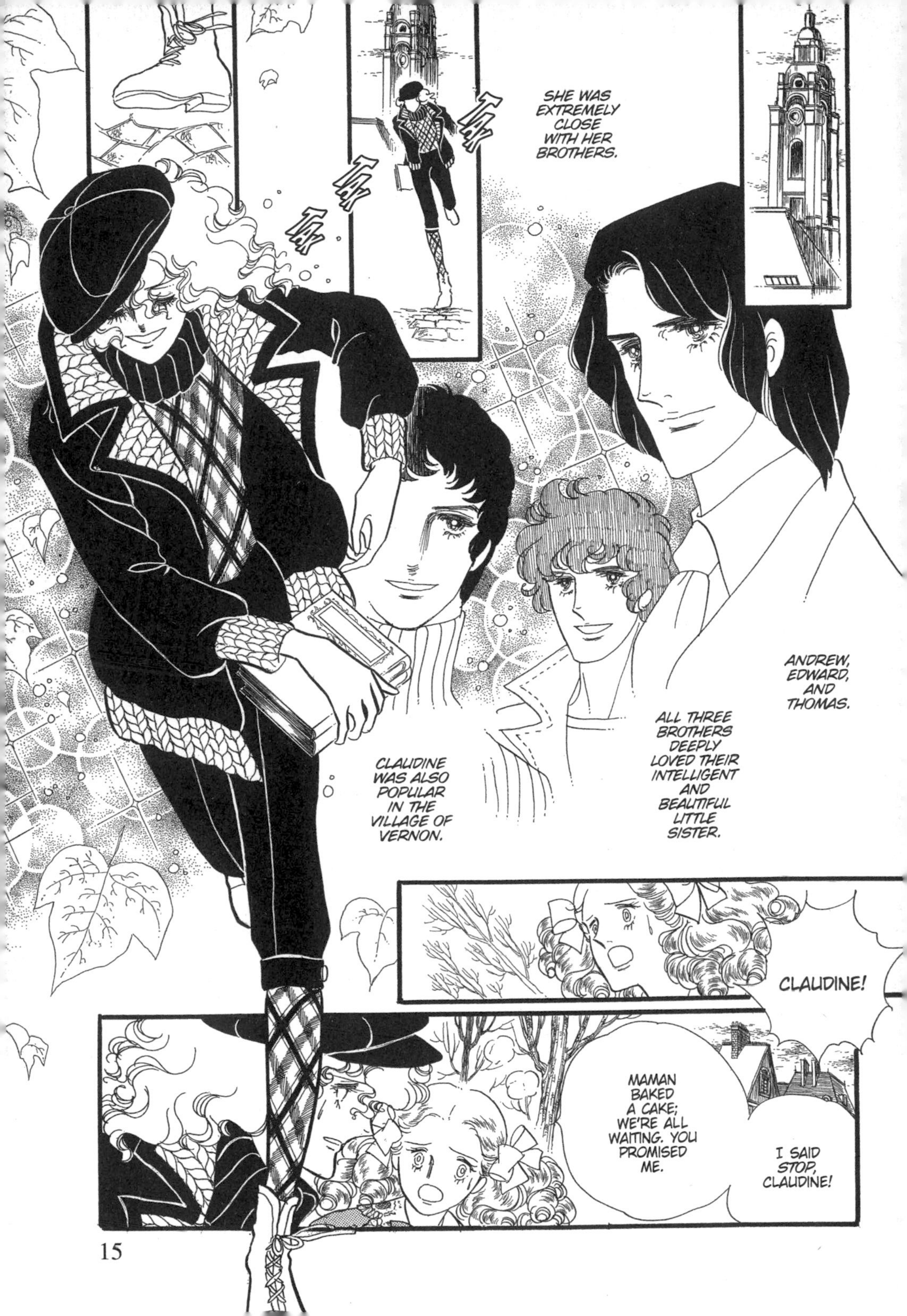
SHE WAS EXTREMELY CLOSE WITH HER BROTHERS.
TAK
TAK
TAK
ANDREW, EDWARD, AND THOMAS.
ALL THREE BROTHERS DEEPLY LOVED THEIR INTELLIGENT AND BEAUTIFUL LITTLE SISTER.
CLAUDINE WAS ALSO POPULAR IN THE VILLAGE OF VERNON.
CLAUDINE!
I SAID STOP, CLAUDINE!
MAMAN BAKED A CAKE; WE'RE ALL WAITING. YOU PROMISED ME.

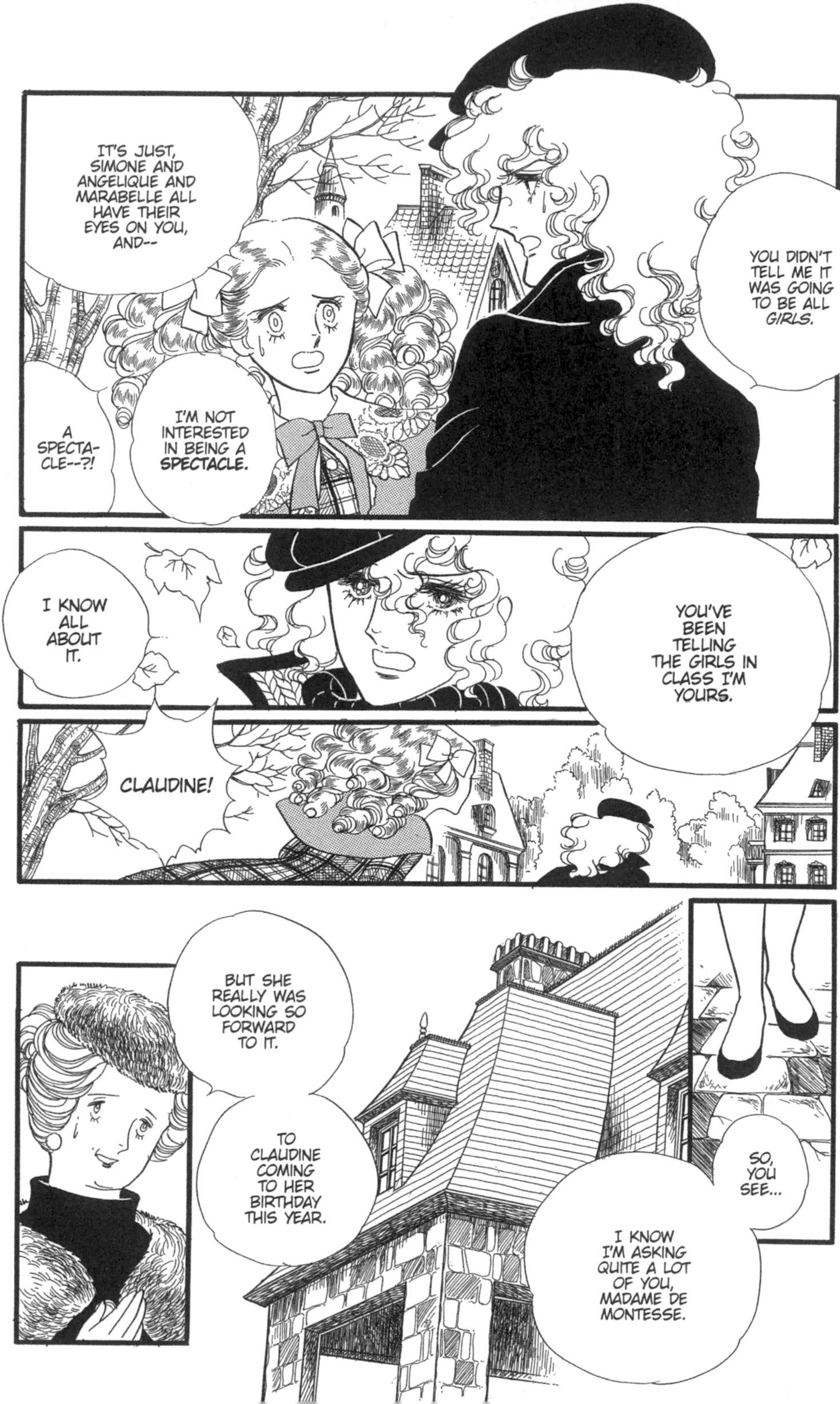
YOU DIDN'T TELL ME IT WAS GOING TO BE ALL *GIRLS.*
IT'S JUST, SIMONE AND ANGELIQUE AND MARABELLE ALL HAVE THEIR EYES ON YOU, AND--
I'M NOT INTERESTED IN BEING A **SPECTACLE.**
A SPECTA-CLE--?!
YOU'VE BEEN TELLING THE GIRLS IN CLASS I'M YOURS.
I KNOW ALL ABOUT IT.
CLAUDINE!
SO, YOU SEE...
I KNOW I'M ASKING QUITE A LOT OF YOU, MADAME DE MONTESSE.
BUT SHE REALLY WAS LOOKING SO FORWARD TO IT.
TO CLAUDINE COMING TO HER BIRTHDAY THIS YEAR.

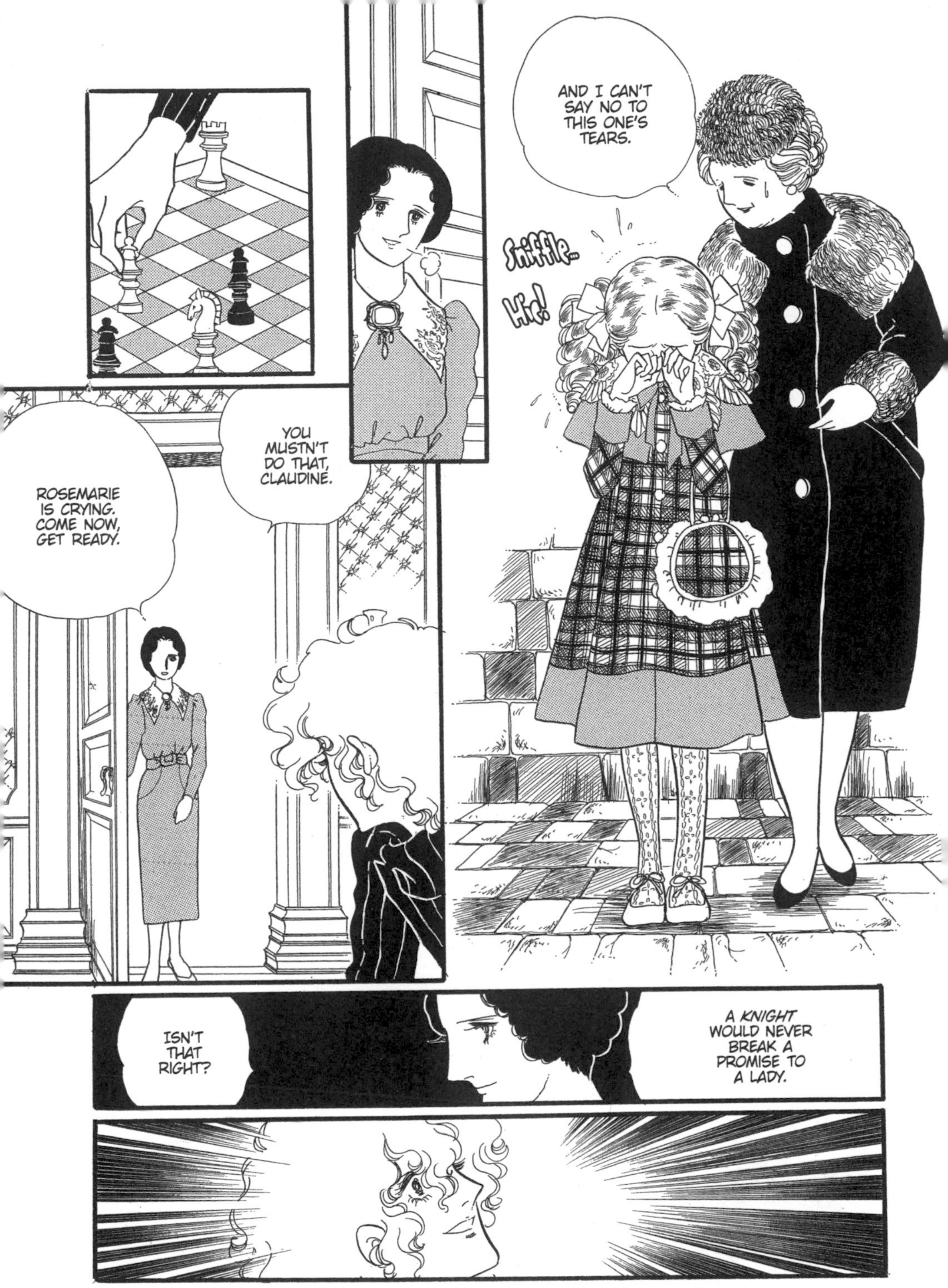
AND I CAN'T SAY NO TO THIS ONE'S TEARS.
Sniffle...
Hic!
YOU MUSTN'T DO THAT, CLAUDINE.
ROSEMARIE IS CRYING. COME NOW, GET READY.
A *KNIGHT* WOULD NEVER BREAK A PROMISE TO A LADY.
ISN'T THAT RIGHT?

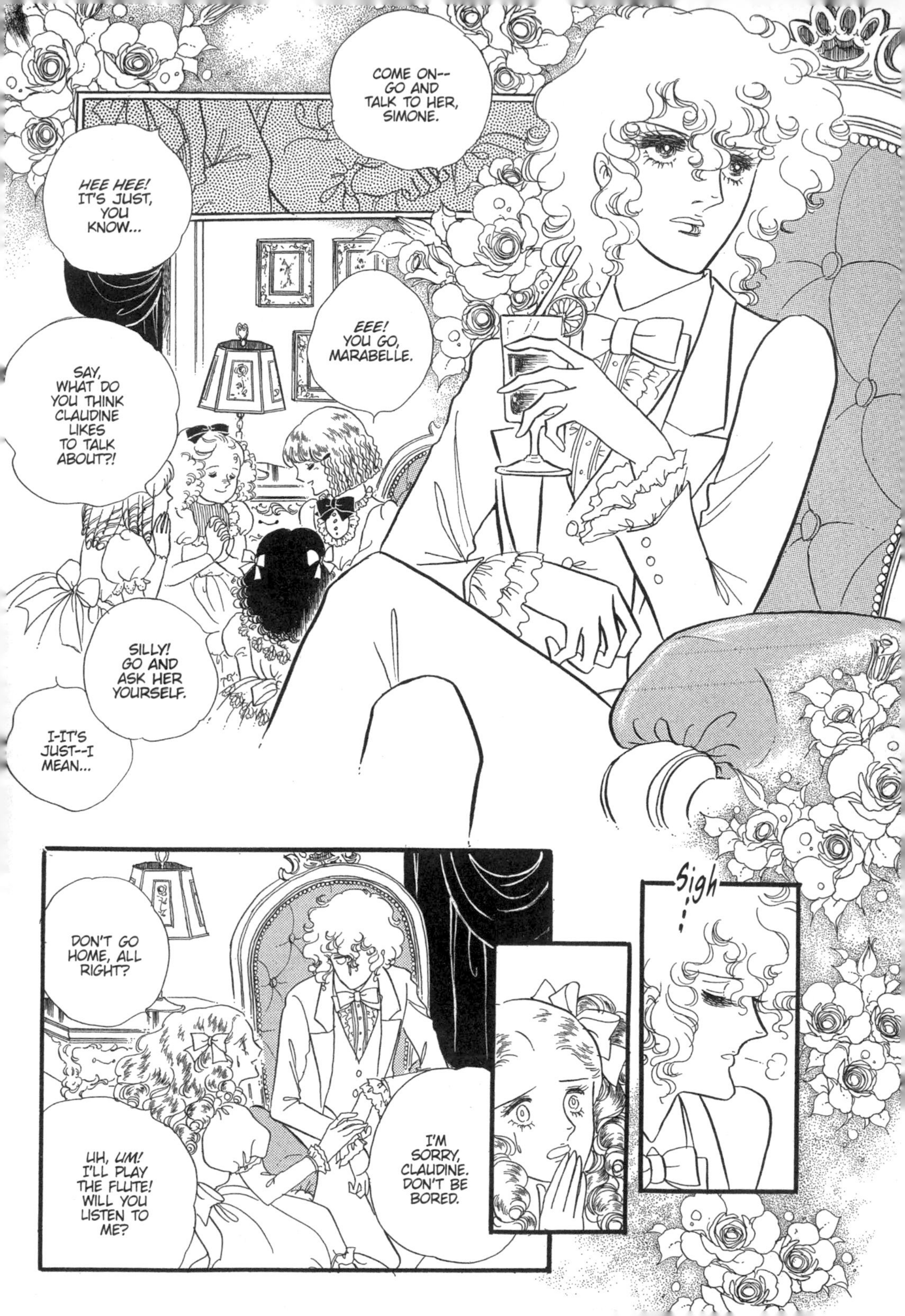
COME ON-- GO AND TALK TO HER, SIMONE.
HEE HEE! IT'S JUST, YOU KNOW...
EEE! YOU GO, MARABELLE.
SAY, WHAT DO YOU THINK CLAUDINE LIKES TO TALK ABOUT?!
SILLY! GO AND ASK HER YOURSELF.
I-IT'S JUST--I MEAN...
Sigh
DON'T GO HOME, ALL RIGHT?
I'M SORRY, CLAUDINE. DON'T BE BORED.
UH, UM! I'LL PLAY THE FLUTE! WILL YOU LISTEN TO ME?

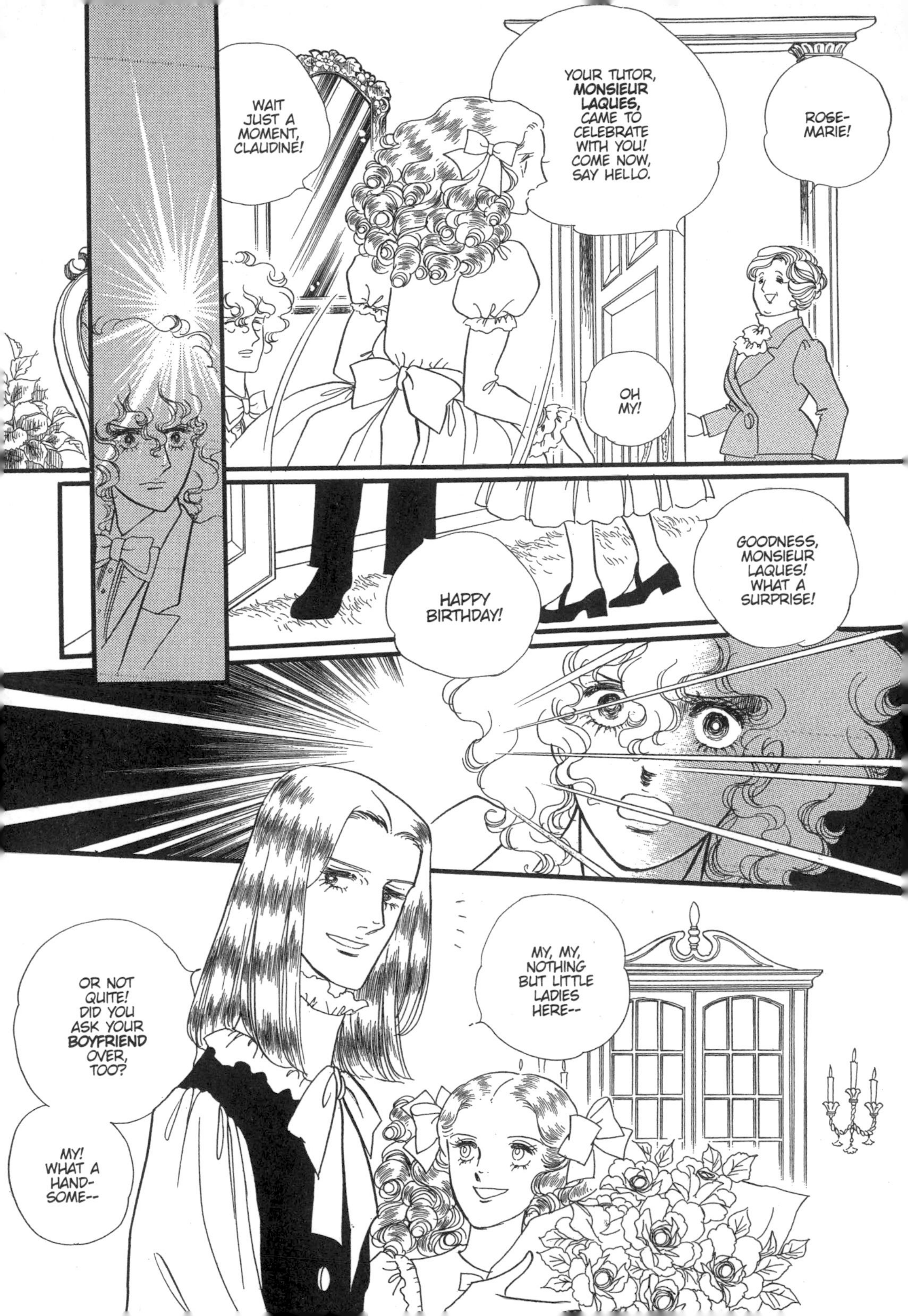
ROSE-MARIE!
YOUR TUTOR, **MONSIEUR LAQUES,** CAME TO CELEBRATE WITH YOU! COME NOW, SAY HELLO.
WAIT JUST A MOMENT, CLAUDINE!
OH MY!
GOODNESS, MONSIEUR LAQUES! WHAT A SURPRISE!
HAPPY BIRTHDAY!
MY, MY, NOTHING BUT LITTLE LADIES HERE--
OR NOT QUITE! DID YOU ASK YOUR **BOYFRIEND** OVER, TOO?
MY! WHAT A HAND-SOME--

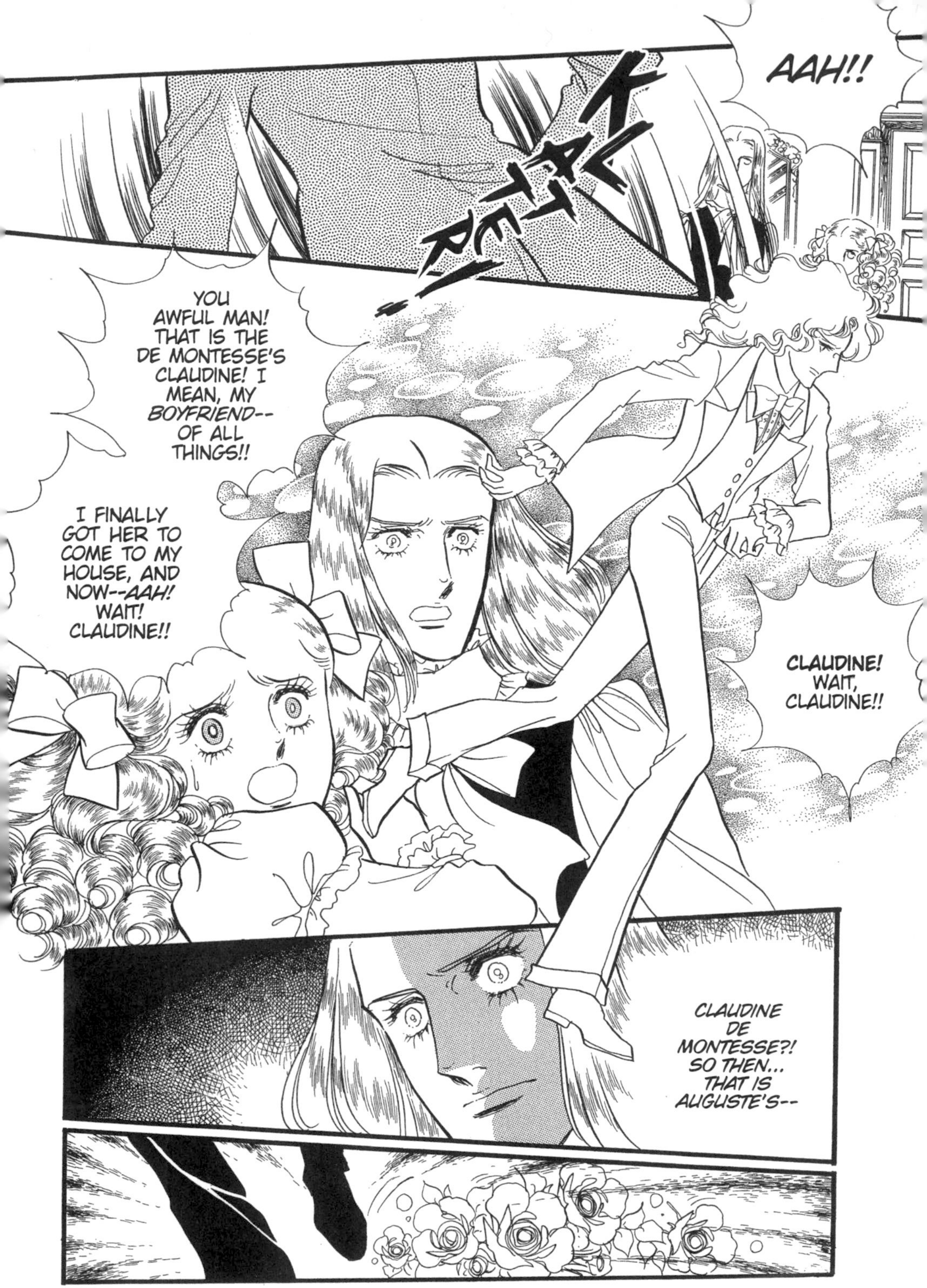
AAH!!
KATTER
YOU AWFUL MAN! THAT IS THE DE MONTESSE'S CLAUDINE! I MEAN, MY *BOYFRIEND*-- OF ALL THINGS!!
I FINALLY GOT HER TO COME TO MY HOUSE, AND NOW--*AAH!* WAIT! CLAUDINE!!
CLAUDINE! WAIT, CLAUDINE!!
CLAUDINE DE MONTESSE?! SO THEN... THAT IS AUGUSTE'S--

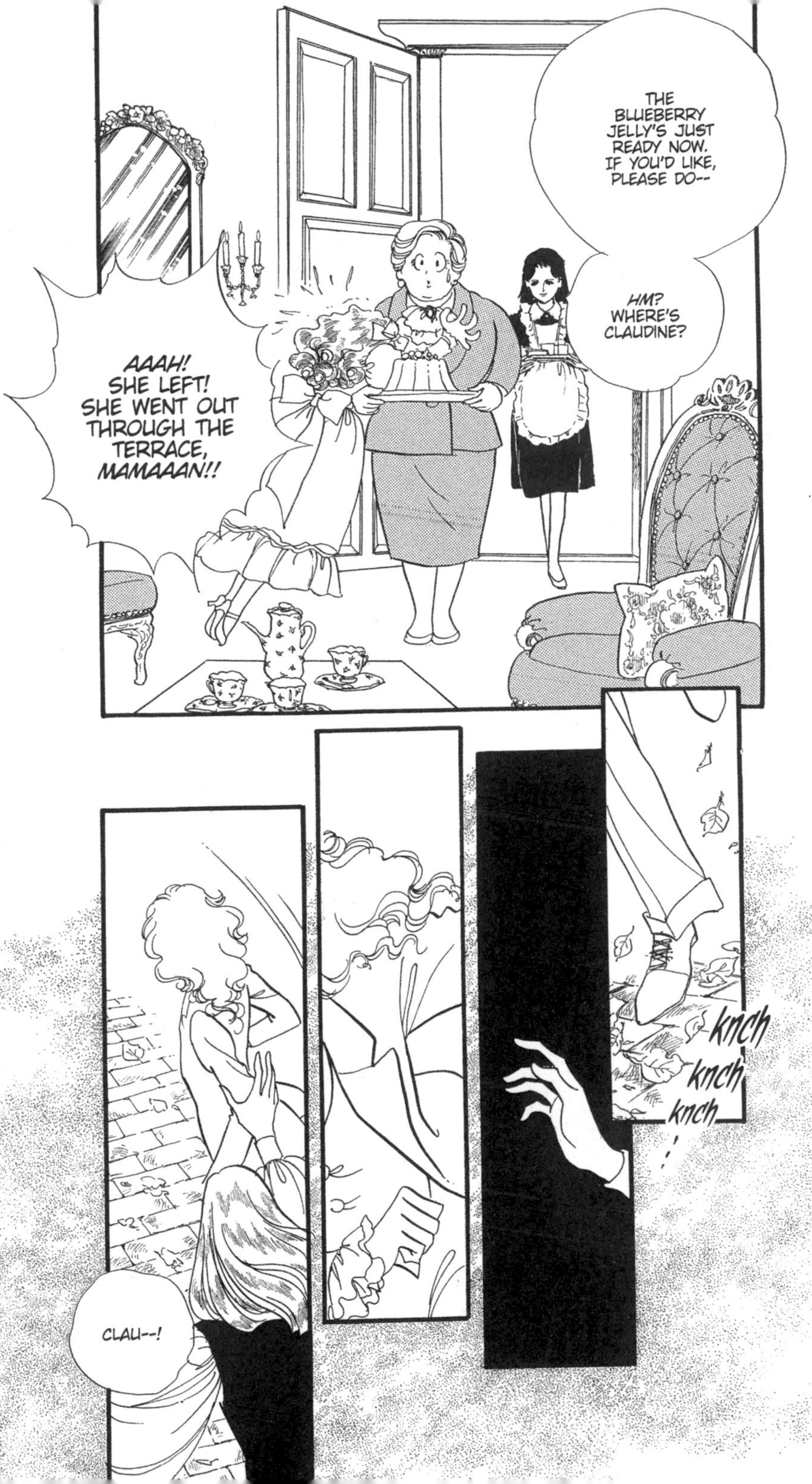
THE BLUEBERRY JELLY'S JUST READY NOW. IF YOU'D LIKE, PLEASE DO--
HM? WHERE'S CLAUDINE?
AAAH! SHE LEFT! SHE WENT OUT THROUGH THE TERRACE, MAMAAAN!!
knch
knch
knch
CLAU--!

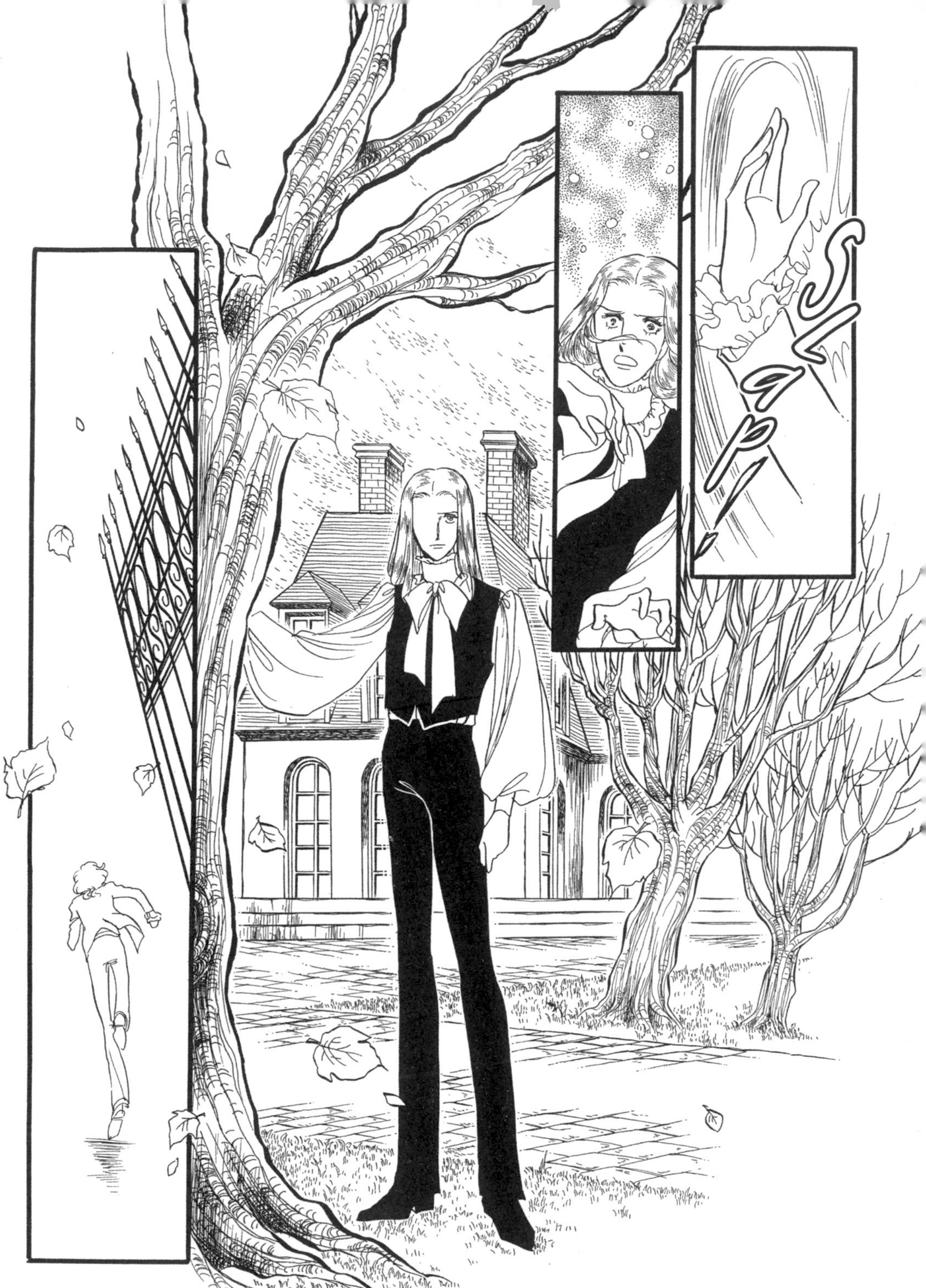
Slap!!

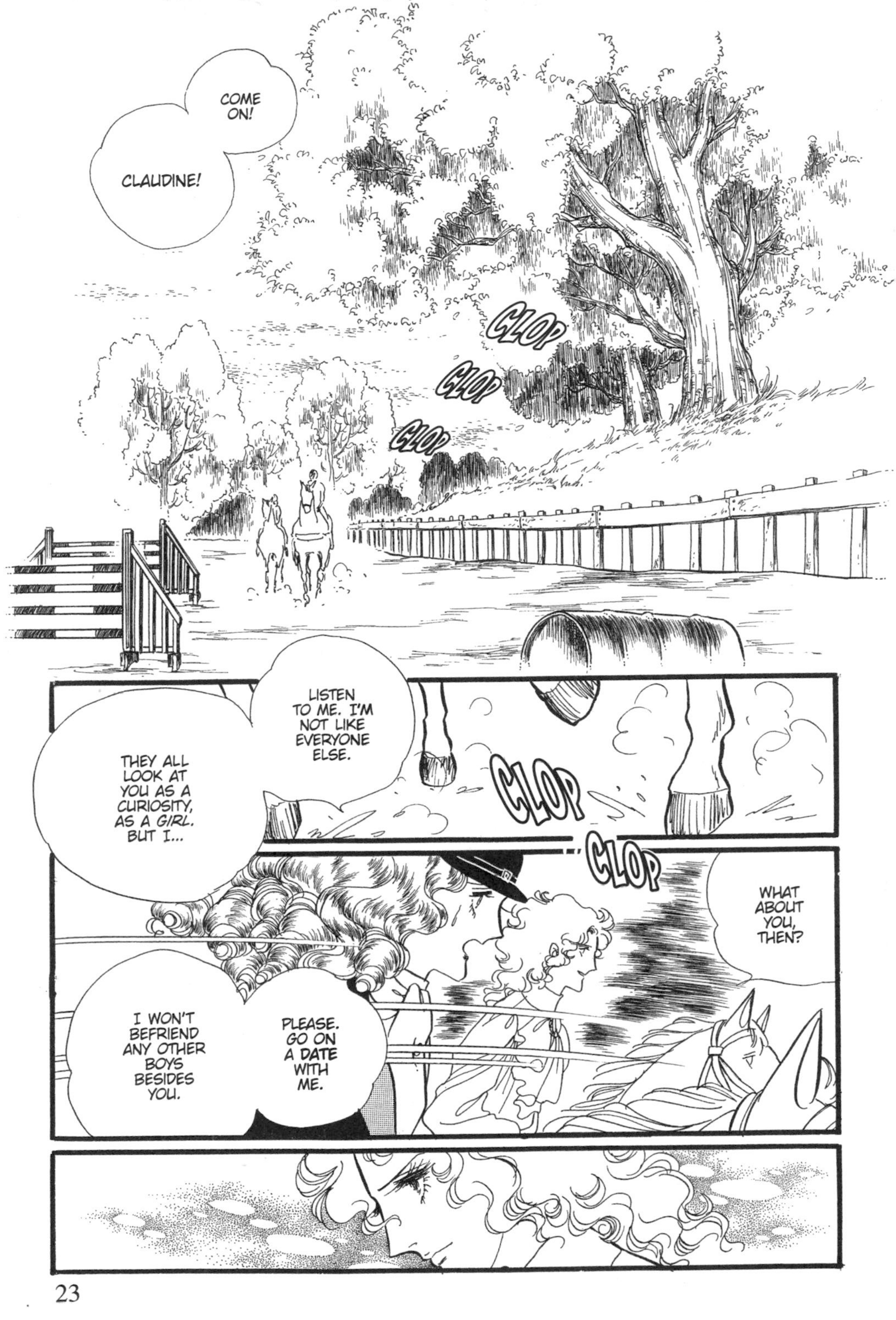
COME ON!
CLAUDINE!
CLOP
CLOP
CLOP
LISTEN TO ME. I'M NOT LIKE EVERYONE ELSE.
THEY ALL LOOK AT YOU AS A CURIOSITY, AS A GIRL. BUT I...
CLOP
CLOP
WHAT ABOUT YOU, THEN?
PLEASE. GO ON A DATE WITH ME.
I WON'T BEFRIEND ANY OTHER BOYS BESIDES YOU.

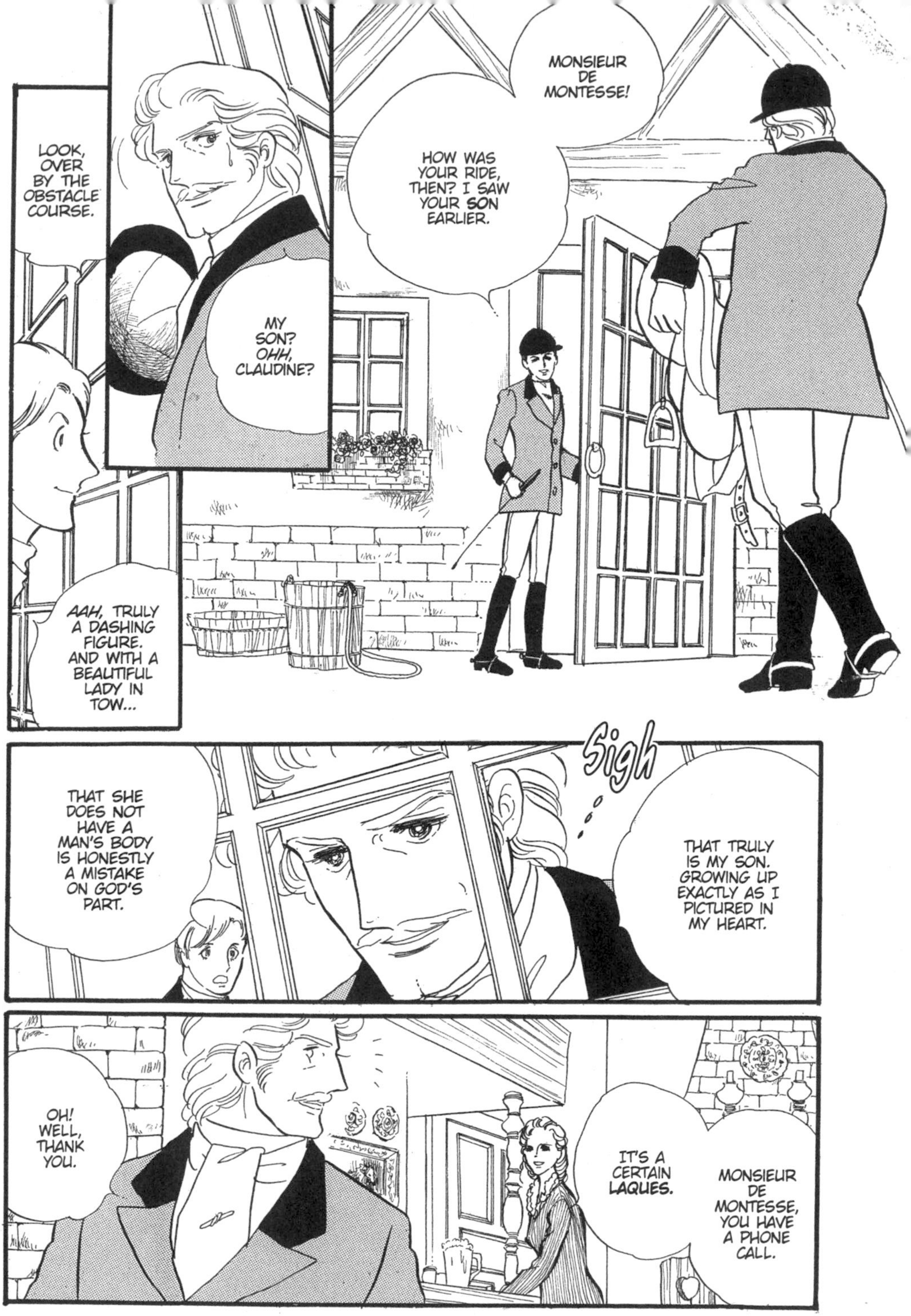
MONSIEUR DE MONTESSE!
HOW WAS YOUR RIDE, THEN? I SAW YOUR SON EARLIER.
MY SON? OHH, CLAUDINE?
LOOK, OVER BY THE OBSTACLE COURSE.
AAH, TRULY A DASHING FIGURE. AND WITH A BEAUTIFUL LADY IN TOW...
Sigh
THAT TRULY IS MY SON. GROWING UP EXACTLY AS I PICTURED IN MY HEART.
THAT SHE DOES NOT HAVE A MAN'S BODY IS HONESTLY A MISTAKE ON GOD'S PART.
MONSIEUR DE MONTESSE, YOU HAVE A PHONE CALL.
IT'S A CERTAIN LAQUES.
OH! WELL, THANK YOU.

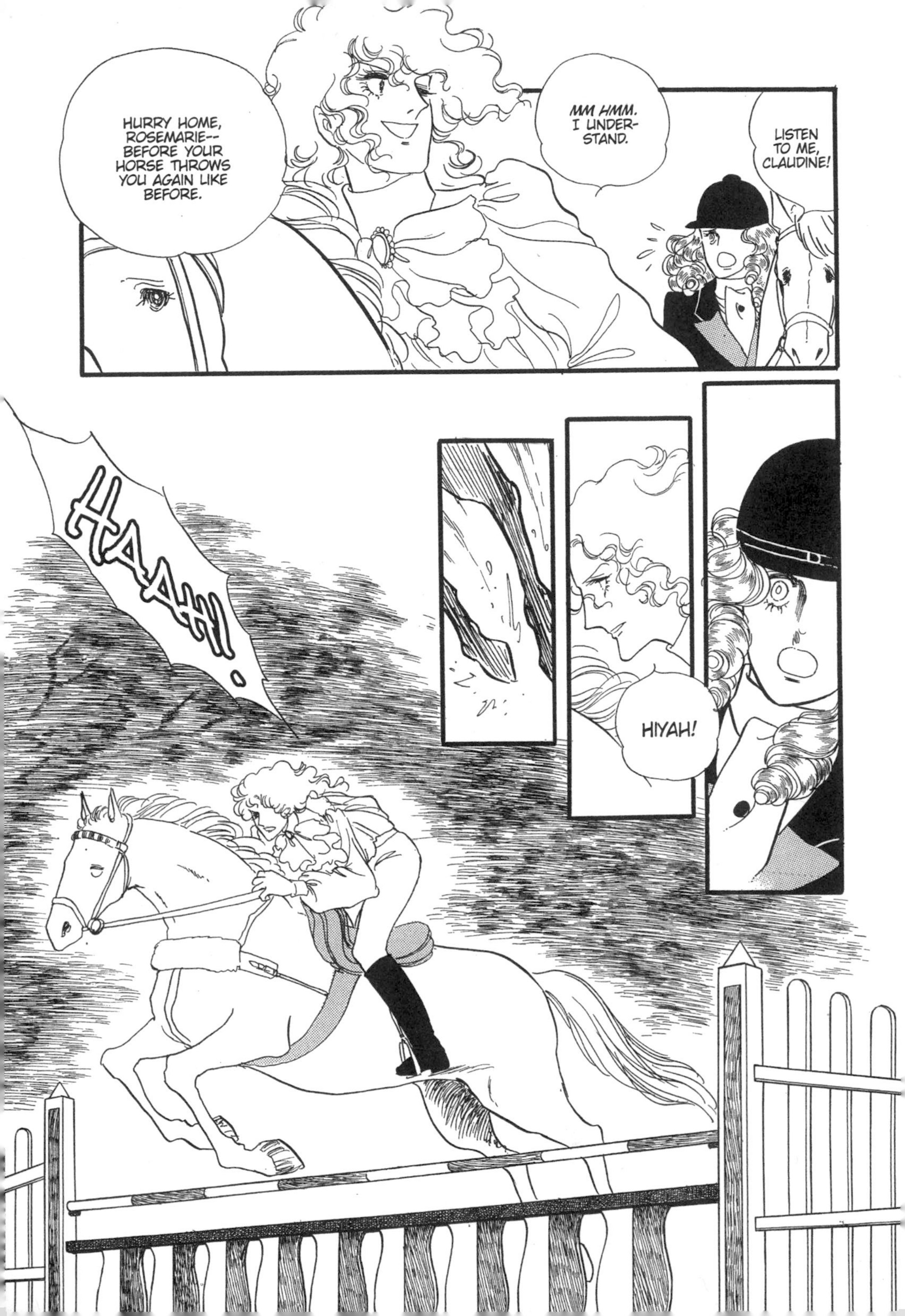
LISTEN TO ME, CLAUDINE!
MM HMM. I UNDER-STAND.
HURRY HOME, ROSEMARIE-- BEFORE YOUR HORSE THROWS YOU AGAIN LIKE BEFORE.
HIYAH!
HAAH!

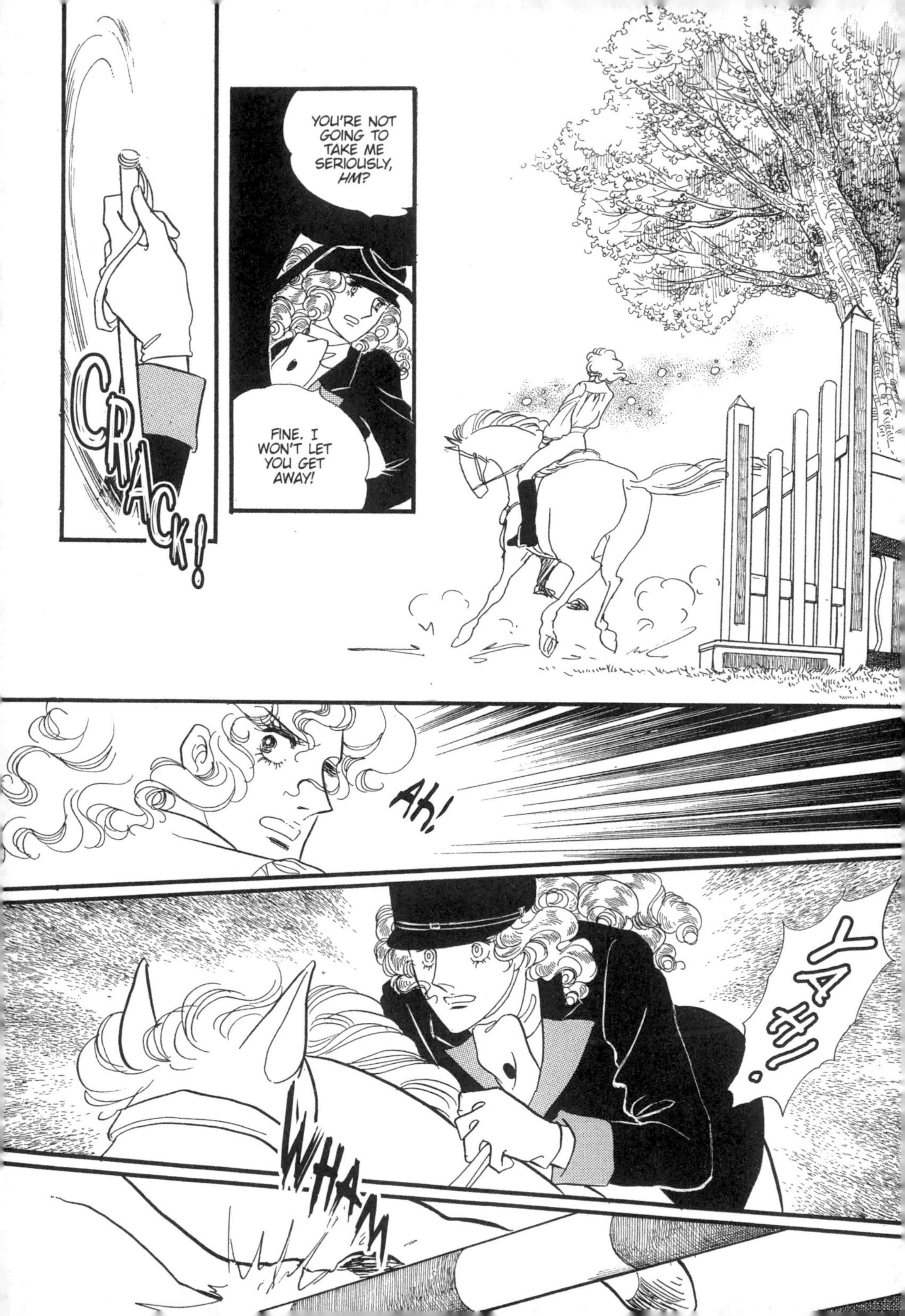
YOU'RE NOT GOING TO TAKE ME SERIOUSLY, HM?
FINE. I WON'T LET YOU GET AWAY!
CRACK!
AH!
YAH!
WHAM

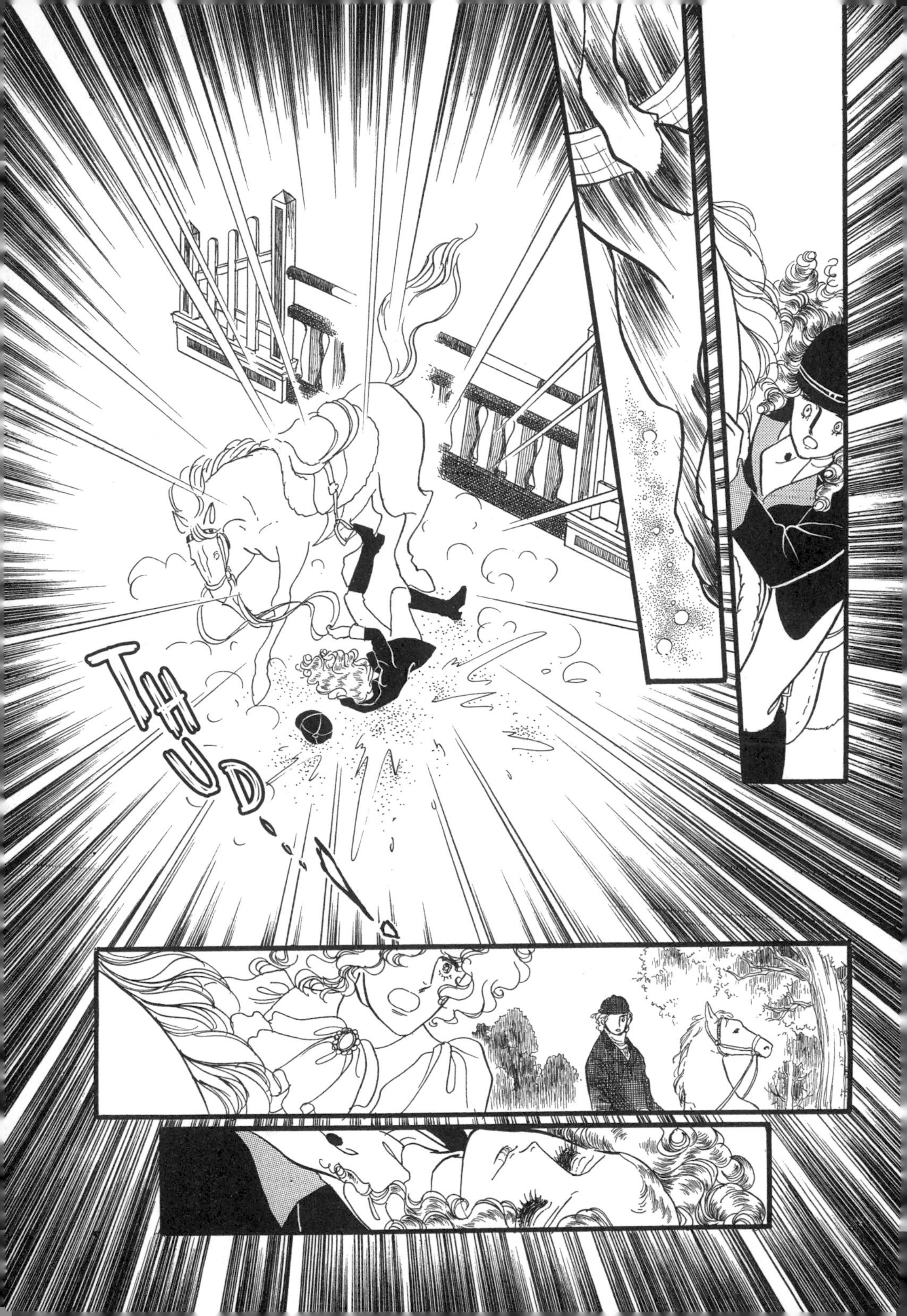
THUD...!

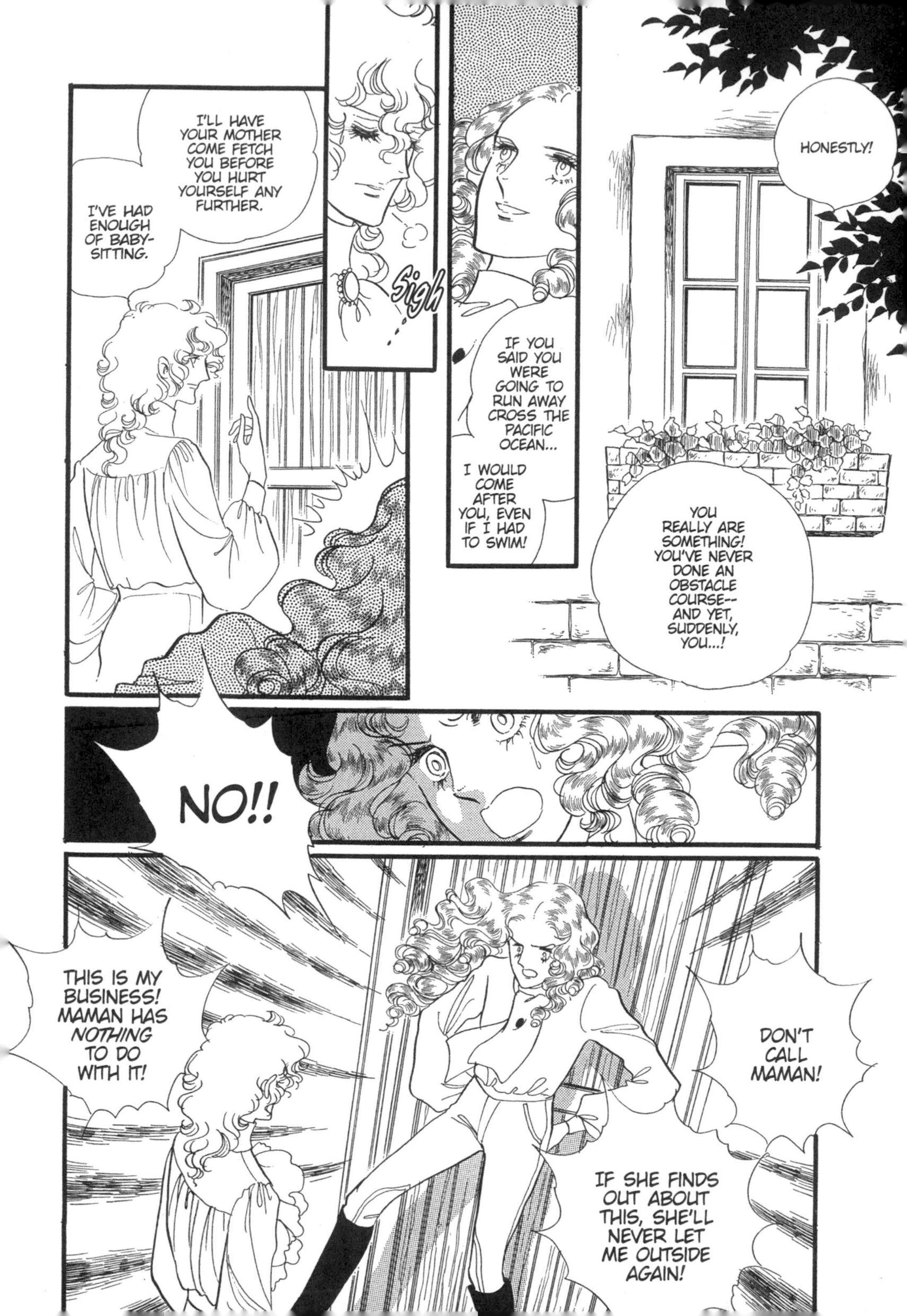
HONESTLY!
YOU REALLY ARE SOMETHING! YOU'VE NEVER DONE AN OBSTACLE COURSE-- AND YET, SUDDENLY, YOU...!
IF YOU SAID YOU WERE GOING TO RUN AWAY CROSS THE PACIFIC OCEAN...
I WOULD COME AFTER YOU, EVEN IF I HAD TO SWIM!
Sigh
I'LL HAVE YOUR MOTHER COME FETCH YOU BEFORE YOU HURT YOURSELF ANY FURTHER.
I'VE HAD ENOUGH OF BABY-SITTING.
NO!!
DON'T CALL MAMAN!
IF SHE FINDS OUT ABOUT THIS, SHE'LL NEVER LET ME OUTSIDE AGAIN!
THIS IS MY BUSINESS! MAMAN HAS *NOTHING* TO DO WITH IT!

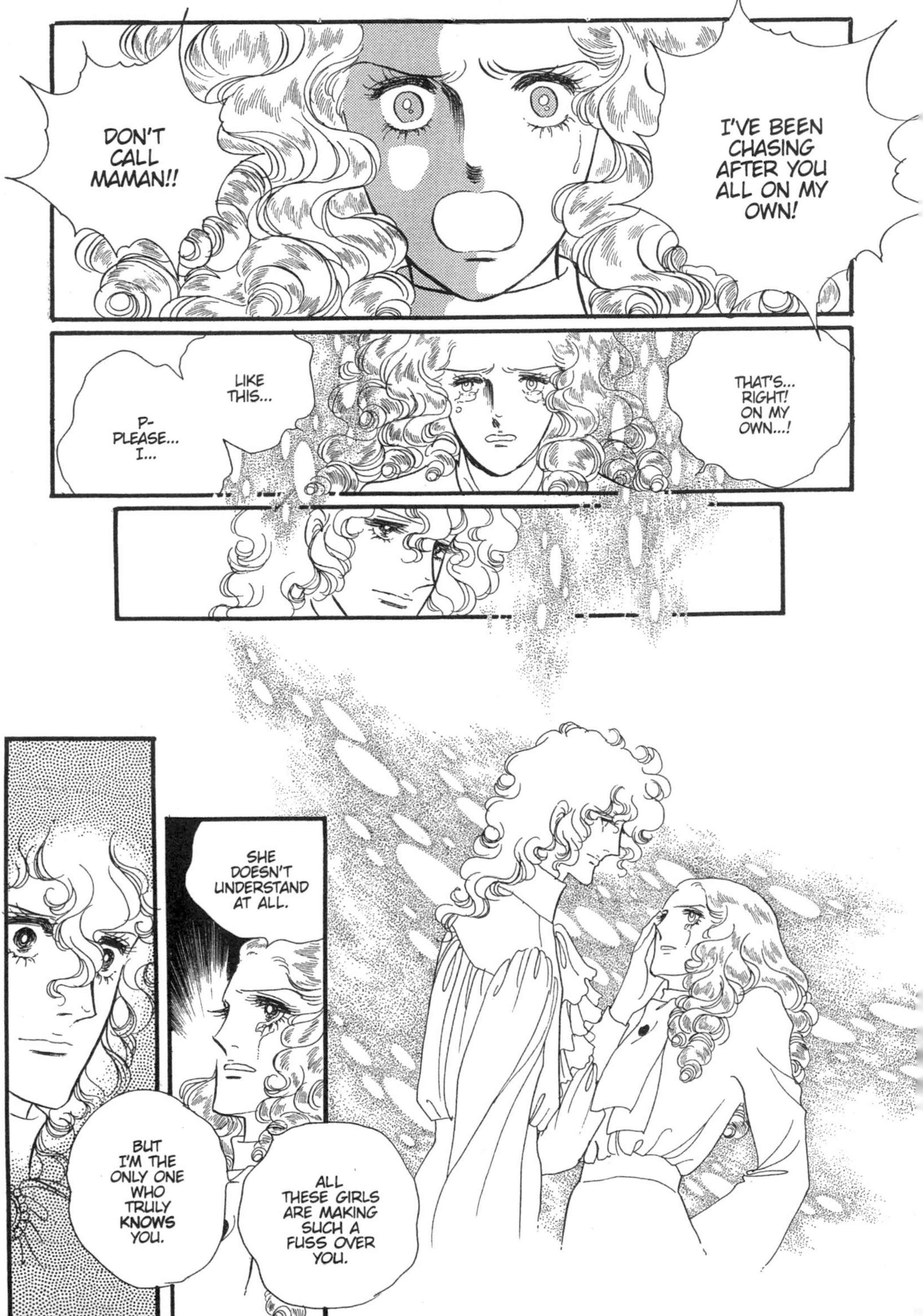
I'VE BEEN CHASING AFTER YOU ALL ON MY OWN!
DON'T CALL MAMAN!!
THAT'S... RIGHT! ON MY OWN...!
LIKE THIS...
P-PLEASE... I...
SHE DOESN'T UNDERSTAND AT ALL.
ALL THESE GIRLS ARE MAKING SUCH A FUSS OVER YOU.
BUT I'M THE ONLY ONE WHO TRULY KNOWS YOU.

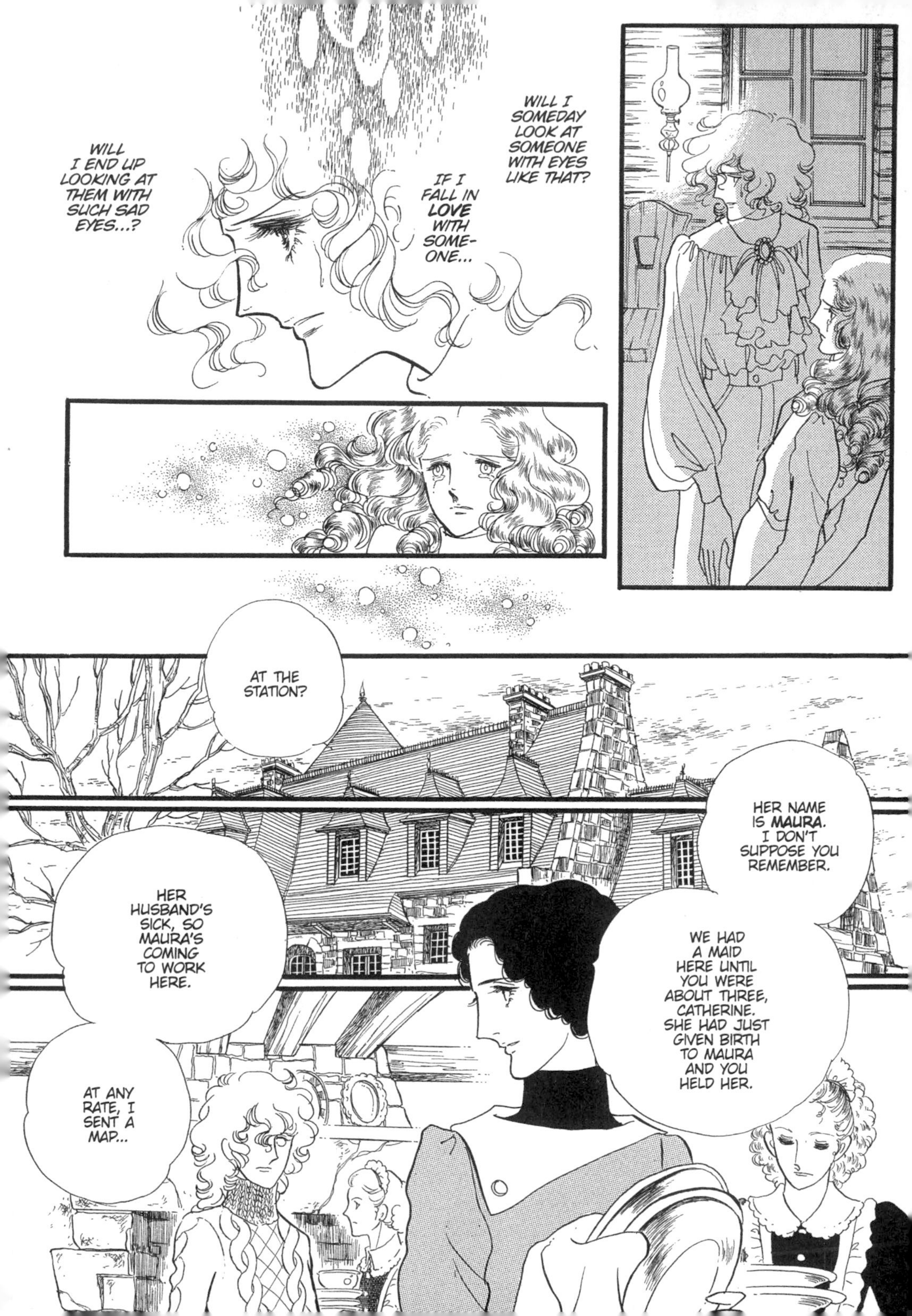
WILL I SOMEDAY LOOK AT SOMEONE WITH EYES LIKE THAT?
IF I FALL IN **LOVE** WITH SOME-ONE...
WILL I END UP LOOKING AT THEM WITH SUCH SAD EYES...?
AT THE STATION?
HER NAME IS **MAURA.** I DON'T SUPPOSE YOU REMEMBER.
HER HUSBAND'S SICK, SO MAURA'S COMING TO WORK HERE.
WE HAD A MAID HERE UNTIL YOU WERE ABOUT THREE, CATHERINE. SHE HAD JUST GIVEN BIRTH TO MAURA AND YOU HELD HER.
AT ANY RATE, I SENT A MAP...

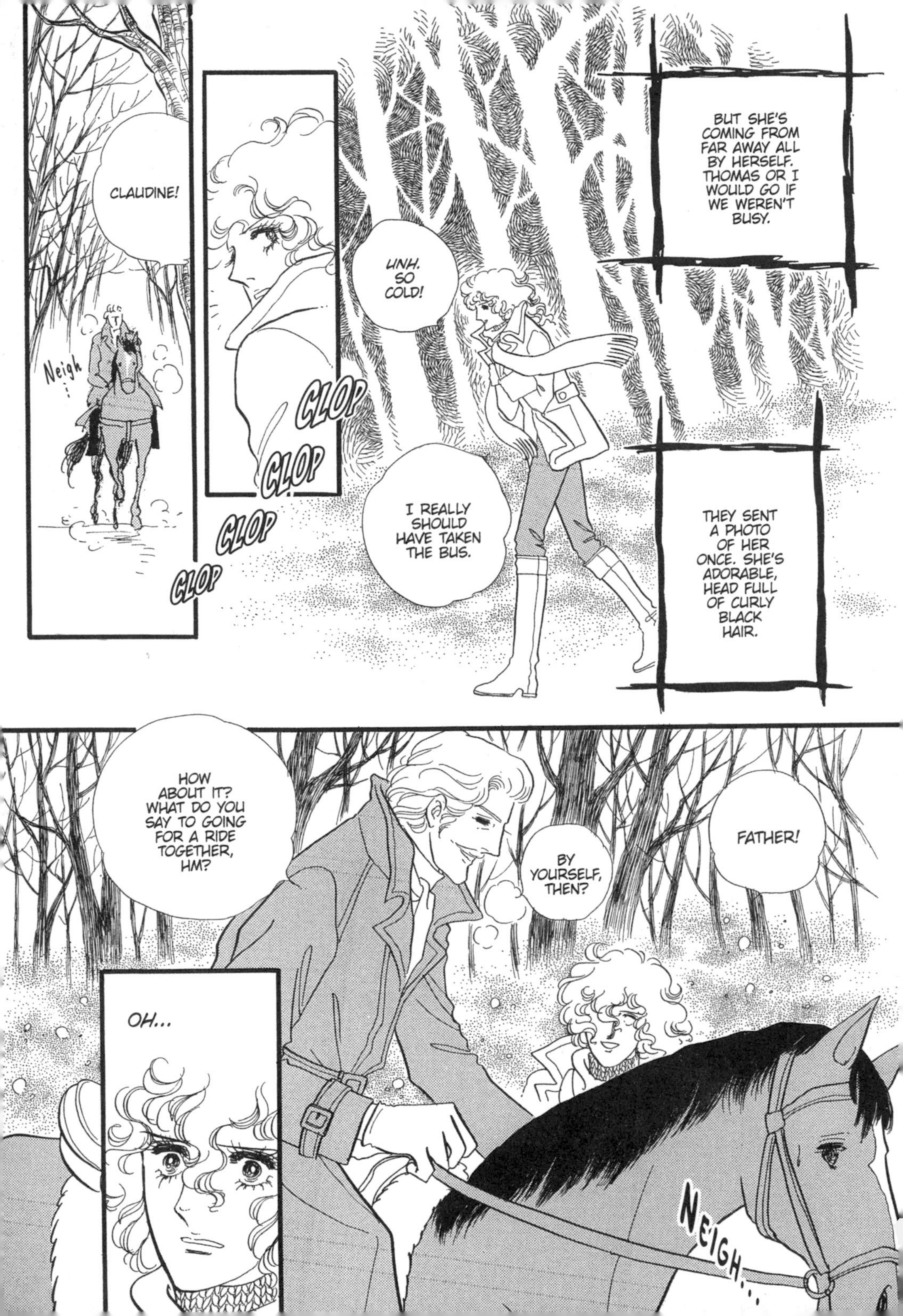
BUT SHE'S COMING FROM FAR AWAY ALL BY HERSELF. THOMAS OR I WOULD GO IF WE WEREN'T BUSY.
THEY SENT A PHOTO OF HER ONCE. SHE'S ADORABLE, HEAD FULL OF CURLY BLACK HAIR.
UNH. SO COLD!
I REALLY SHOULD HAVE TAKEN THE BUS.
CLOP
CLOP
CLOP
CLOP
CLAUDINE!
Neigh
FATHER!
BY YOURSELF, THEN?
HOW ABOUT IT? WHAT DO YOU SAY TO GOING FOR A RIDE TOGETHER, HM?
NEIGH...
OH...

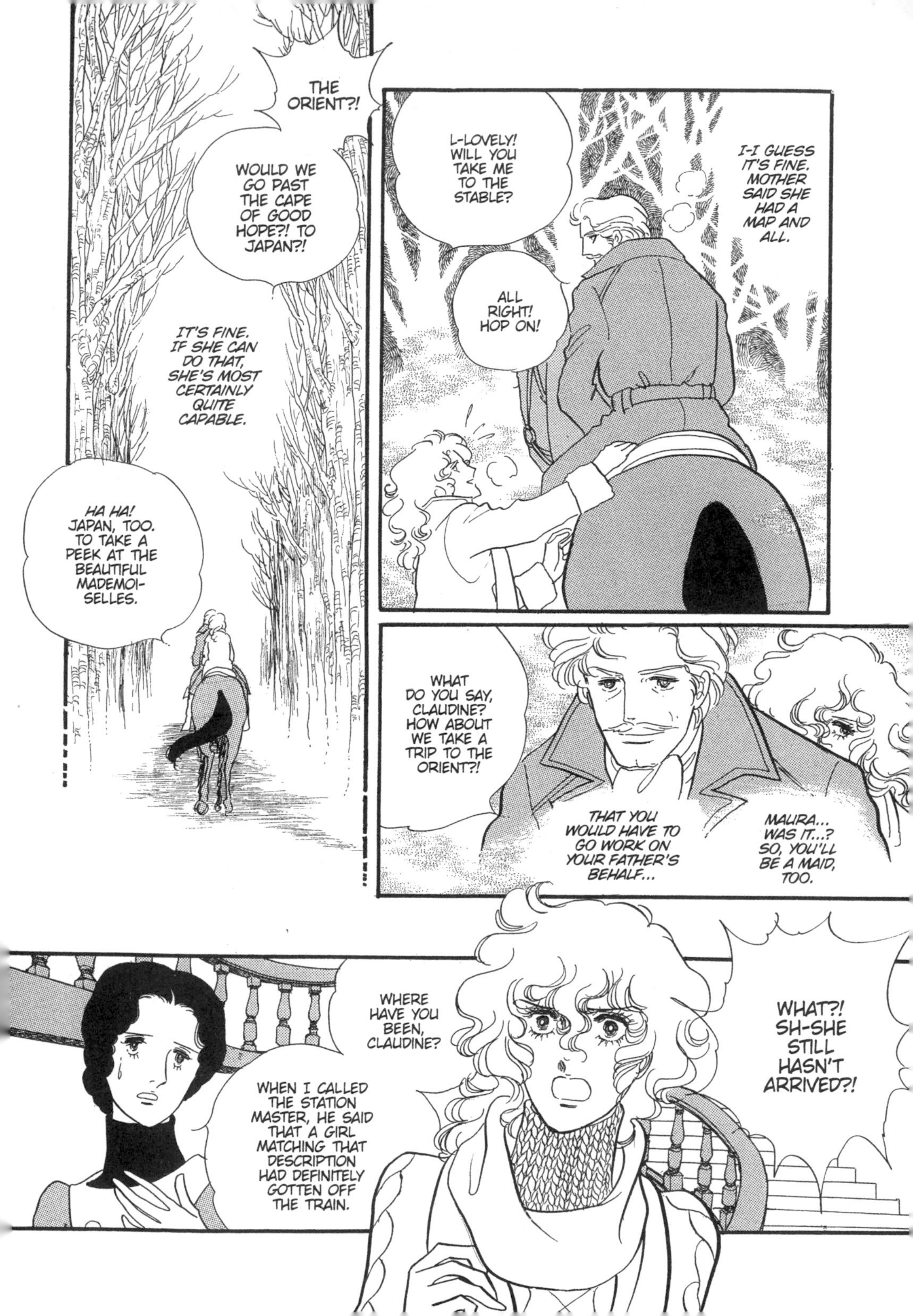
I-I GUESS IT'S FINE. MOTHER SAID SHE HAD A MAP AND ALL.
L-LOVELY! WILL YOU TAKE ME TO THE STABLE?
ALL RIGHT! HOP ON!
MAURA... WAS IT...? SO, YOU'LL BE A MAID, TOO.
THAT YOU WOULD HAVE TO GO WORK ON YOUR FATHER'S BEHALF...
WHAT DO YOU SAY, CLAUDINE? HOW ABOUT WE TAKE A TRIP TO THE ORIENT?!
THE ORIENT?!
WOULD WE GO PAST THE CAPE OF GOOD HOPE?! TO JAPAN?!
IT'S FINE. IF SHE CAN DO THAT, SHE'S MOST CERTAINLY QUITE CAPABLE.
HA HA! JAPAN, TOO. TO TAKE A PEEK AT THE BEAUTIFUL MADEMOISELLES.
WHAT?! SH-SHE STILL HASN'T ARRIVED?!
WHERE HAVE YOU BEEN, CLAUDINE?
WHEN I CALLED THE STATION MASTER, HE SAID THAT A GIRL MATCHING THAT DESCRIPTION HAD DEFINITELY GOTTEN OFF THE TRAIN.

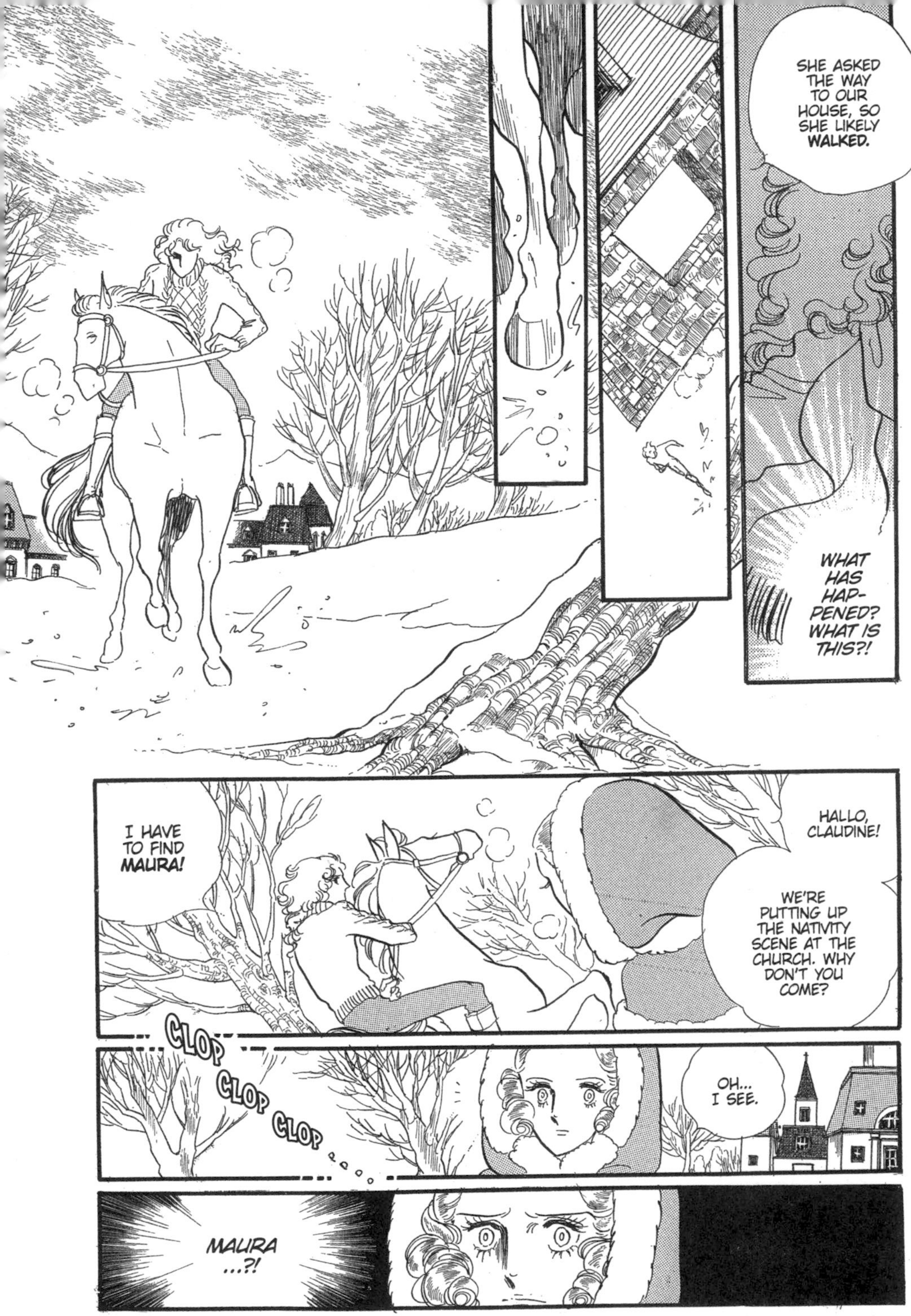
SHE ASKED THE WAY TO OUR HOUSE, SO SHE LIKELY WALKED.
WHAT HAS HAP-PENED? WHAT IS THIS?!
HALLO, CLAUDINE!
WE'RE PUTTING UP THE NATIVITY SCENE AT THE CHURCH. WHY DON'T YOU COME?
I HAVE TO FIND MAURA!
OH... I SEE.
CLOP CLOP CLOP
MAURA ...?!

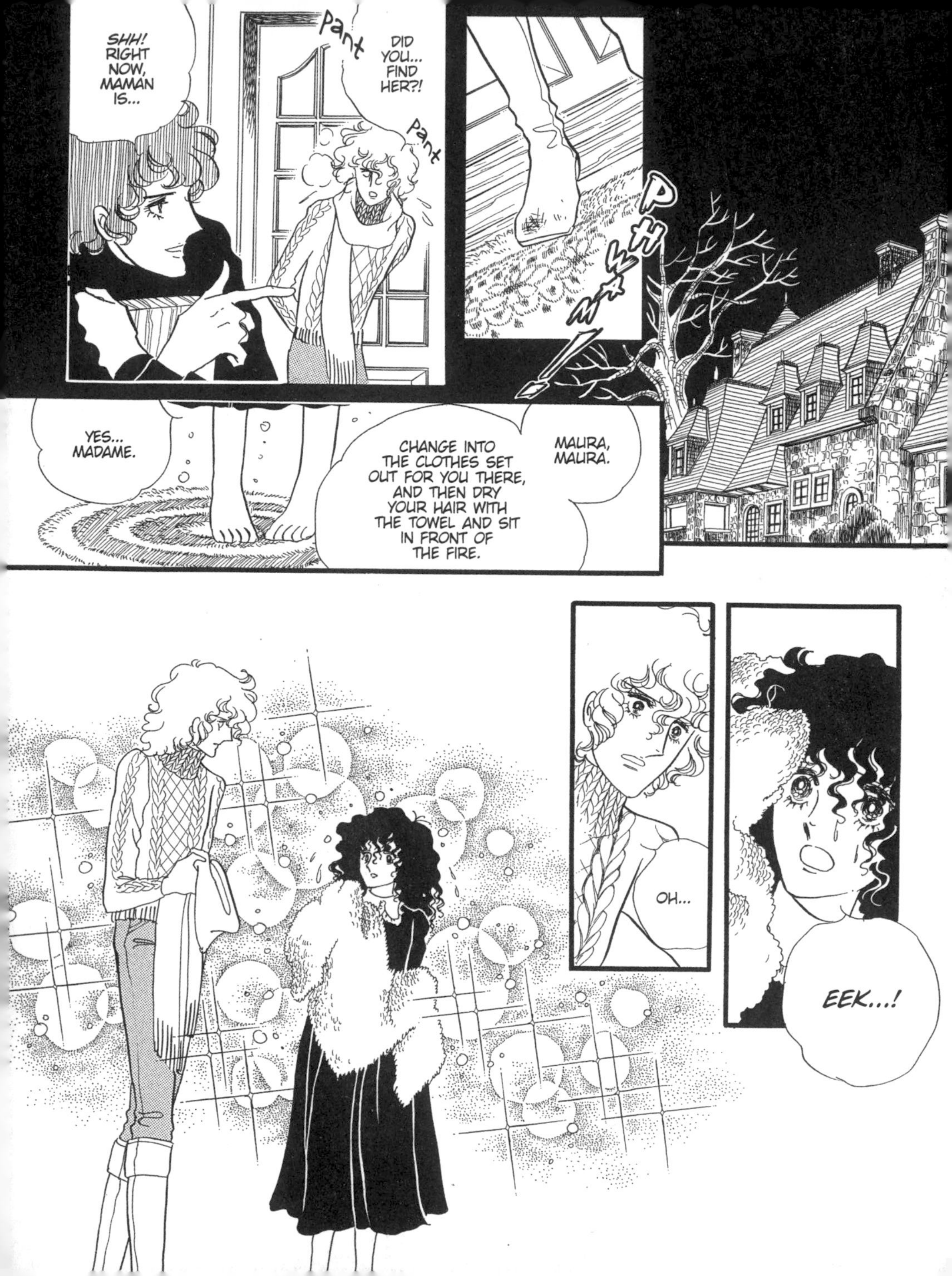
PHWAM!
Pant
DID YOU... FIND HER?!
Pant
SHH! RIGHT NOW, MAMAN IS...
MAURA, MAURA.
CHANGE INTO THE CLOTHES SET OUT FOR YOU THERE, AND THEN DRY YOUR HAIR WITH THE TOWEL AND SIT IN FRONT OF THE FIRE.
YES... MADAME.
EEK...!
OH...

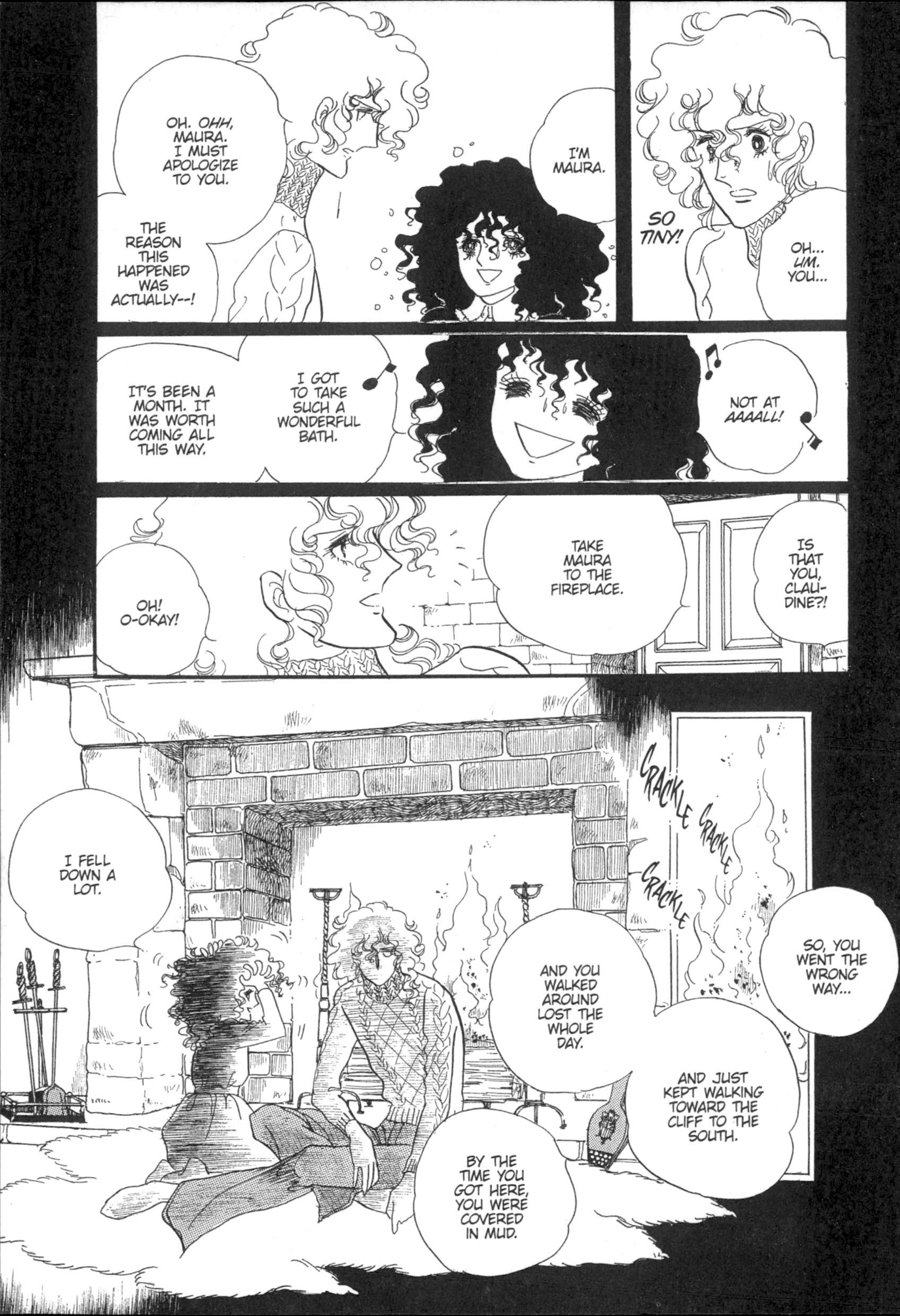
OH... UM. YOU...
SO TINY!
I'M MAURA.
OH. OHH, MAURA. I MUST APOLOGIZE TO YOU.
THE REASON THIS HAPPENED WAS ACTUALLY--!
NOT AT AAAALL!
I GOT TO TAKE SUCH A WONDERFUL BATH.
IT'S BEEN A MONTH. IT WAS WORTH COMING ALL THIS WAY.
IS THAT YOU, CLAUDINE?!
TAKE MAURA TO THE FIREPLACE.
OH! O-OKAY!
CRACKLE CRACKLE
CRACKLE
SO, YOU WENT THE WRONG WAY...
AND YOU WALKED AROUND LOST THE WHOLE DAY.
AND JUST KEPT WALKING TOWARD THE CLIFF TO THE SOUTH.
BY THE TIME YOU GOT HERE, YOU WERE COVERED IN MUD.
I FELL DOWN A LOT.

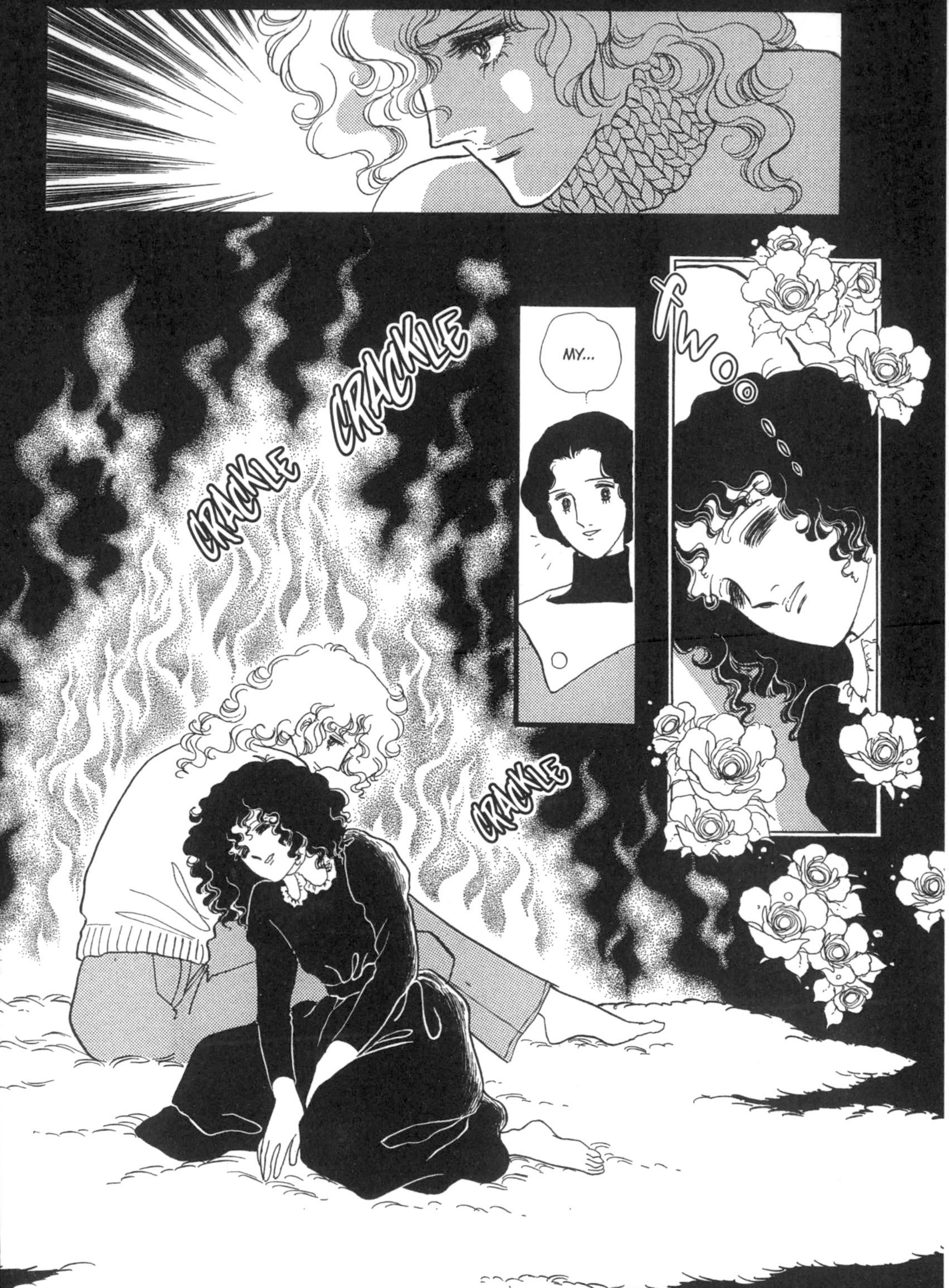
FWOO...
MY...
CRACKLE
CRACKLE
CRACKLE
CRACKLE

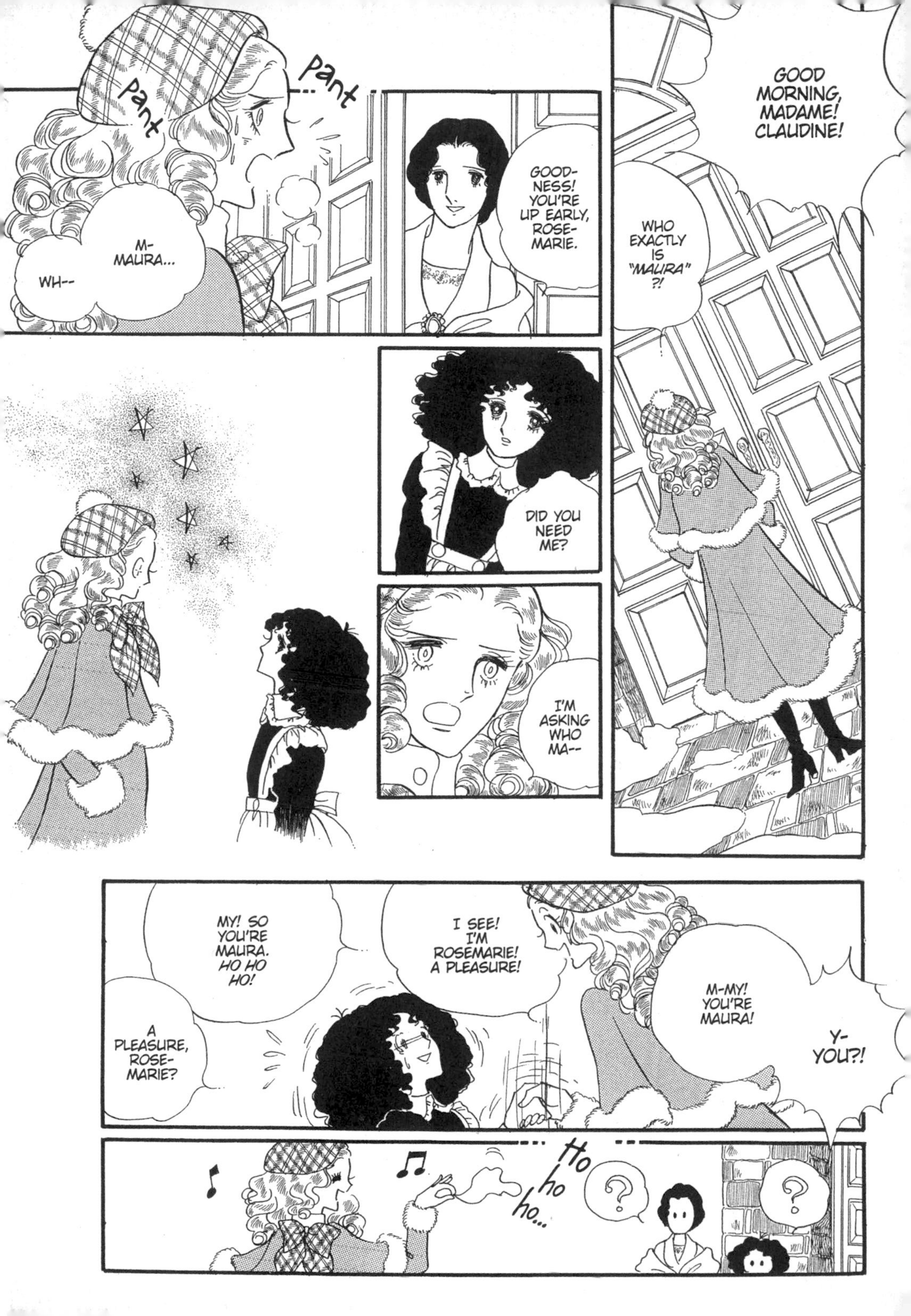
GOOD MORNING, MADAME! CLAUDINE!
WHO EXACTLY IS "MAURA" ?!
GOOD-NESS! YOU'RE UP EARLY, ROSE-MARIE.
Pant
Pant
M-MAURA...
WH--
DID YOU NEED ME?
I'M ASKING WHO MA--
Y-YOU?!
M-MY! YOU'RE MAURA!
I SEE! I'M ROSEMARIE! A PLEASURE!
MY! SO YOU'RE MAURA. HO HO HO!
A PLEASURE, ROSE-MARIE?
Ho ho ho...
?
?

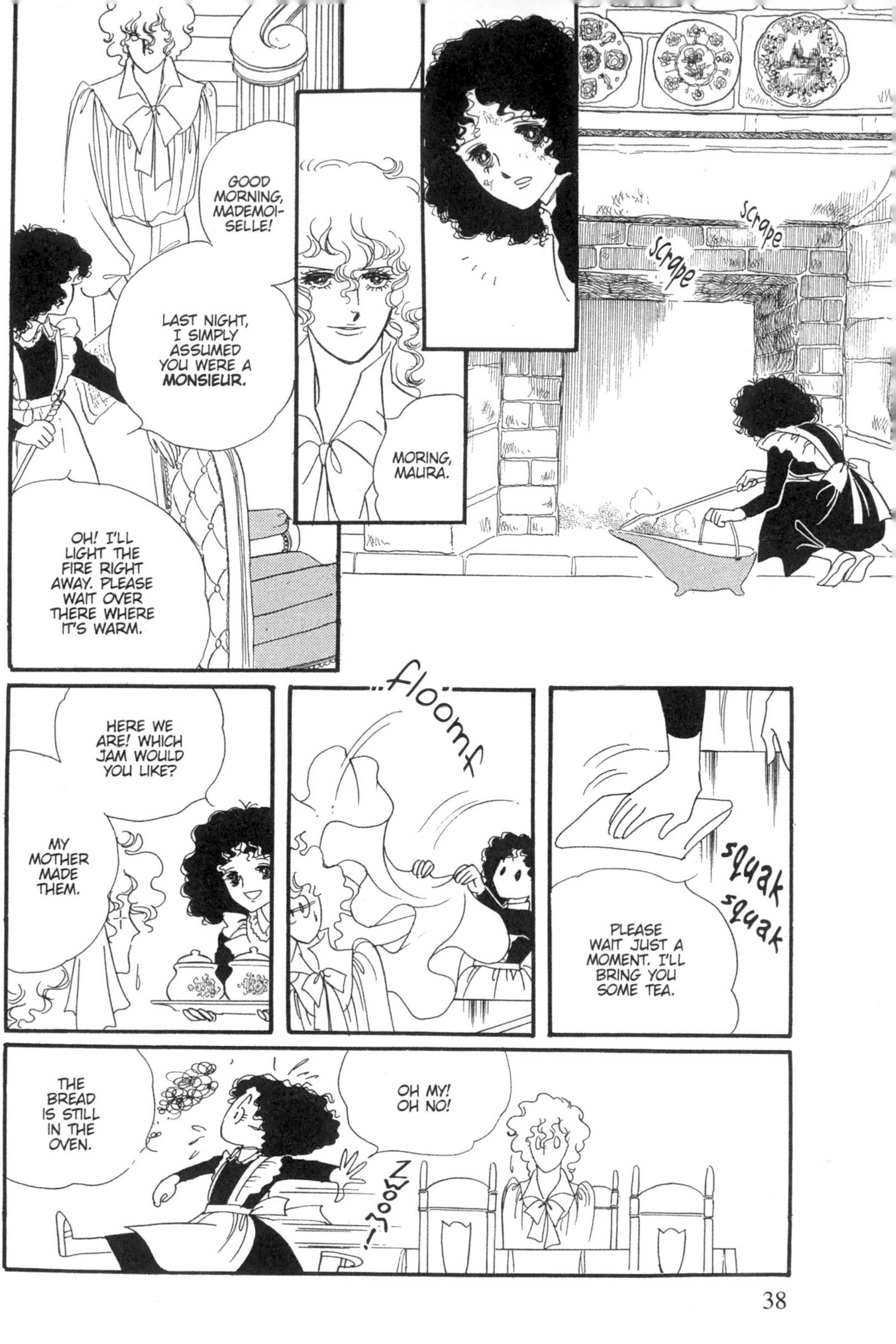
SCRAPE
SCRAPE
MORING, MAURA.
GOOD MORNING, MADEMOISELLE!
LAST NIGHT, I SIMPLY ASSUMED YOU WERE A **MONSIEUR.**
OH! I'LL LIGHT THE FIRE RIGHT AWAY. PLEASE WAIT OVER THERE WHERE IT'S WARM.
SQUAK
SQUAK
PLEASE WAIT JUST A MOMENT. I'LL BRING YOU SOME TEA.
FLOOMF
HERE WE ARE! WHICH JAM WOULD YOU LIKE?
MY MOTHER MADE THEM.
OH MY! OH NO!
THE BREAD IS STILL IN THE OVEN.
ZWOOP!

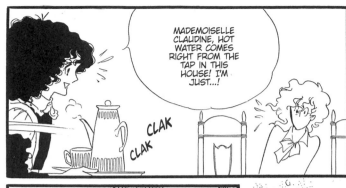

MADEMOISELLE CLAUDINE, HOT WATER COMES RIGHT FROM THE TAP IN THIS HOUSE! I'M JUST...!
CLAK CLAK
UM. IS SOME-THING...?
MM HMM.
YOU REALLY MOVE, HM?
AND THE WAY YOU TALK IS LIKE A GROWN-UP, VERY IMPRESSIVE.
WELL! I'M NOT A *CHILD*, YOU KNOW.
I GOT MY PERIOD ALREADY. I CAN DO ANY JOB. MY BODY'S JUST TINY.
OH. I SEE.

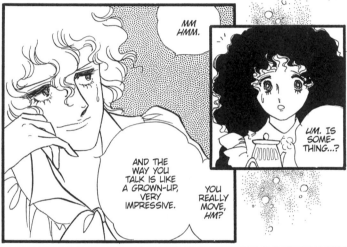

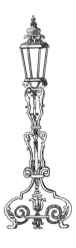

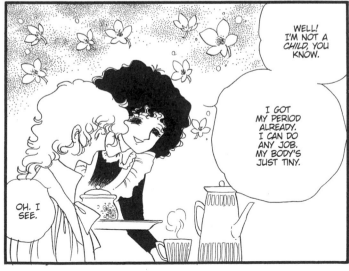

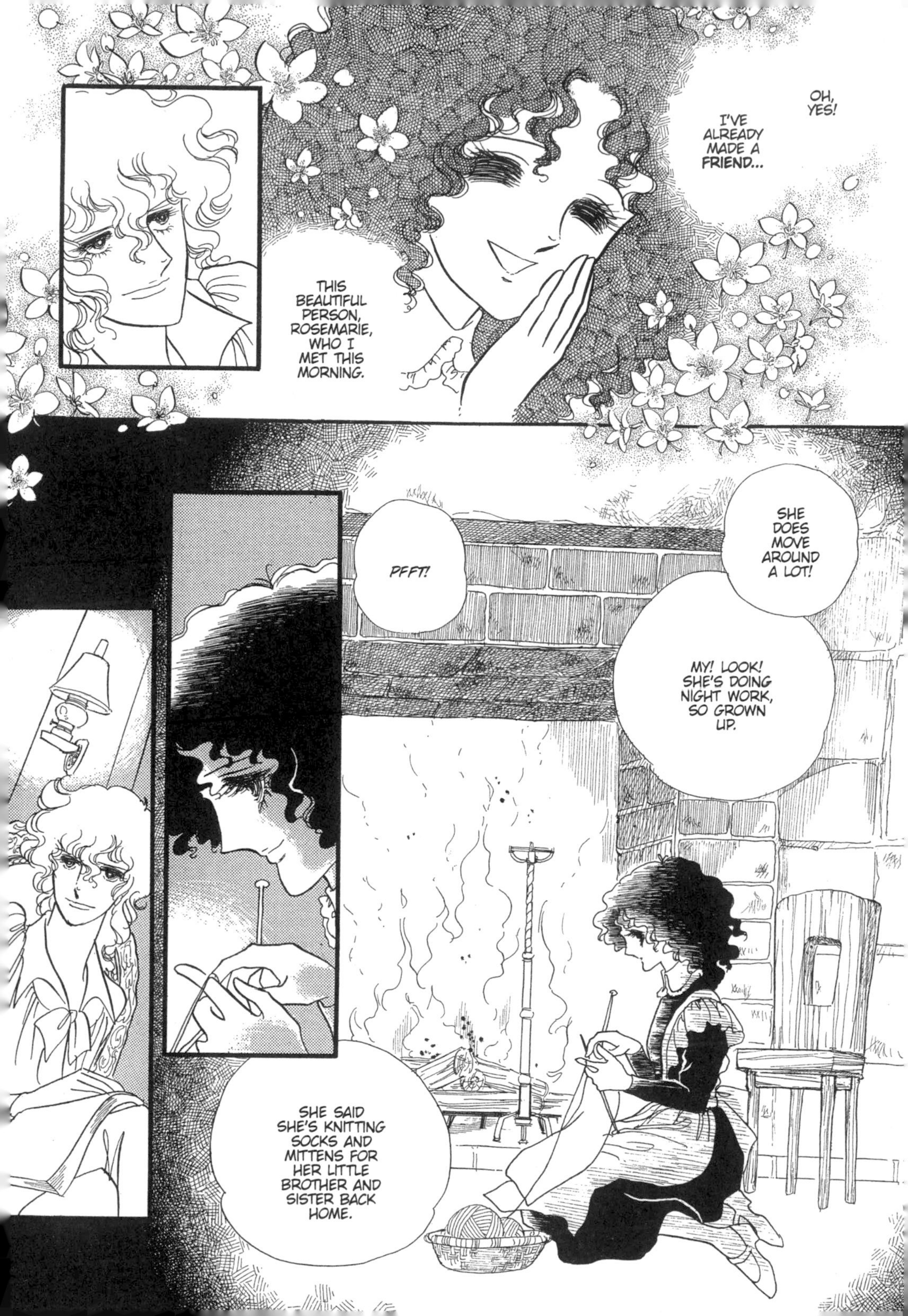
OH, YES!
I'VE ALREADY MADE A FRIEND...
THIS BEAUTIFUL PERSON, ROSEMARIE, WHO I MET THIS MORNING.
SHE DOES MOVE AROUND A LOT!
MY! LOOK! SHE'S DOING NIGHT WORK, SO GROWN UP.
PFFT!
SHE SAID SHE'S KNITTING SOCKS AND MITTENS FOR HER LITTLE BROTHER AND SISTER BACK HOME.

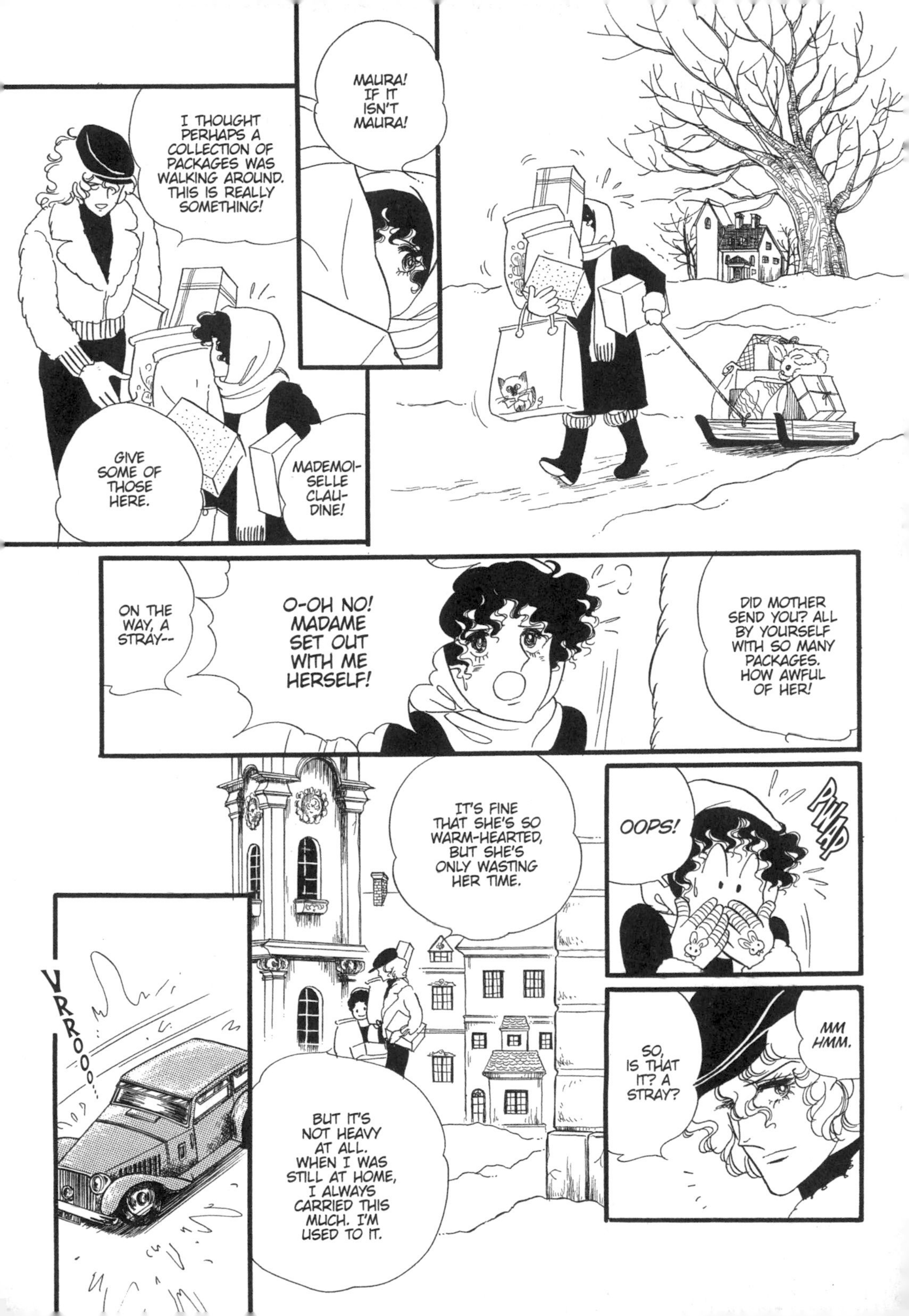
MAURA! IF IT ISN'T MAURA!
I THOUGHT PERHAPS A COLLECTION OF PACKAGES WAS WALKING AROUND. THIS IS REALLY SOMETHING!
MADEMOI-SELLE CLAU-DINE!
GIVE SOME OF THOSE HERE.
DID MOTHER SEND YOU? ALL BY YOURSELF WITH SO MANY PACKAGES. HOW AWFUL OF HER!
O-OH NO! MADAME SET OUT WITH ME HERSELF!
ON THE WAY, A STRAY--
PWAP
OOPS!
MM HMM.
SO, IS THAT IT? A STRAY?
IT'S FINE THAT SHE'S SO WARM-HEARTED, BUT SHE'S ONLY WASTING HER TIME.
BUT IT'S NOT HEAVY AT ALL. WHEN I WAS STILL AT HOME, I ALWAYS CARRIED THIS MUCH. I'M USED TO IT.
VRROOO...

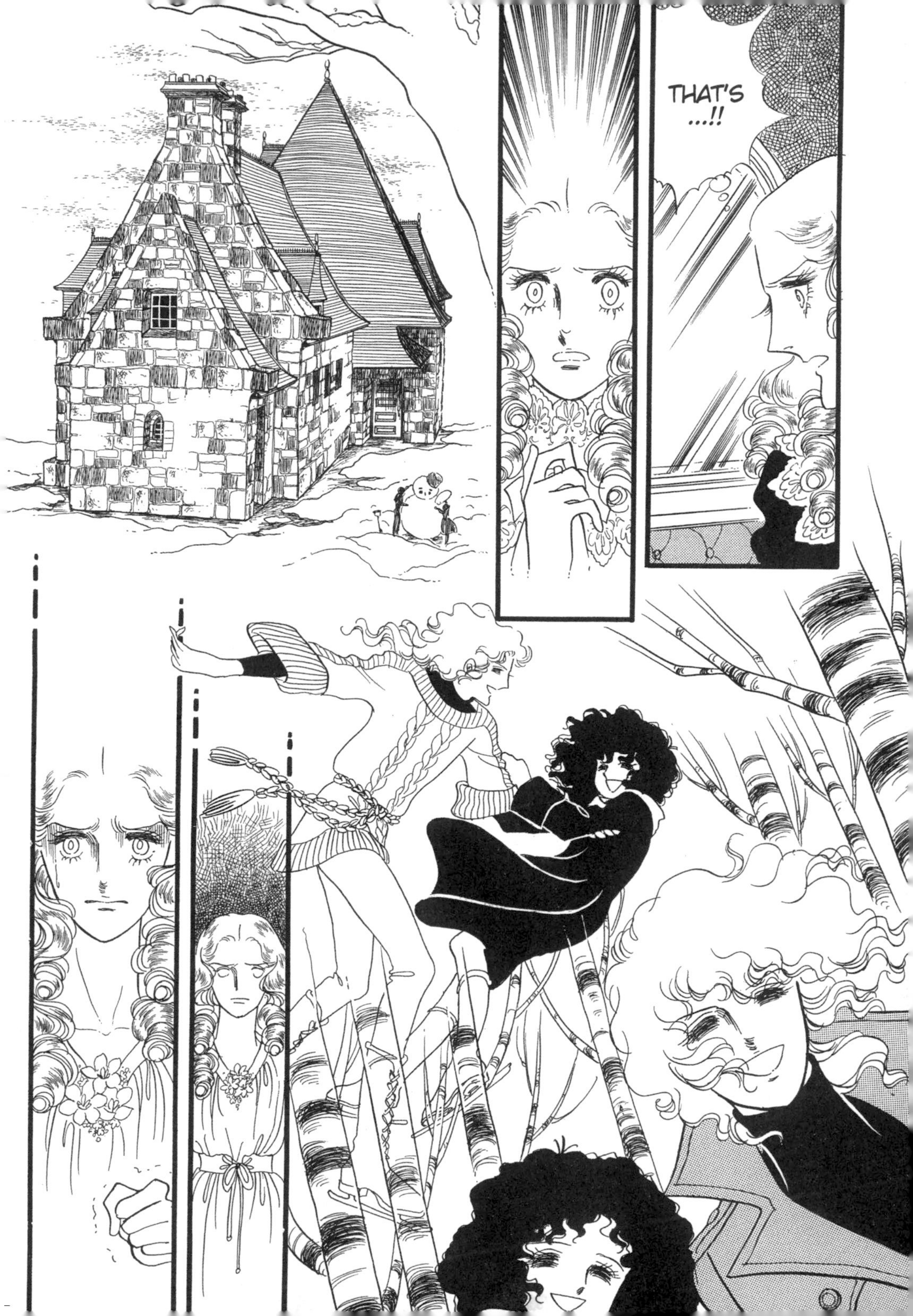
THAT'S ...!!

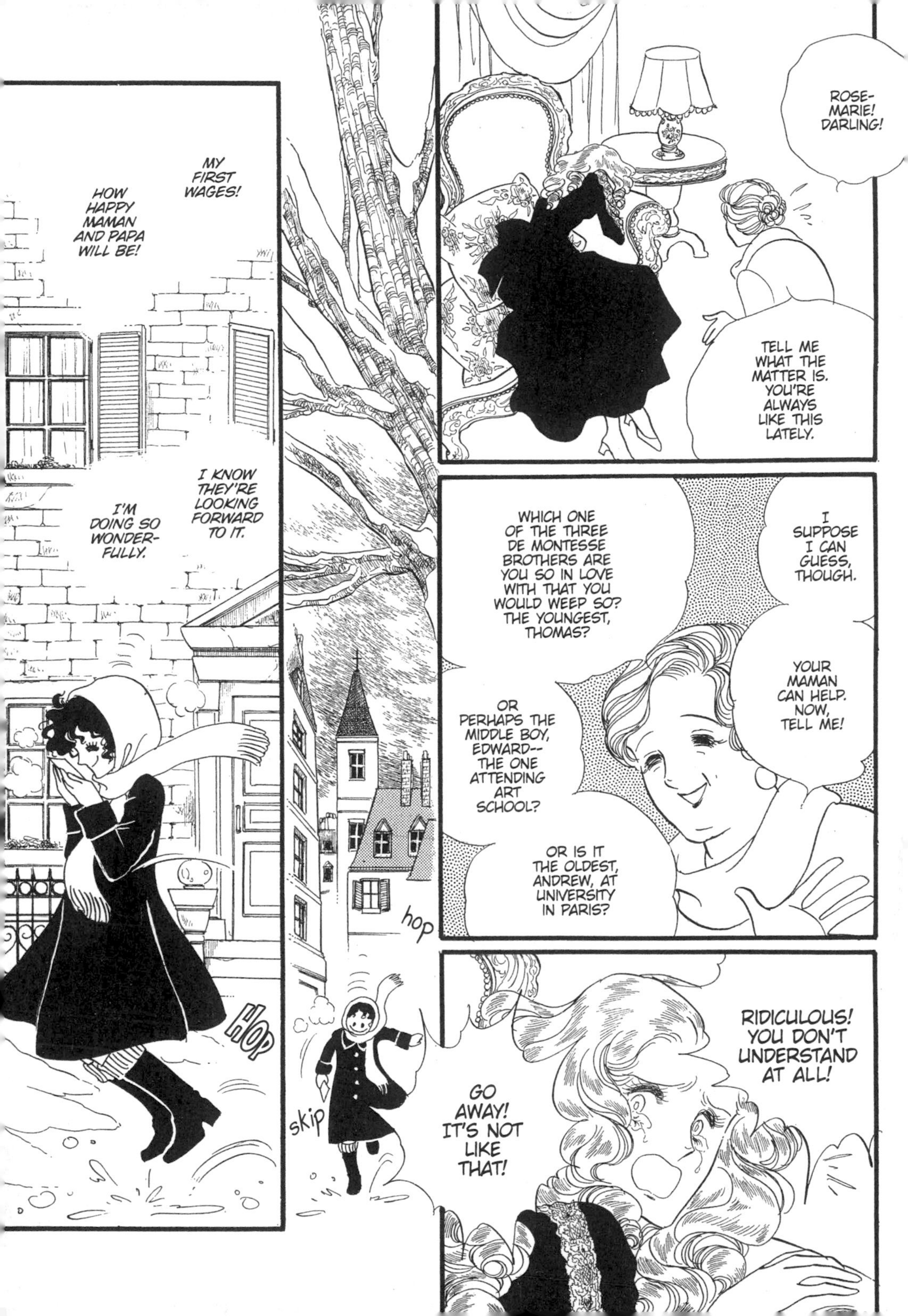
ROSE-MARIE! DARLING!
TELL ME WHAT THE MATTER IS. YOU'RE ALWAYS LIKE THIS LATELY.
I SUPPOSE I CAN GUESS, THOUGH.
WHICH ONE OF THE THREE DE MONTESSE BROTHERS ARE YOU SO IN LOVE WITH THAT YOU WOULD WEEP SO? THE YOUNGEST, THOMAS?
OR PERHAPS THE MIDDLE BOY, EDWARD-- THE ONE ATTENDING ART SCHOOL?
OR IS IT THE OLDEST, ANDREW, AT UNIVERSITY IN PARIS?
YOUR MAMAN CAN HELP. NOW, TELL ME!
RIDICULOUS! YOU DON'T UNDERSTAND AT ALL!
GO AWAY! IT'S NOT LIKE THAT!
hop
skip
MY FIRST WAGES!
HOW HAPPY MAMAN AND PAPA WILL BE!
I KNOW THEY'RE LOOKING FORWARD TO IT.
I'M DOING SO WONDERFULLY.
HOP

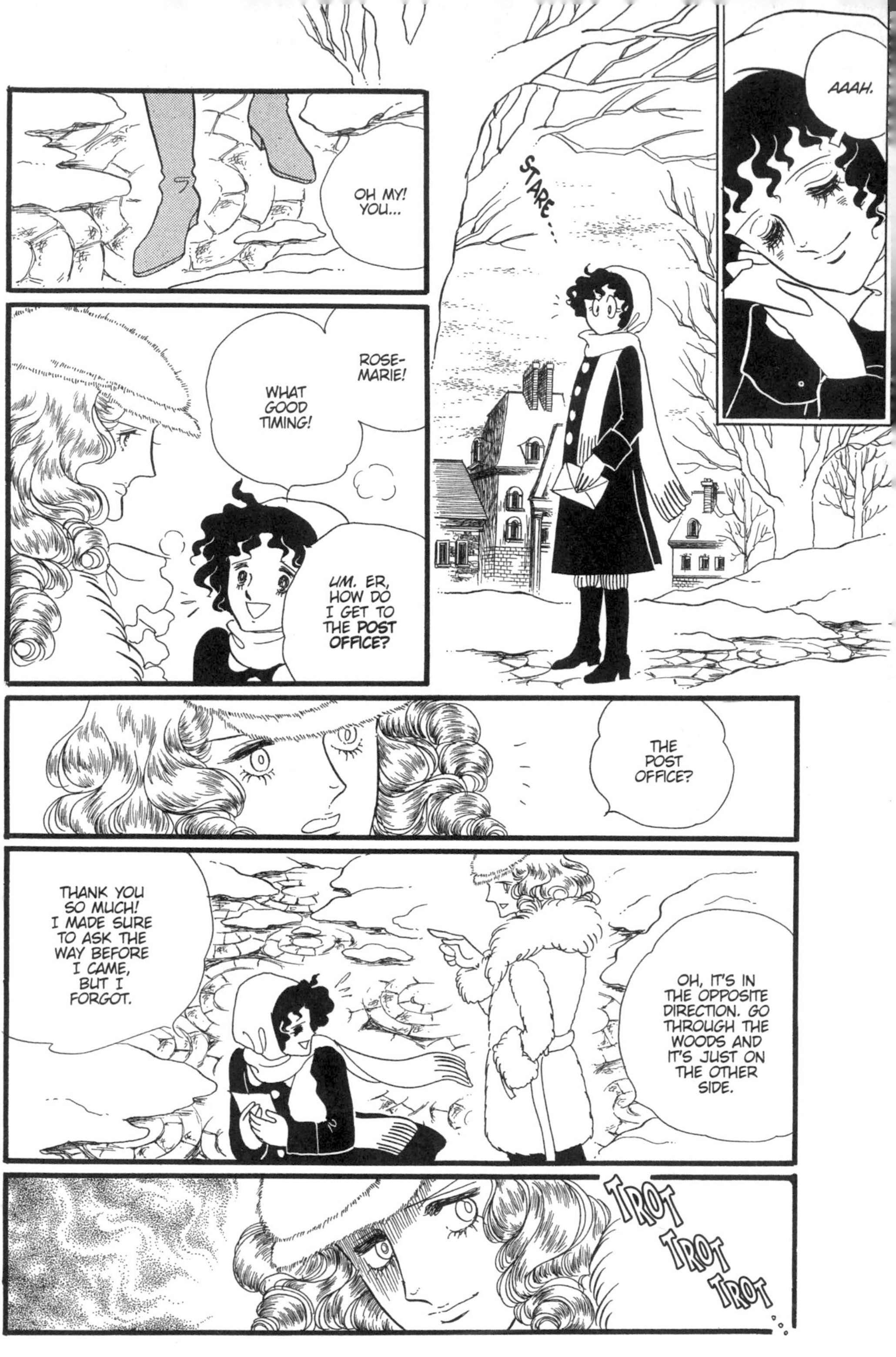
AAAH.
STARE...
OH MY! YOU...
ROSE-MARIE!
WHAT GOOD TIMING!
UM. ER, HOW DO I GET TO THE POST OFFICE?
THE POST OFFICE?
OH, IT'S IN THE OPPOSITE DIRECTION. GO THROUGH THE WOODS AND IT'S JUST ON THE OTHER SIDE.
THANK YOU SO MUCH! I MADE SURE TO ASK THE WAY BEFORE I CAME, BUT I FORGOT.
TROT TROT TROT

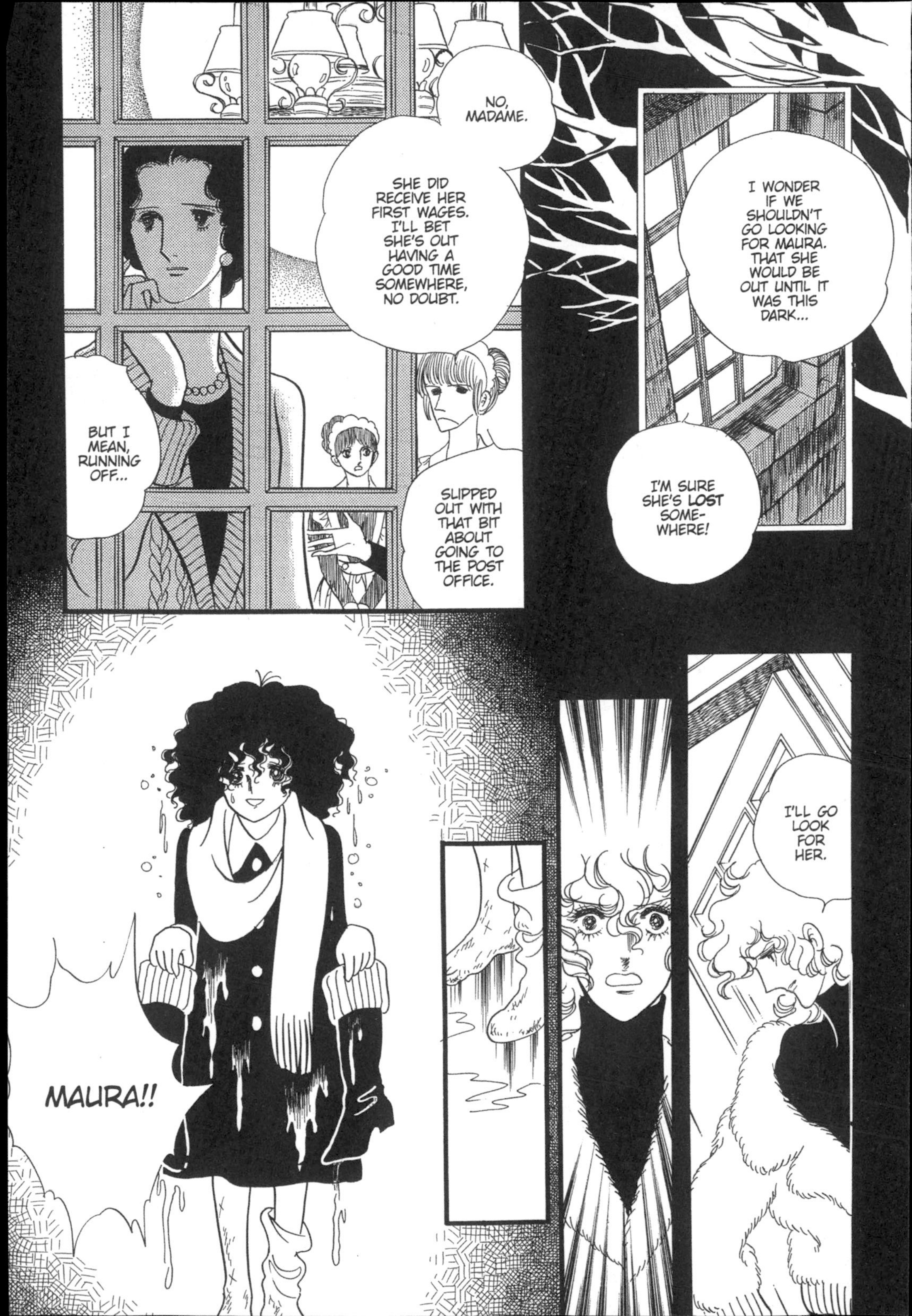
I WONDER IF WE SHOULDN'T GO LOOKING FOR MAURA. THAT SHE WOULD BE OUT UNTIL IT WAS THIS DARK...
I'M SURE SHE'S **LOST** SOME-WHERE!
NO, MADAME.
SHE DID RECEIVE HER FIRST WAGES. I'LL BET SHE'S OUT HAVING A GOOD TIME SOMEWHERE, NO DOUBT.
BUT I MEAN, RUNNING OFF...
SLIPPED OUT WITH THAT BIT ABOUT GOING TO THE POST OFFICE.
I'LL GO LOOK FOR HER.
MAURA!!

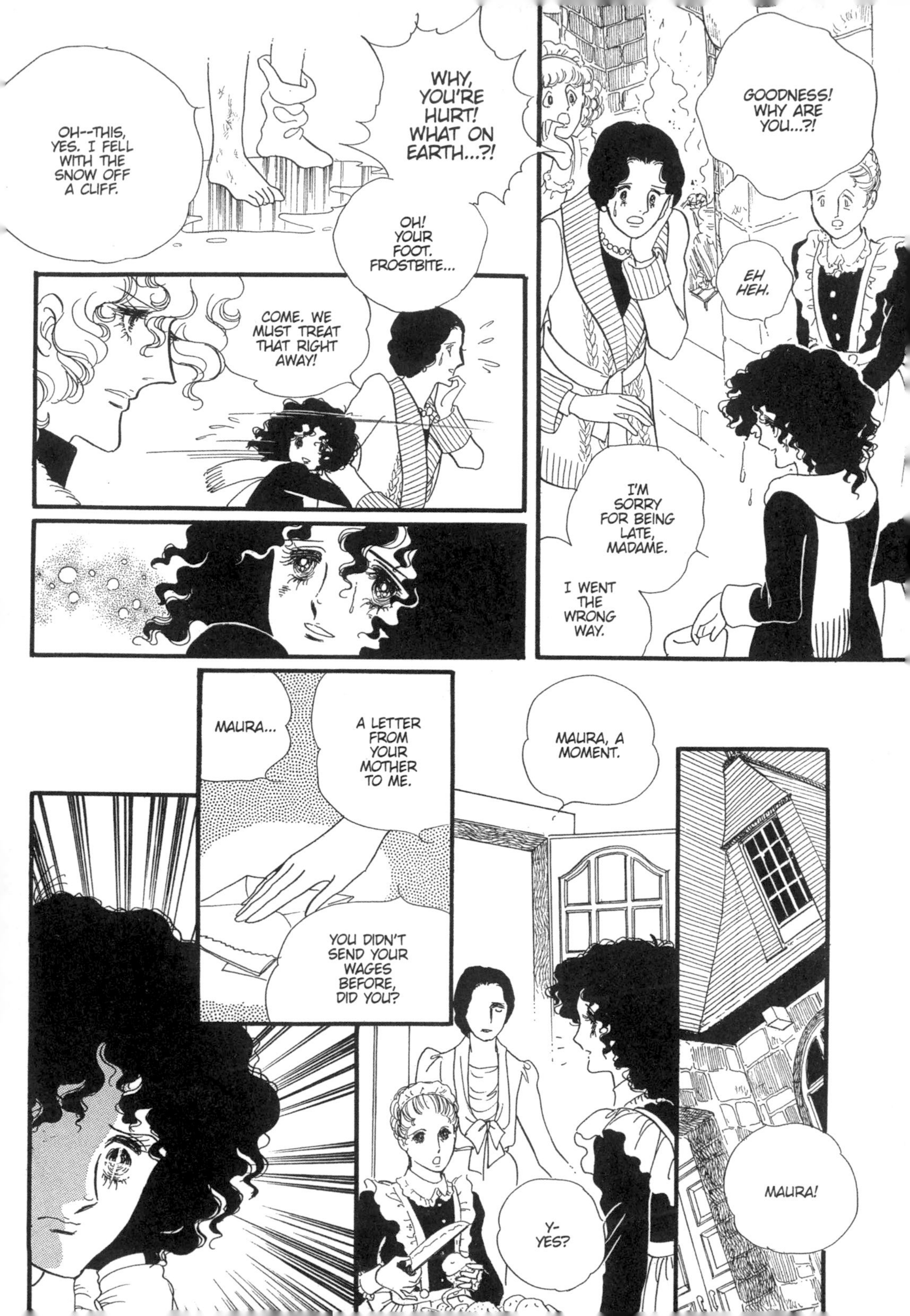
GOODNESS! WHY ARE YOU...?!
EH HEH.
I'M SORRY FOR BEING LATE, MADAME.
I WENT THE WRONG WAY.
WHY, YOU'RE HURT! WHAT ON EARTH...?!
OH--THIS, YES. I FELL WITH THE SNOW OFF A CLIFF.
OH! YOUR FOOT. FROSTBITE...
COME. WE MUST TREAT THAT RIGHT AWAY!
MAURA!
MAURA, A MOMENT.
Y-YES?
MAURA...
A LETTER FROM YOUR MOTHER TO ME.
YOU DIDN'T SEND YOUR WAGES BEFORE, DID YOU?

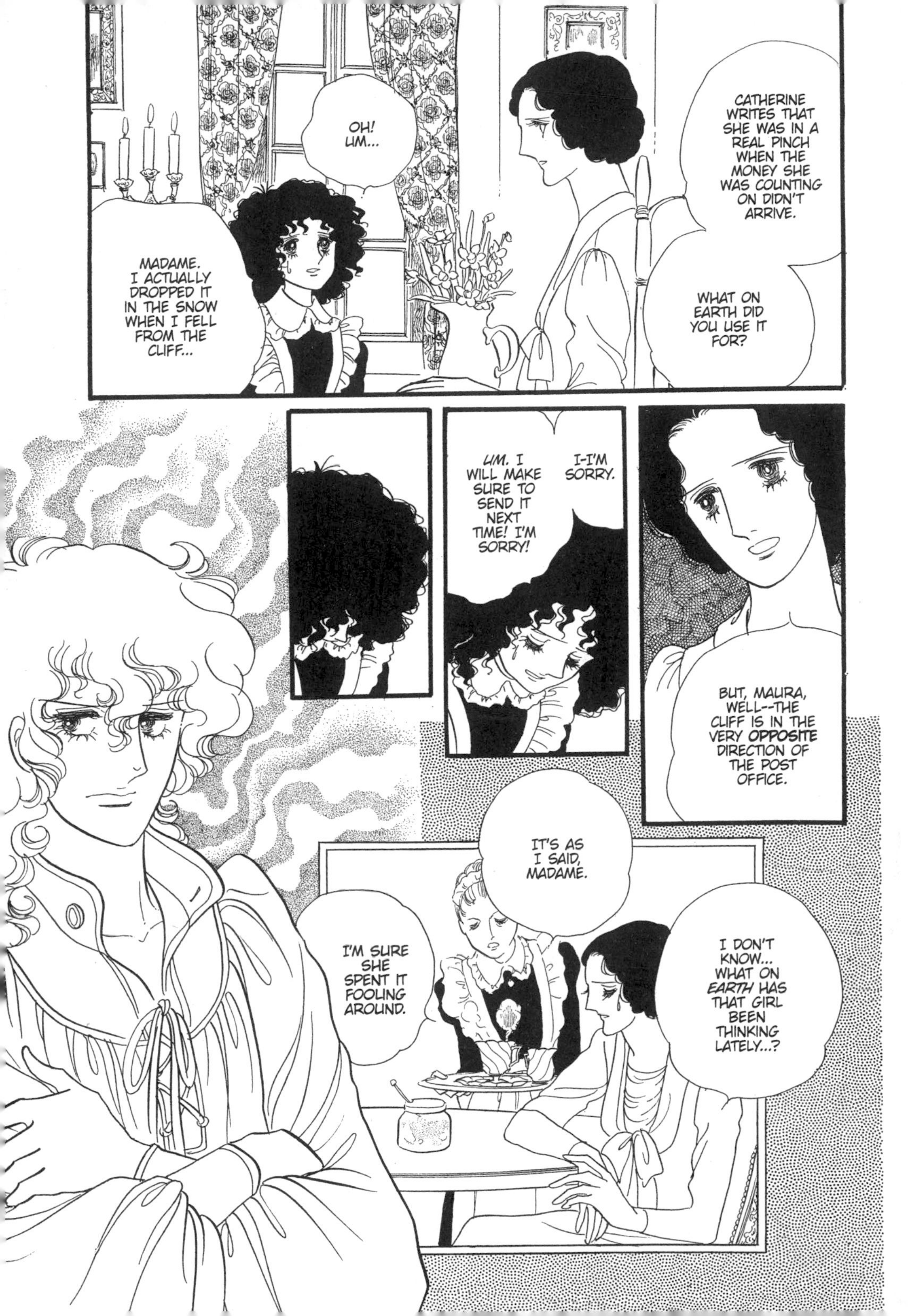
CATHERINE WRITES THAT SHE WAS IN A REAL PINCH WHEN THE MONEY SHE WAS COUNTING ON DIDN'T ARRIVE.
WHAT ON EARTH DID YOU USE IT FOR?
OH! UM...
MADAME. I ACTUALLY DROPPED IT IN THE SNOW WHEN I FELL FROM THE CLIFF...
BUT, MAURA, WELL--THE CLIFF IS IN THE VERY **OPPOSITE** DIRECTION OF THE POST OFFICE.
I-I'M SORRY.
UM. I WILL MAKE SURE TO SEND IT NEXT TIME! I'M SORRY!
IT'S AS I SAID, MADAME.
I'M SURE SHE SPENT IT FOOLING AROUND.
I DON'T KNOW... WHAT ON *EARTH* HAS THAT GIRL BEEN THINKING LATELY...?

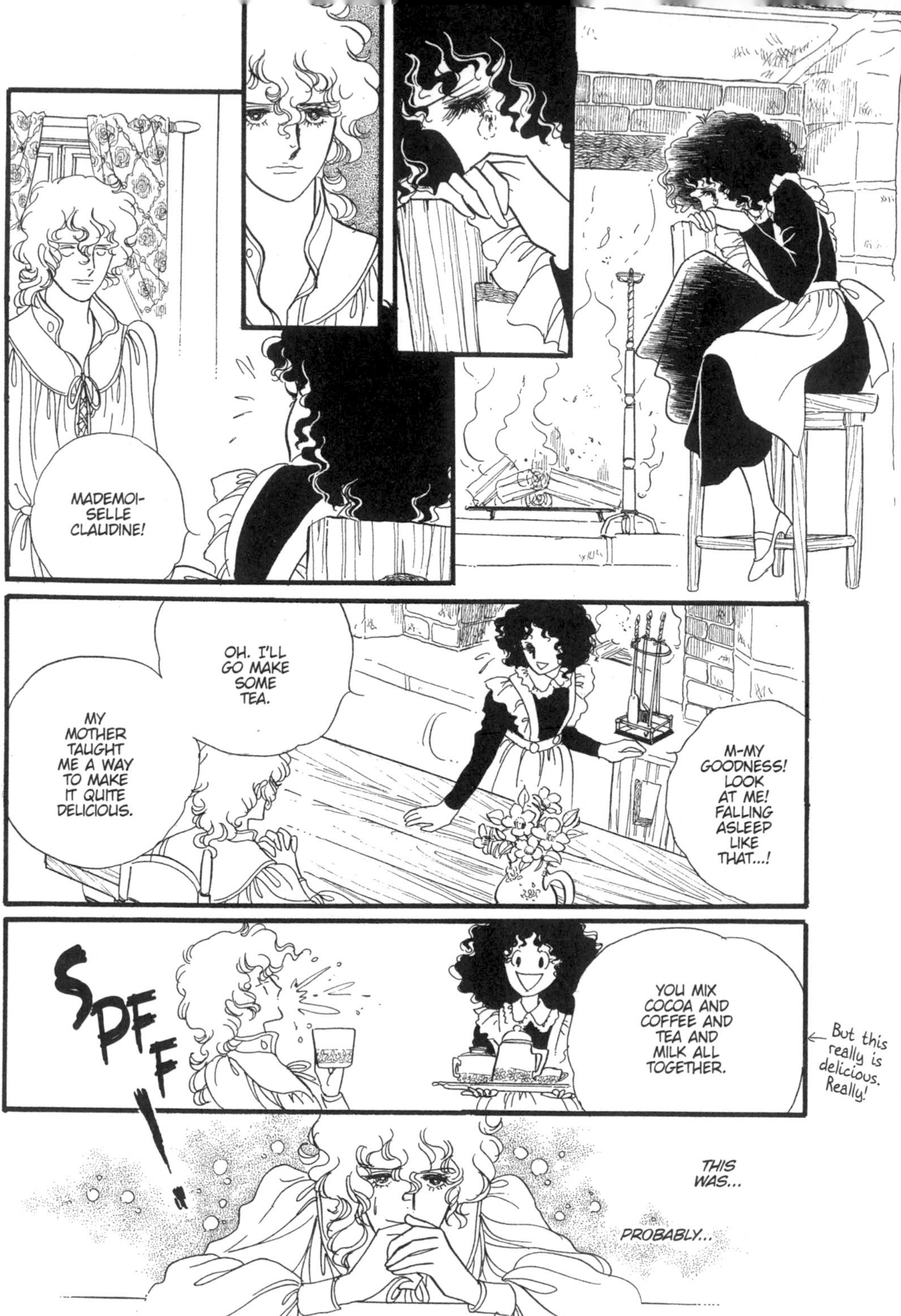
MADEMOI-SELLE CLAUDINE!
M-MY GOODNESS! LOOK AT ME! FALLING ASLEEP LIKE THAT...!
OH. I'LL GO MAKE SOME TEA.
MY MOTHER TAUGHT ME A WAY TO MAKE IT QUITE DELICIOUS.
But this really is delicious. Really!
YOU MIX COCOA AND COFFEE AND TEA AND MILK ALL TOGETHER.
SPFF!!
THIS WAS...
PROBABLY...

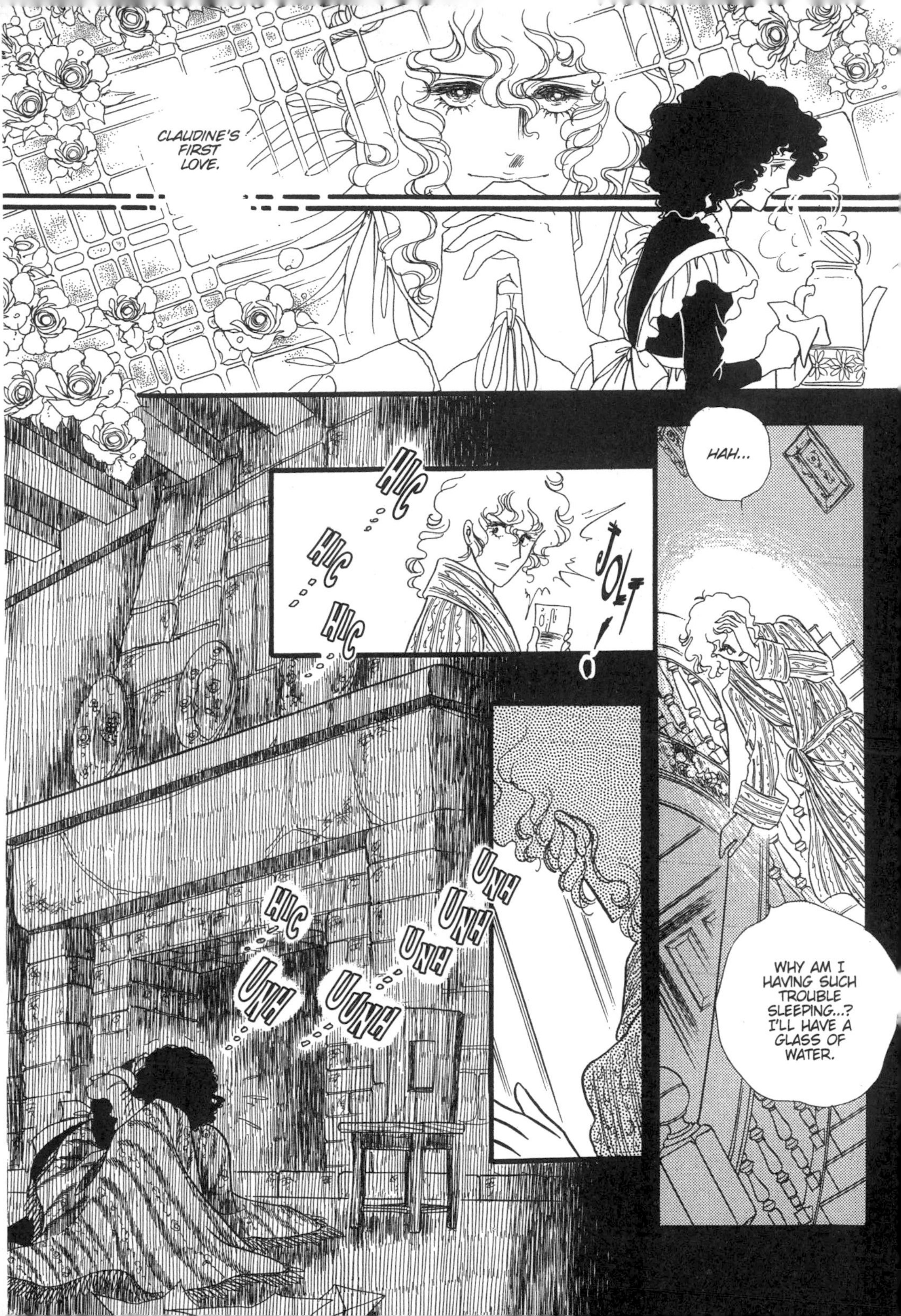
CLAUDINE'S FIRST LOVE.
HAH...
WHY AM I HAVING SUCH TROUBLE SLEEPING...? I'LL HAVE A GLASS OF WATER.
JOLT!
HIC
HIC
HIC
UNH
UNH
UNH
HIC
UUNH
UNH

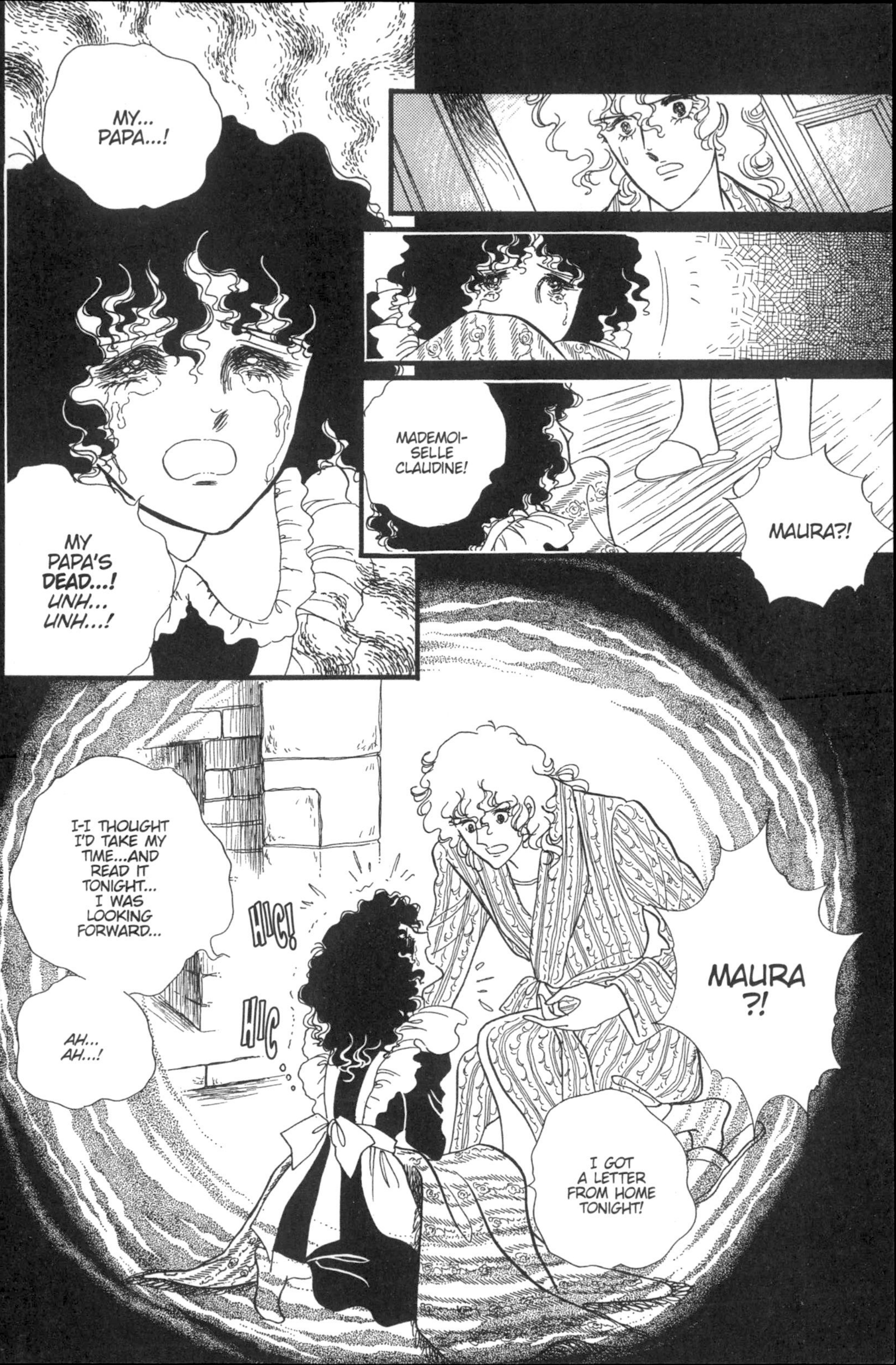
MAURA?!
MADEMOI-SELLE CLAUDINE!
MY... PAPA...!
MY PAPA'S DEAD...! UNH... UNH...!
MAURA ?!
I GOT A LETTER FROM HOME TONIGHT!
HIC!
HIC
I-I THOUGHT I'D TAKE MY TIME...AND READ IT TONIGHT... I WAS LOOKING FORWARD...
AH... AH...!

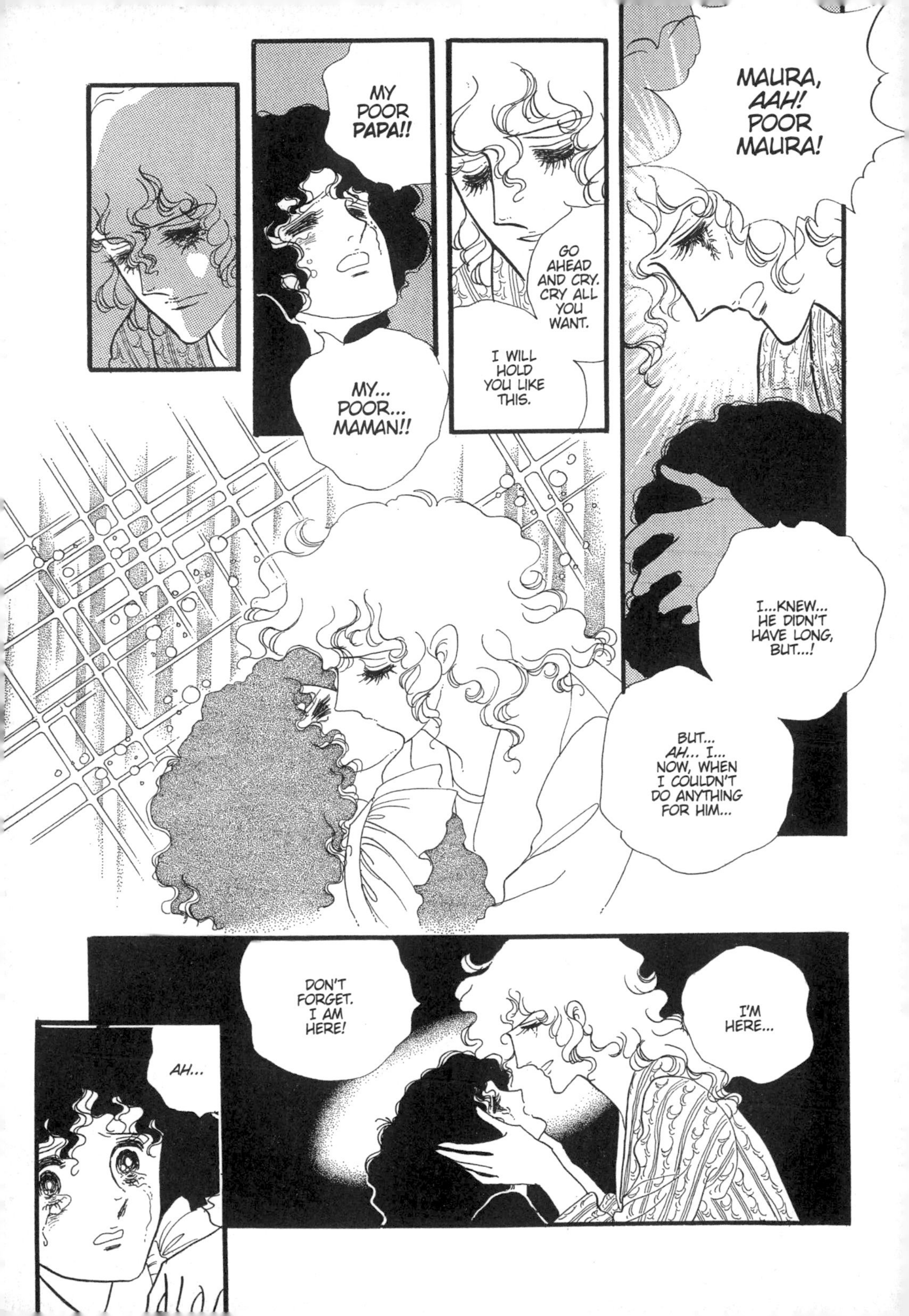
MAURA, *AAH!* POOR MAURA!
I...KNEW... HE DIDN'T HAVE LONG, BUT...!
BUT... *AH...* I... NOW, WHEN I COULDN'T DO ANYTHING FOR HIM...
GO AHEAD AND CRY. CRY ALL YOU WANT.
I WILL HOLD YOU LIKE THIS.
MY POOR PAPA!!
MY... POOR... MAMAN!!
I'M HERE...
DON'T FORGET. I AM HERE!
AH...

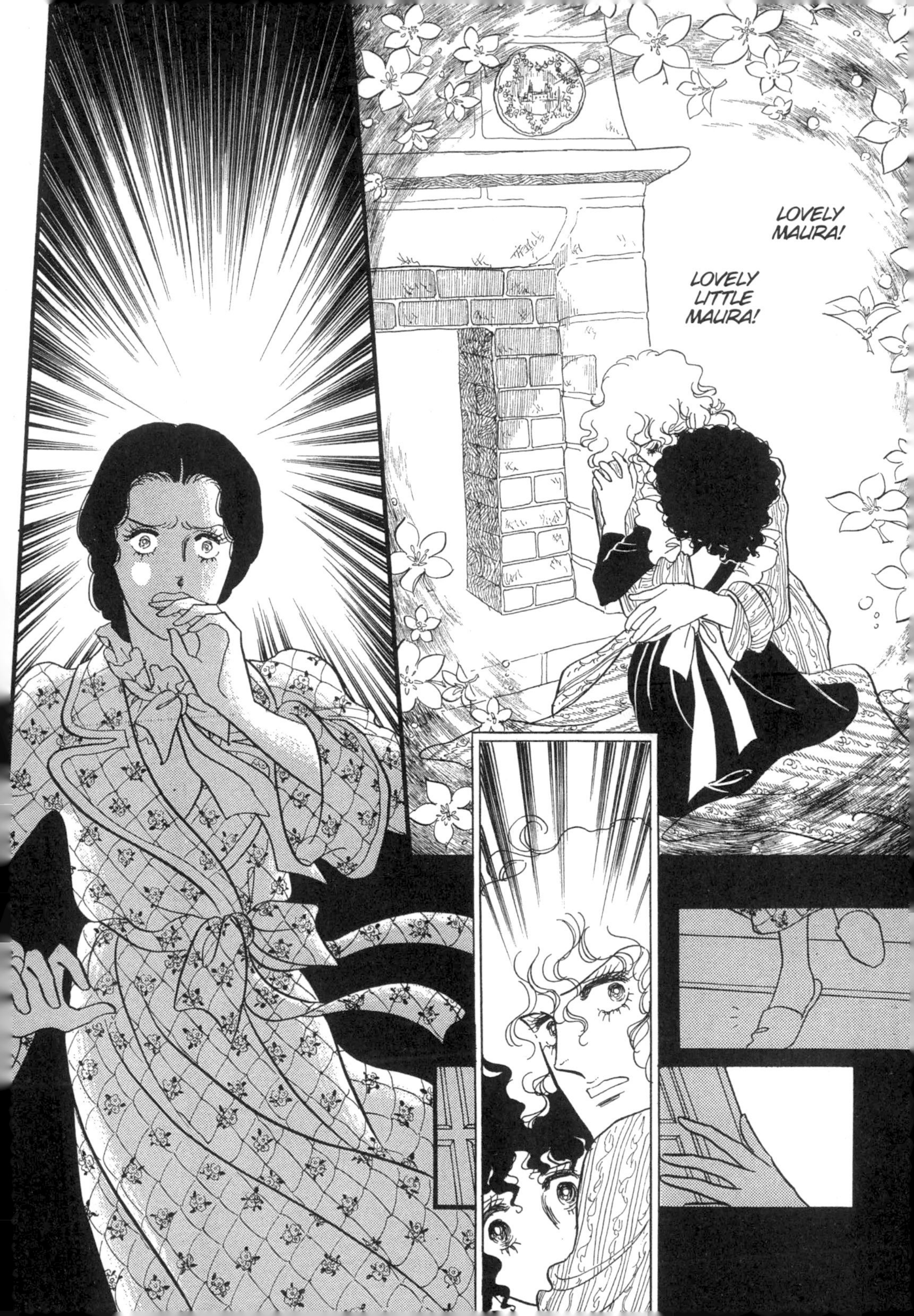
LOVELY MAURA!
LOVELY LITTLE MAURA!

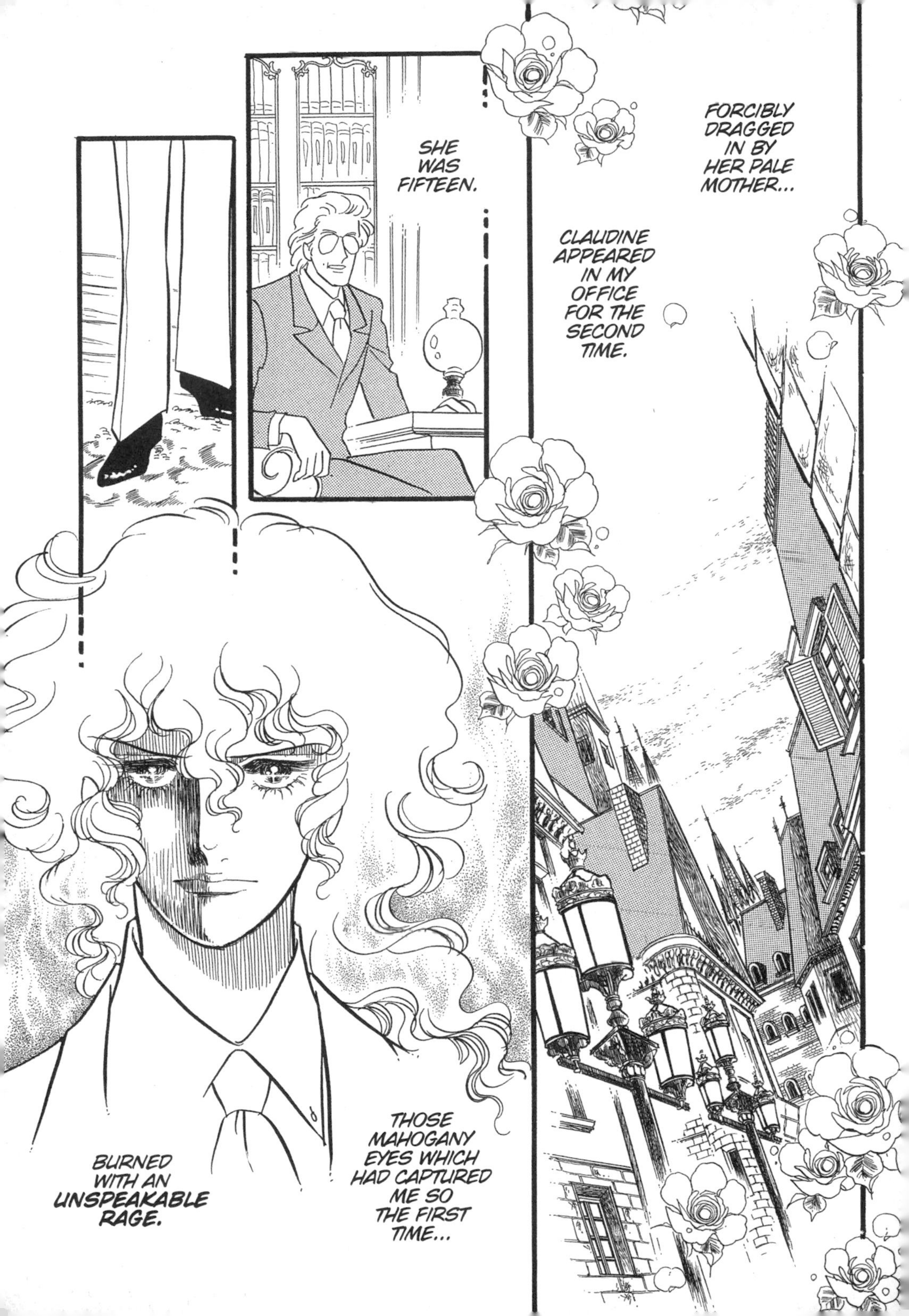
FORCIBLY DRAGGED IN BY HER PALE MOTHER...
CLAUDINE APPEARED IN MY OFFICE FOR THE SECOND TIME.
SHE WAS FIFTEEN.
THOSE MAHOGANY EYES WHICH HAD CAPTURED ME SO THE FIRST TIME...
BURNED WITH AN UNSPEAKABLE RAGE.

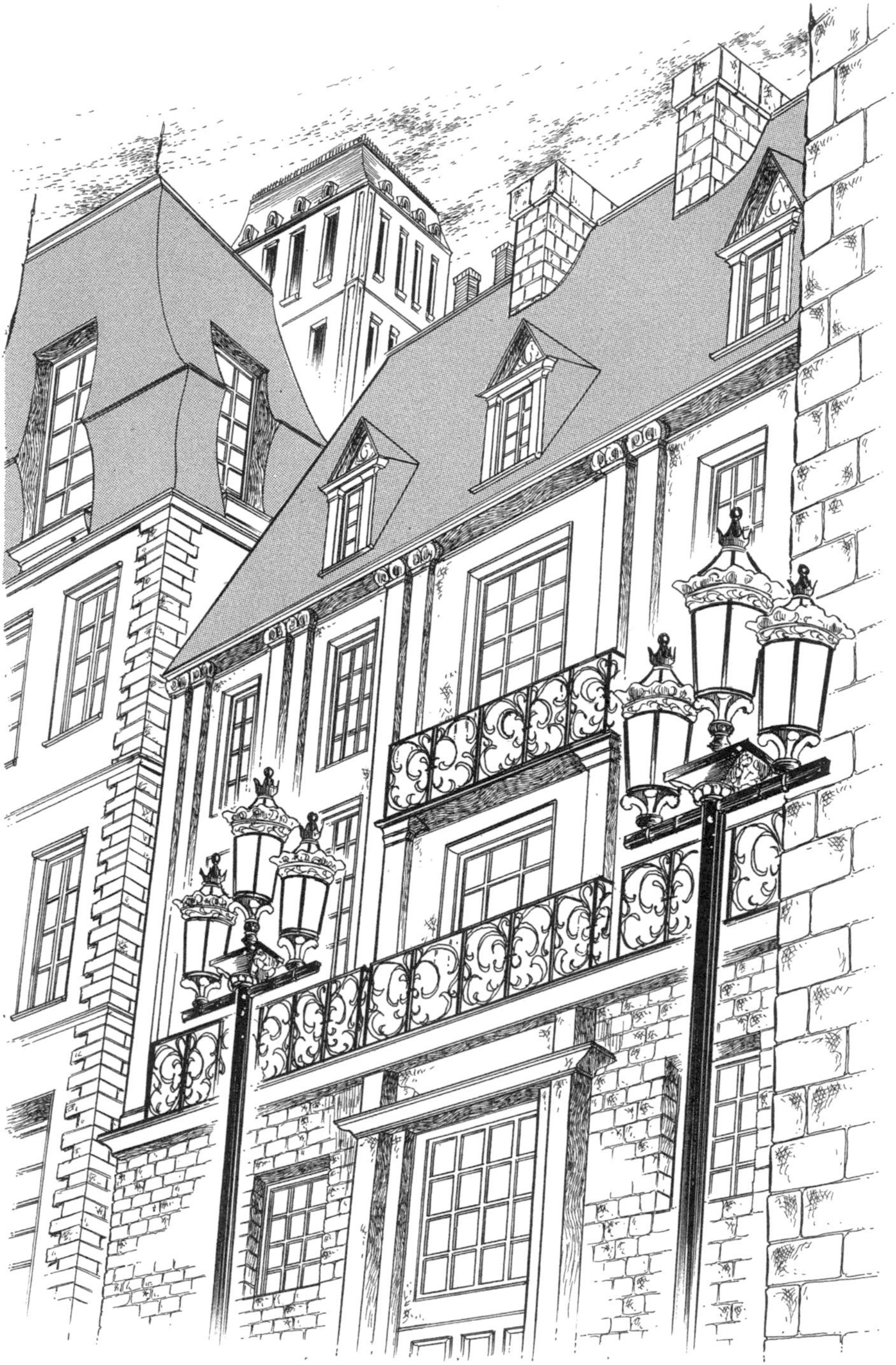

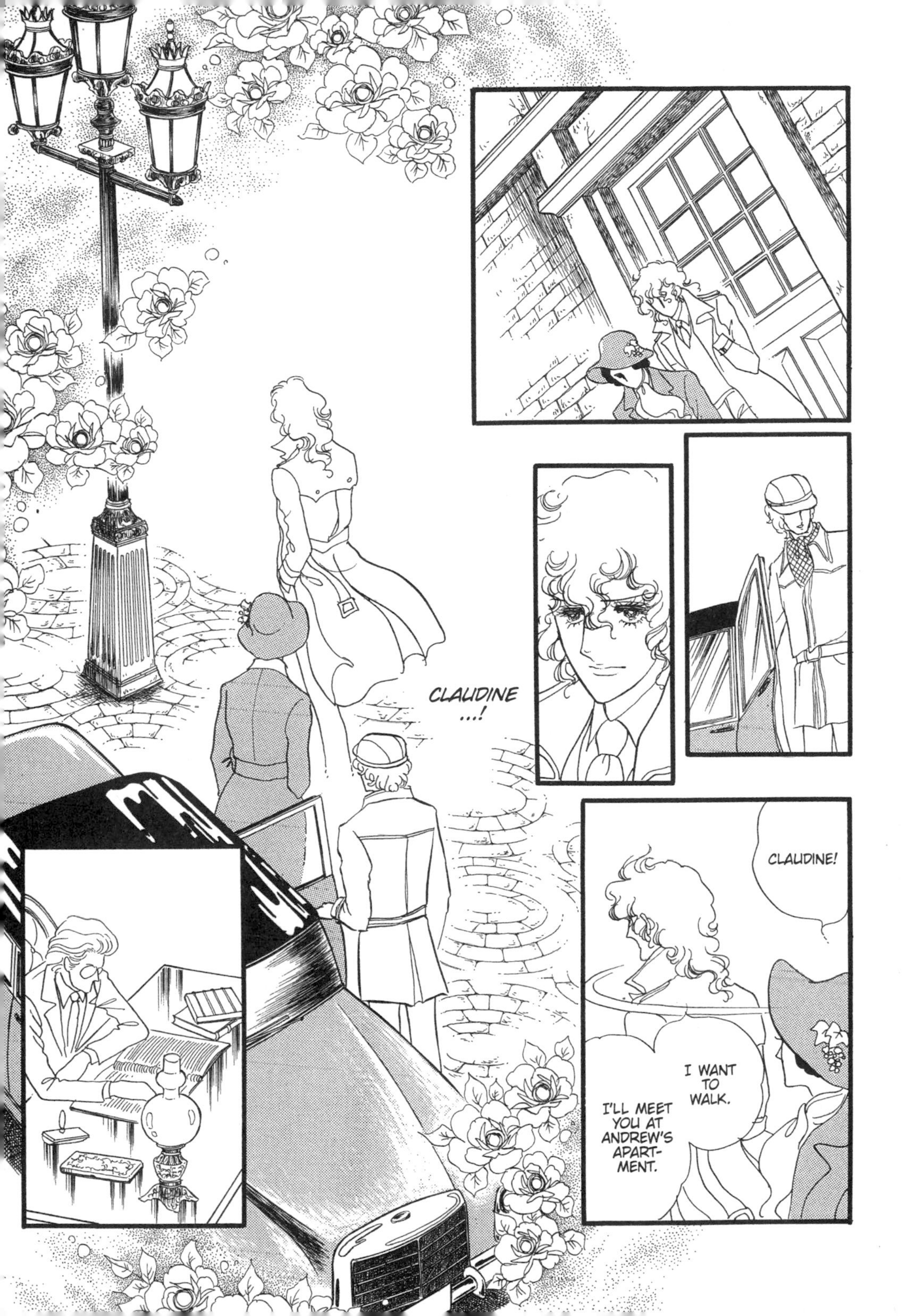
CLAUDINE ...!
CLAUDINE!
I WANT TO WALK.
I'LL MEET YOU AT ANDREW'S APART-MENT.

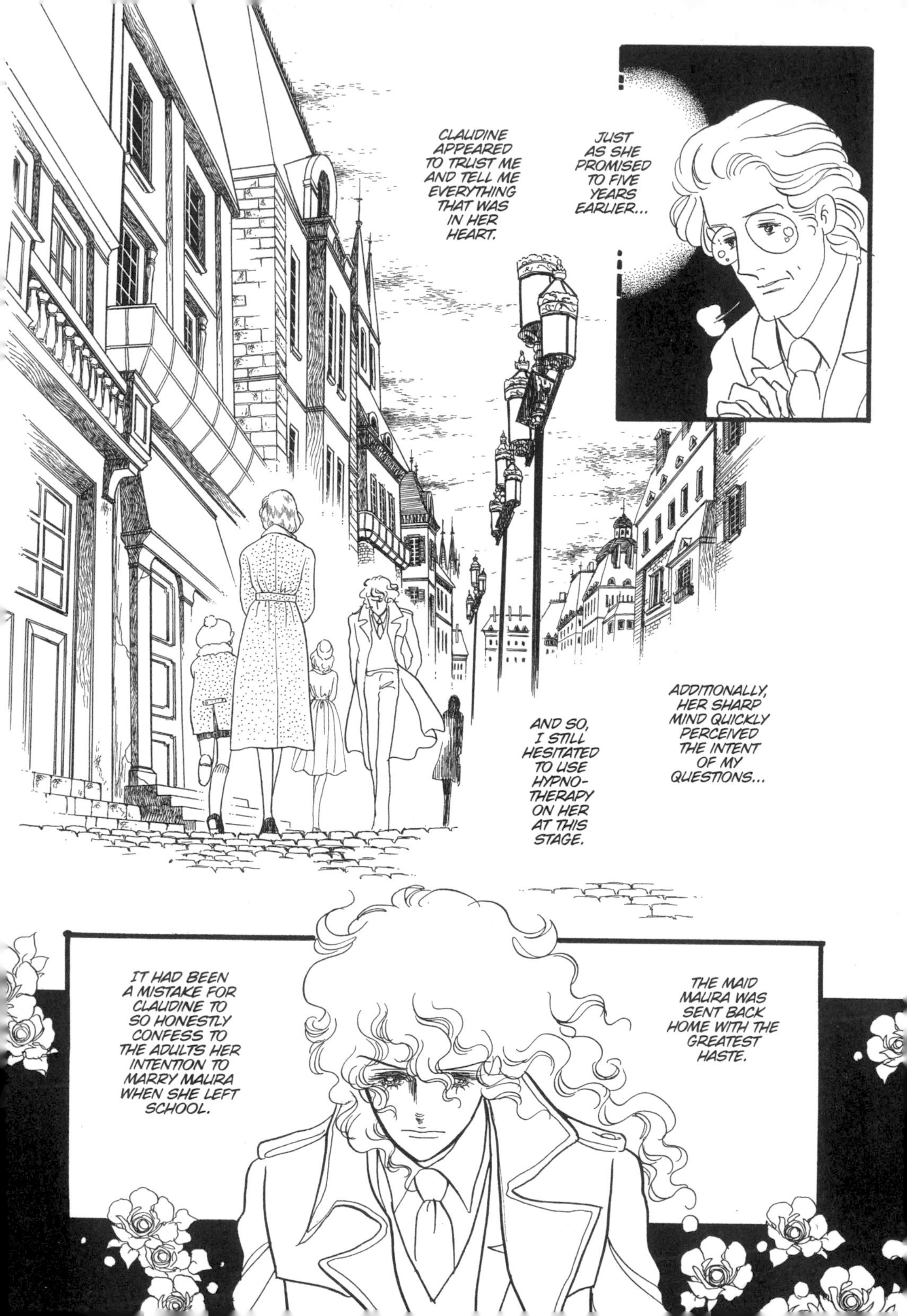
JUST AS SHE PROMISED TO FIVE YEARS EARLIER...
CLAUDINE APPEARED TO TRUST ME AND TELL ME EVERYTHING THAT WAS IN HER HEART.
ADDITIONALLY, HER SHARP MIND QUICKLY PERCEIVED THE INTENT OF MY QUESTIONS...
AND SO, I STILL HESITATED TO USE HYPNO-THERAPY ON HER AT THIS STAGE.
THE MAID MAURA WAS SENT BACK HOME WITH THE GREATEST HASTE.
IT HAD BEEN A MISTAKE FOR CLAUDINE TO SO HONESTLY CONFESS TO THE ADULTS HER INTENTION TO MARRY MAURA WHEN SHE LEFT SCHOOL.

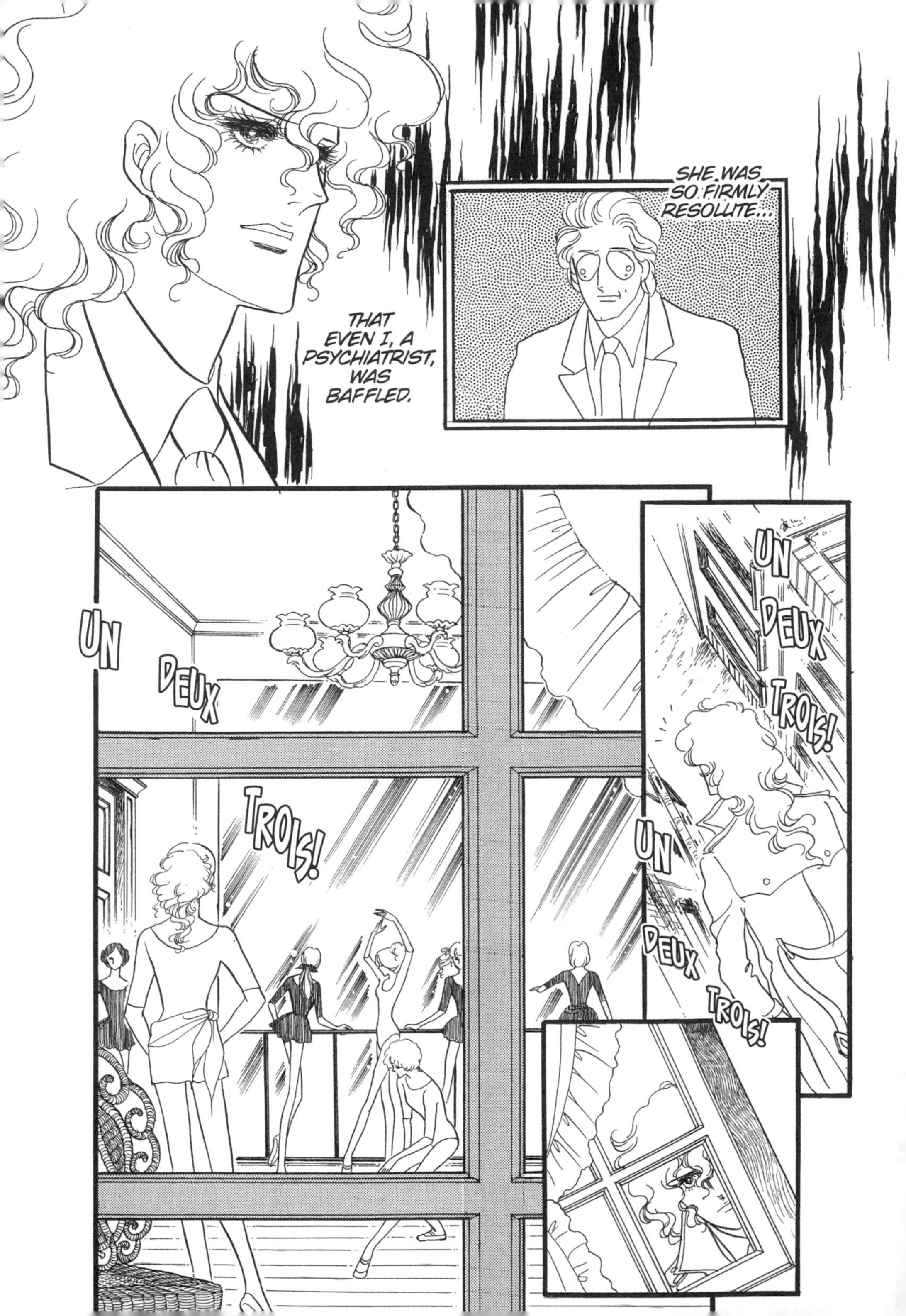
SHE WAS SO FIRMLY RESOLUTE...
THAT EVEN I, A PSYCHIATRIST, WAS BAFFLED.
UN
DEUX
TROIS!
UN
DEUX
TROIS!
UN
DEUX
TROIS!

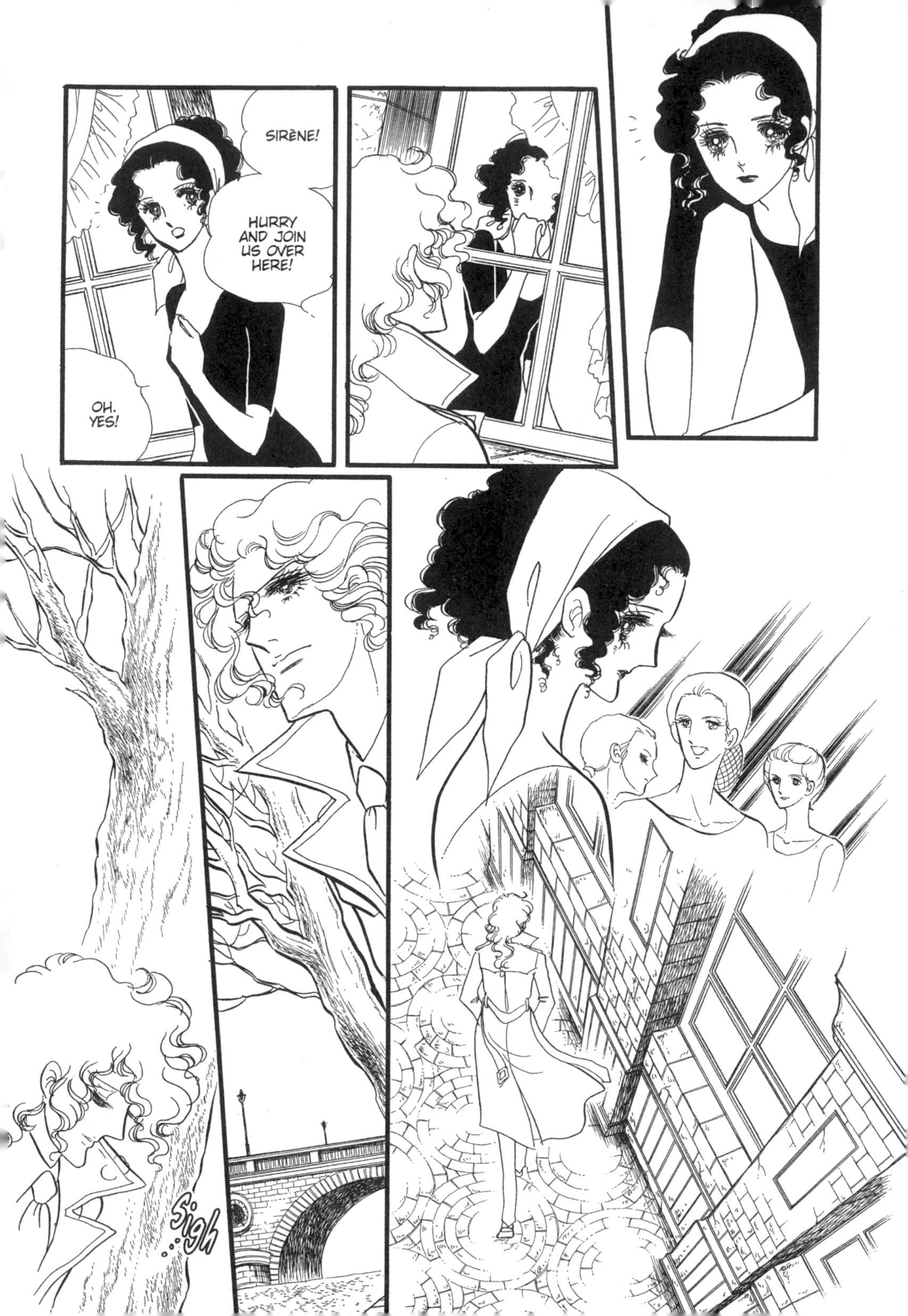
SIRÈNE!
HURRY AND JOIN US OVER HERE!
OH. YES!
Sigh

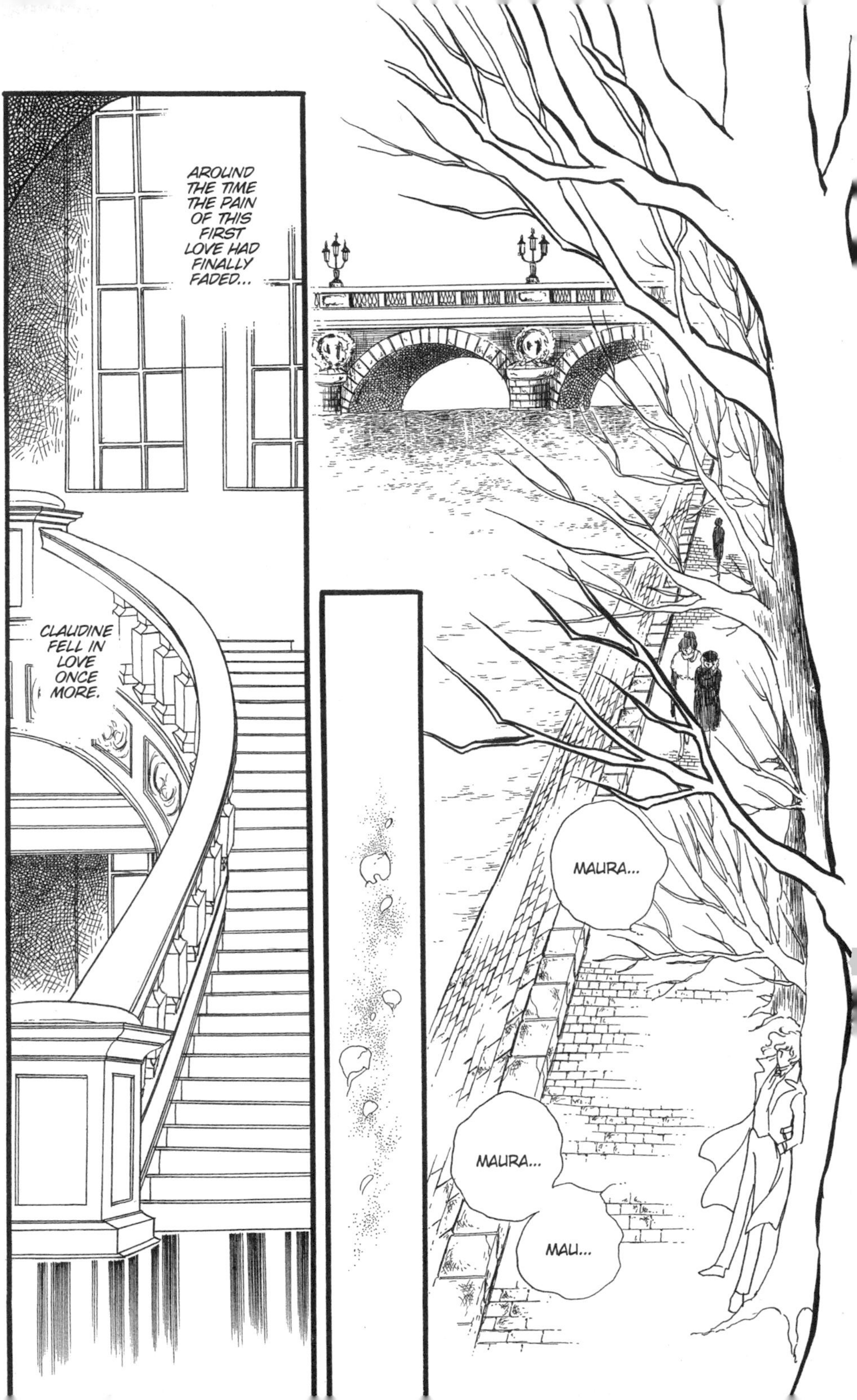
MAURA...
MAURA...
MAU...
AROUND THE TIME THE PAIN OF THIS FIRST LOVE HAD FINALLY FADED...
CLAUDINE FELL IN LOVE ONCE MORE.

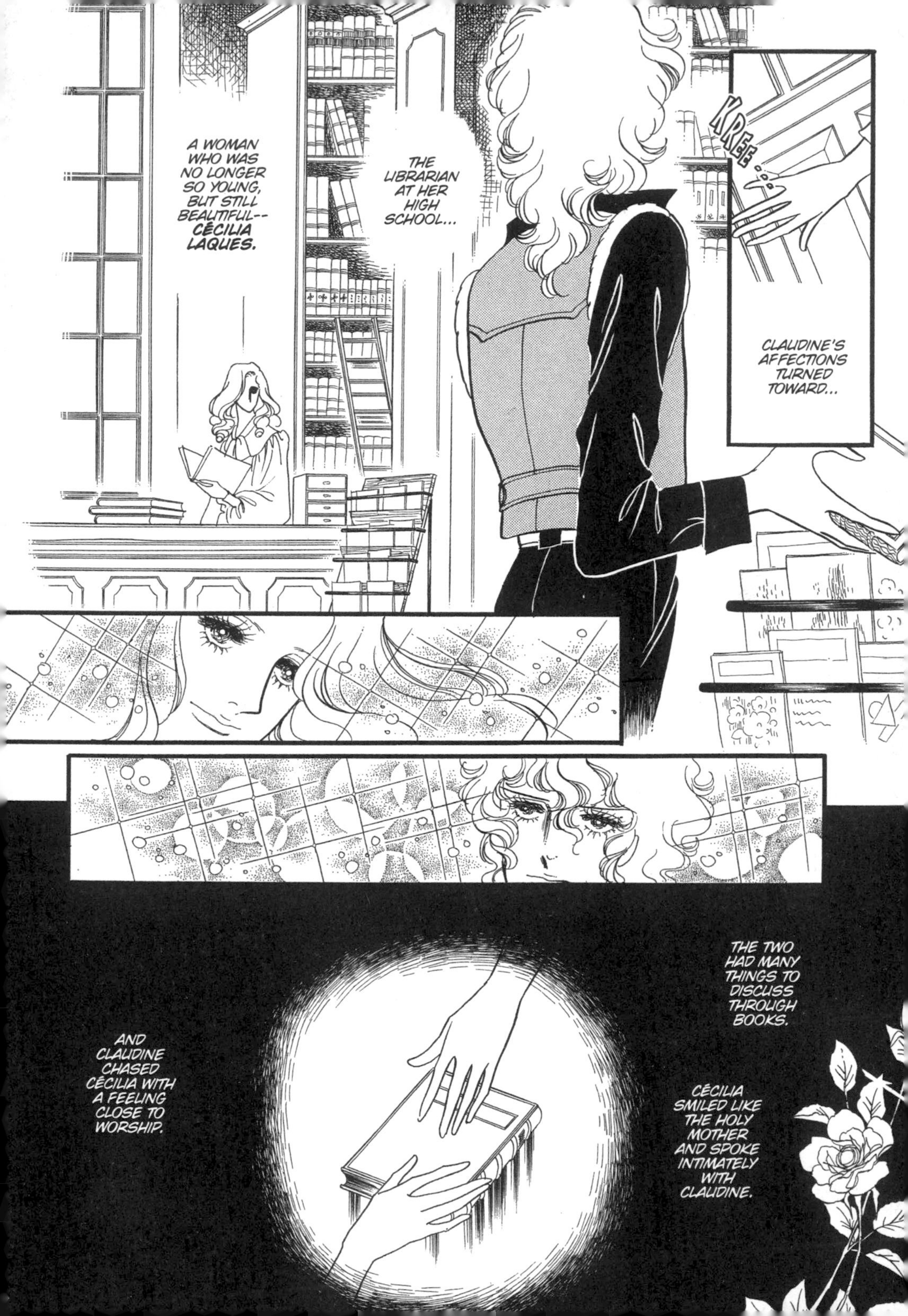
KREE...
CLAUDINE'S AFFECTIONS TURNED TOWARD...
THE LIBRARIAN AT HER HIGH SCHOOL...
A WOMAN WHO WAS NO LONGER SO YOUNG, BUT STILL BEAUTIFUL-- **CÉCILIA LAQUES.**
THE TWO HAD MANY THINGS TO DISCUSS THROUGH BOOKS.
CÉCILIA SMILED LIKE THE HOLY MOTHER AND SPOKE INTIMATELY WITH CLAUDINE.
AND CLAUDINE CHASED CÉCILIA WITH A FEELING CLOSE TO WORSHIP.

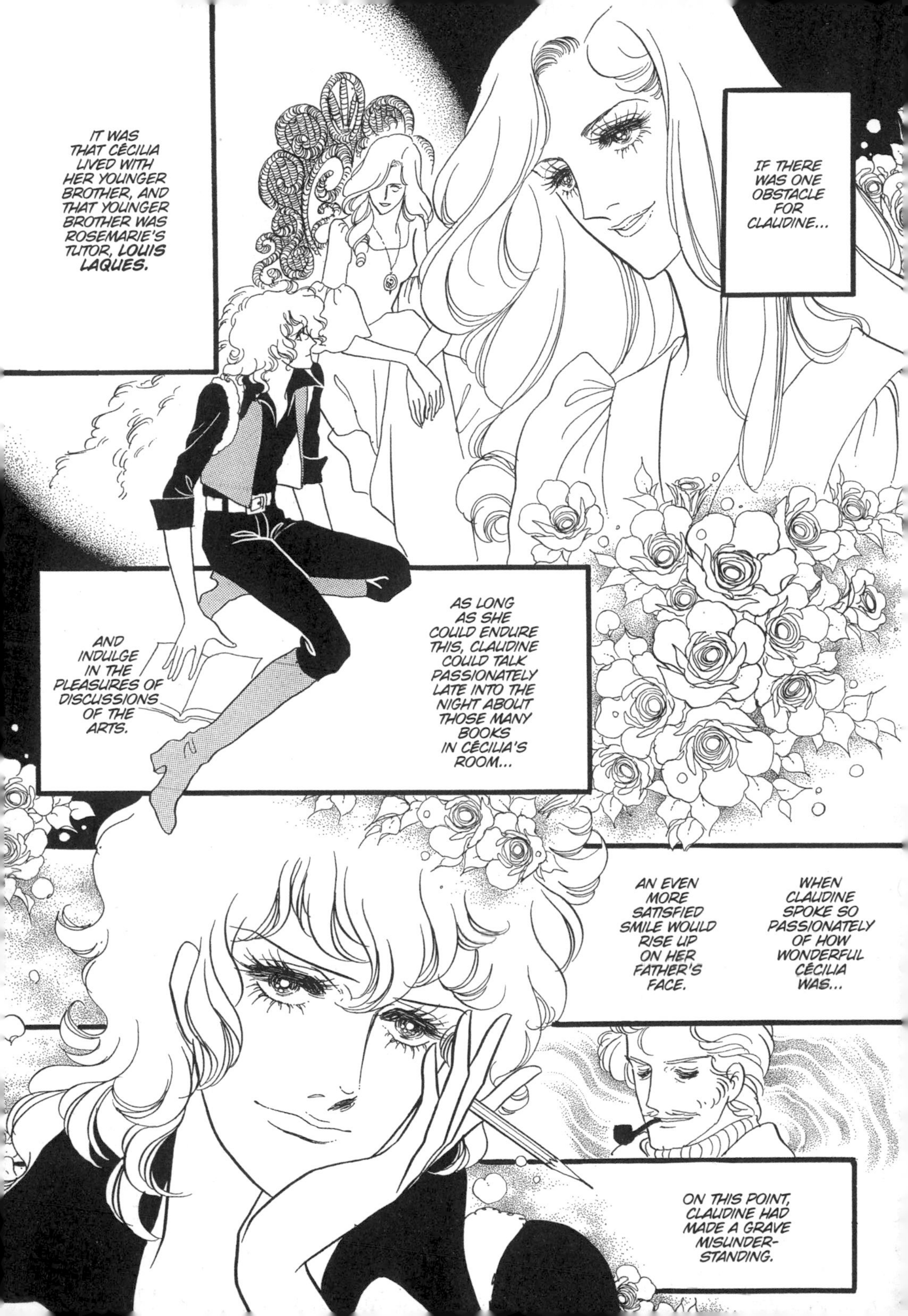
IF THERE WAS ONE OBSTACLE FOR CLAUDINE...
IT WAS THAT CÉCILIA LIVED WITH HER YOUNGER BROTHER, AND THAT YOUNGER BROTHER WAS ROSEMARIE'S TUTOR, **LOUIS LAQUES.**
AS LONG AS SHE COULD ENDURE THIS, CLAUDINE COULD TALK PASSIONATELY LATE INTO THE NIGHT ABOUT THOSE MANY BOOKS IN CÉCILIA'S ROOM...
AND INDULGE IN THE PLEASURES OF DISCUSSIONS OF THE ARTS.
WHEN CLAUDINE SPOKE SO PASSIONATELY OF HOW WONDERFUL CÉCILIA WAS...
AN EVEN MORE SATISFIED SMILE WOULD RISE UP ON HER FATHER'S FACE.
ON THIS POINT, CLAUDINE HAD MADE A GRAVE MISUNDER-STANDING.

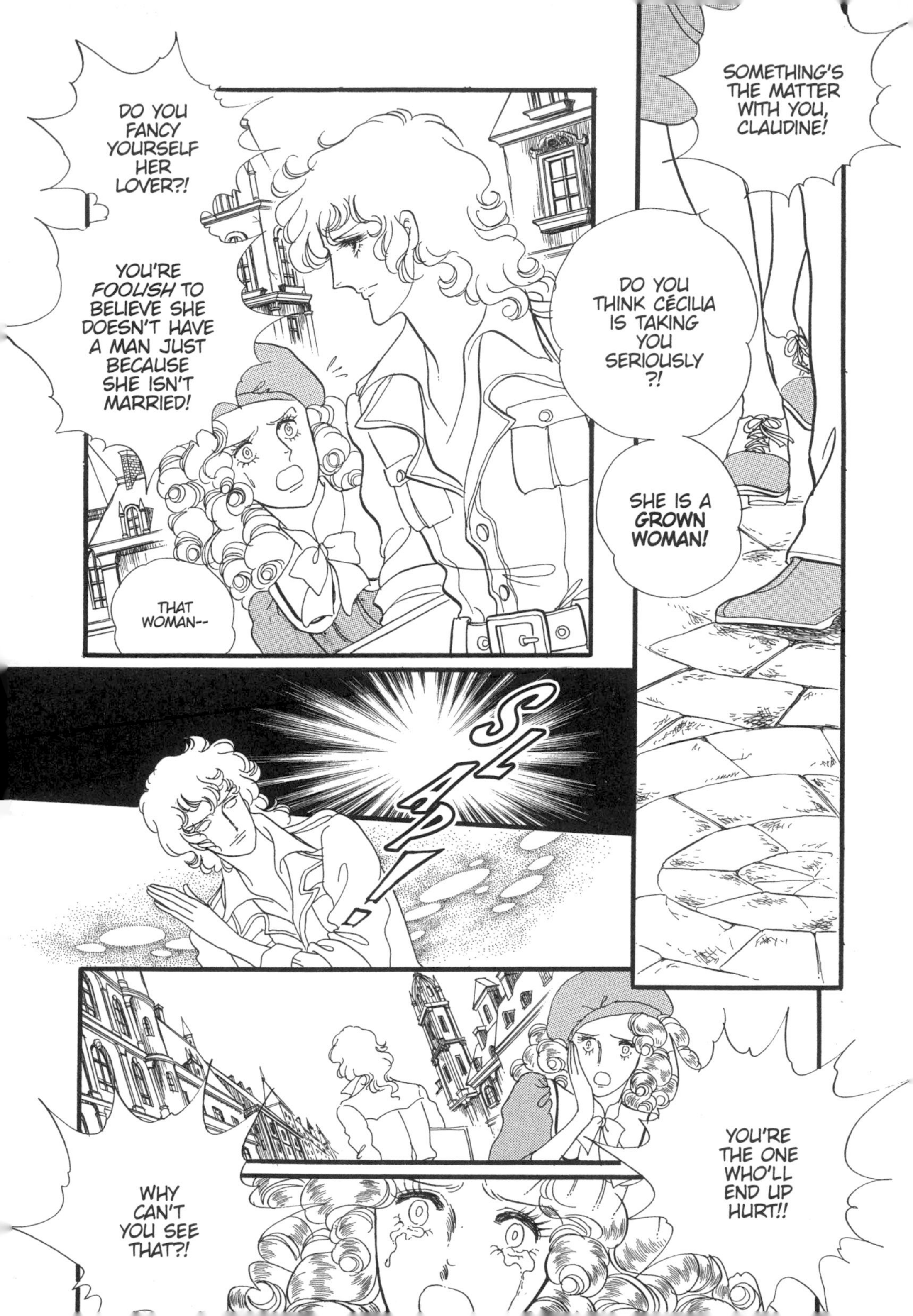
SOMETHING'S THE MATTER WITH YOU, CLAUDINE!
DO YOU THINK CÉCILIA IS TAKING YOU SERIOUSLY?!
SHE IS A **GROWN WOMAN!**
DO YOU FANCY YOURSELF HER LOVER?!
YOU'RE *FOOLISH* TO BELIEVE SHE DOESN'T HAVE A MAN JUST BECAUSE SHE ISN'T MARRIED!
THAT WOMAN--
SLAP!
YOU'RE THE ONE WHO'LL END UP HURT!!
WHY CAN'T YOU SEE THAT?!

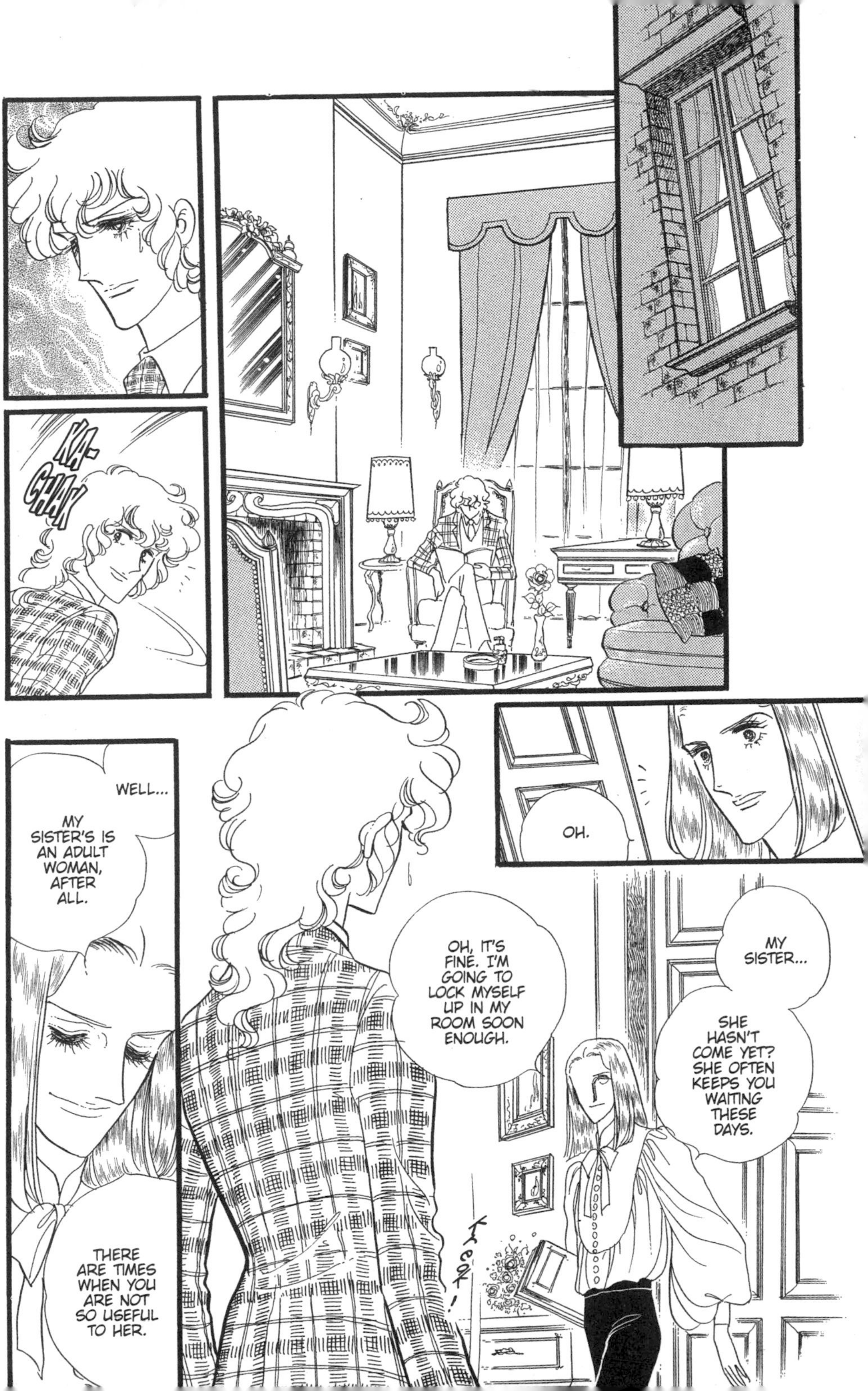
KA-CHAK
OH.
MY SISTER...
SHE HASN'T COME YET? SHE OFTEN KEEPS YOU WAITING THESE DAYS.
KREAK!
OH, IT'S FINE. I'M GOING TO LOCK MYSELF UP IN MY ROOM SOON ENOUGH.
WELL...
MY SISTER'S IS AN ADULT WOMAN, AFTER ALL.
THERE ARE TIMES WHEN YOU ARE NOT SO USEFUL TO HER.

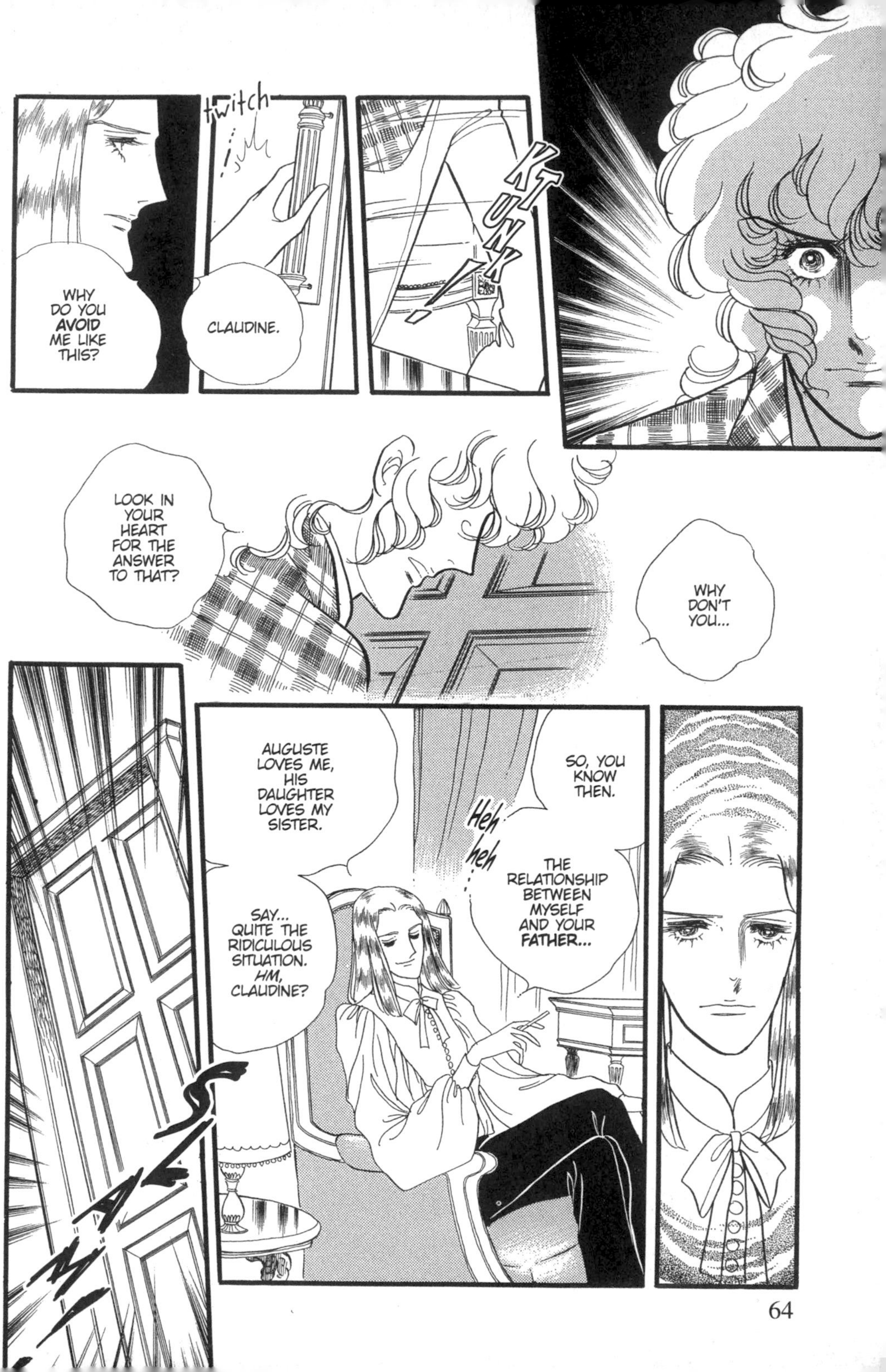
KTUNK!
twitch
CLAUDINE.
WHY DO YOU AVOID ME LIKE THIS?
WHY DON'T YOU...
LOOK IN YOUR HEART FOR THE ANSWER TO THAT?
SO, YOU KNOW THEN.
Heh heh
THE RELATIONSHIP BETWEEN MYSELF AND YOUR FATHER...
AUGUSTE LOVES ME, HIS DAUGHTER LOVES MY SISTER.
SAY... QUITE THE RIDICULOUS SITUATION. HM, CLAUDINE?
SLAM!

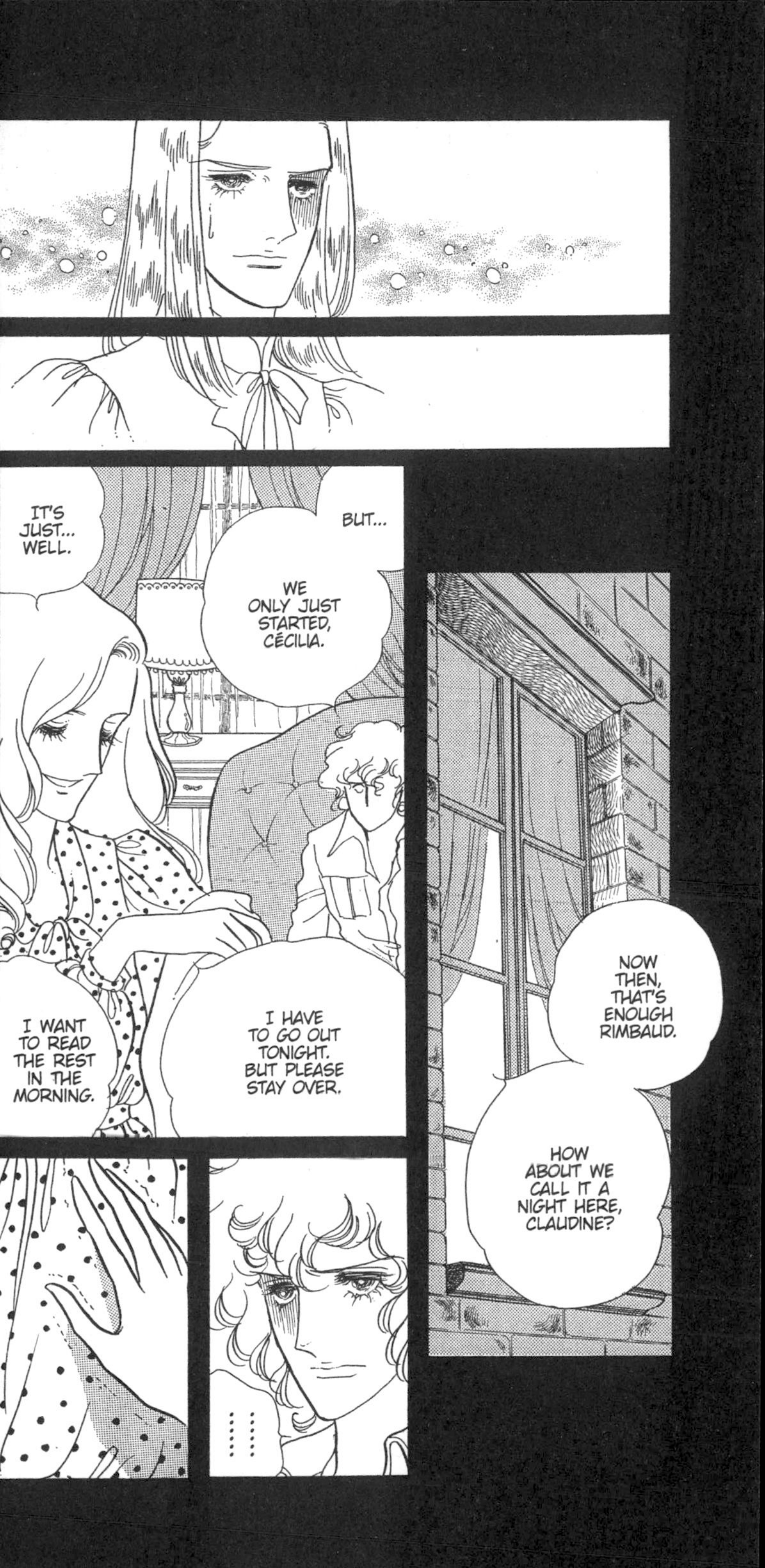
NOW THEN, THAT'S ENOUGH RIMBAUD.
HOW ABOUT WE CALL IT A NIGHT HERE, CLAUDINE?
BUT...
WE ONLY JUST STARTED, CÉCILIA.
IT'S JUST... WELL.
I HAVE TO GO OUT TONIGHT. BUT PLEASE STAY OVER.
I WANT TO READ THE REST IN THE MORNING.
......

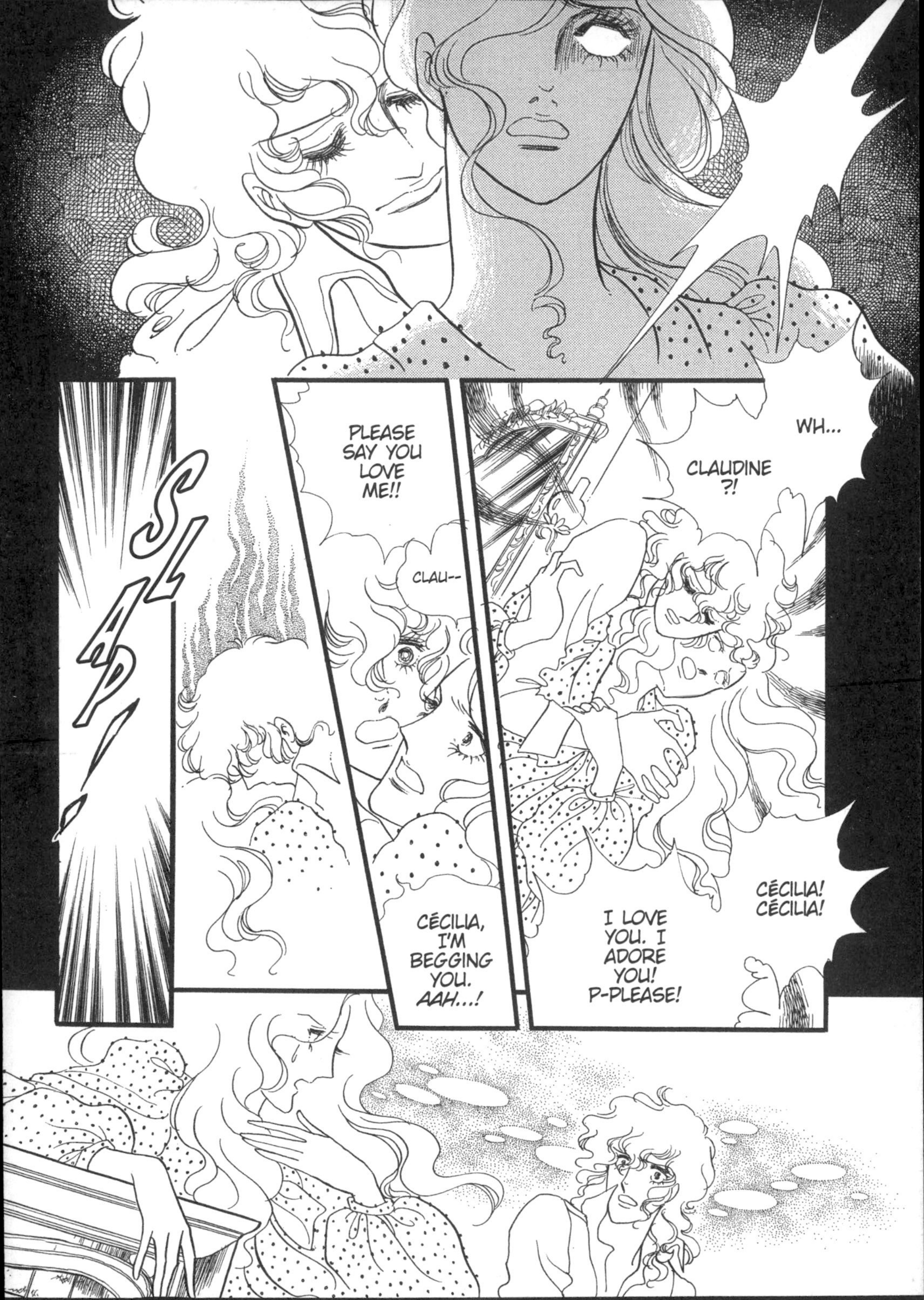
WH...
CLAUDINE ?!
CÉCILIA! CÉCILIA!
I LOVE YOU. I ADORE YOU! P-PLEASE!
PLEASE SAY YOU LOVE ME!!
CLAU--
CÉCILIA, I'M BEGGING YOU. AAH...!
SLAP!

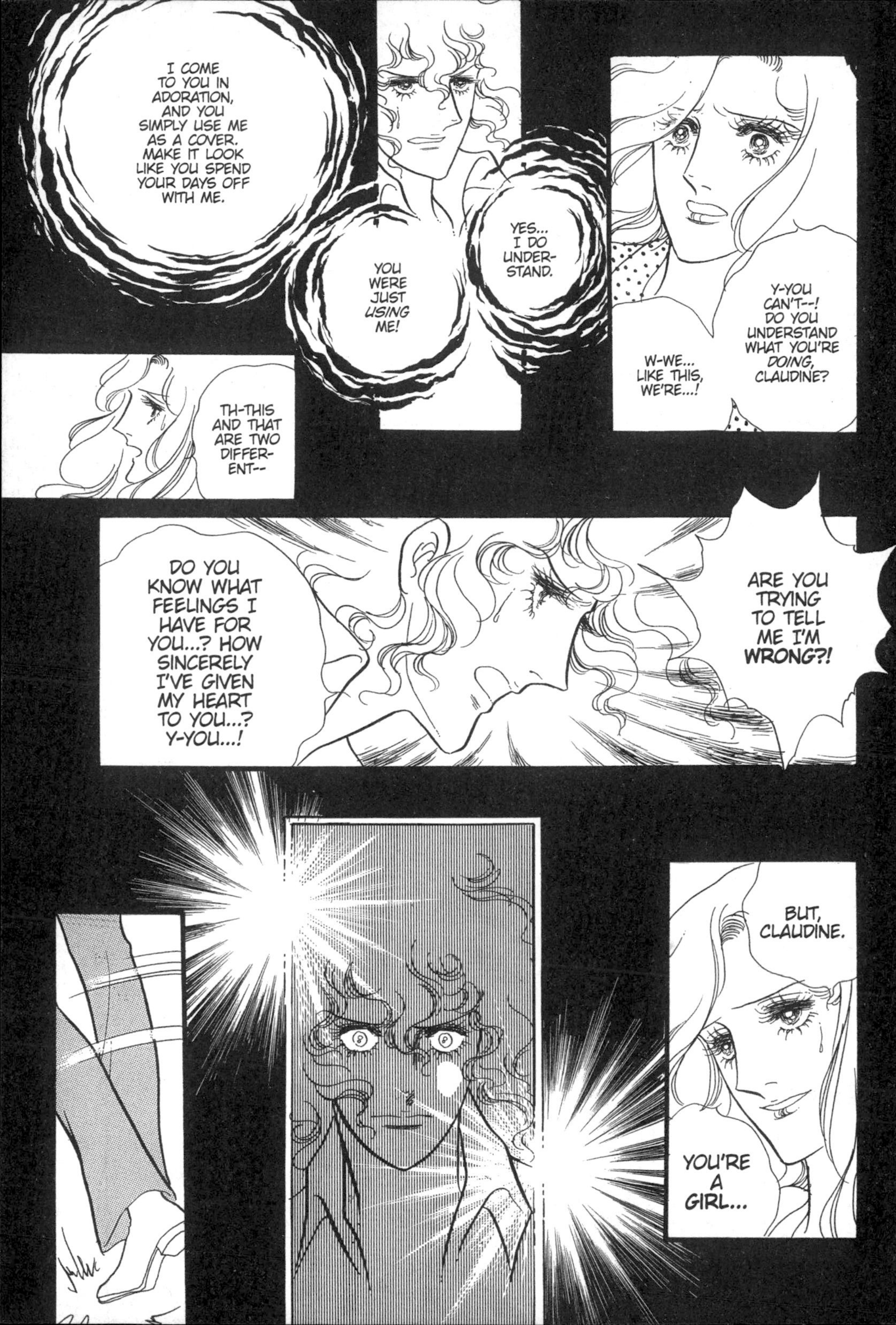
Y-YOU CAN'T--! DO YOU UNDERSTAND WHAT YOU'RE *DOING*, CLAUDINE?
W-WE... LIKE THIS, WE'RE...!
YES... I DO UNDER-STAND.
YOU WERE JUST *USING* ME!
I COME TO YOU IN ADORATION, AND YOU SIMPLY USE ME AS A COVER. MAKE IT LOOK LIKE YOU SPEND YOUR DAYS OFF WITH ME.
TH-THIS AND THAT ARE TWO DIFFER-ENT--
ARE YOU TRYING TO TELL ME I'M **WRONG?!**
DO YOU KNOW WHAT FEELINGS I HAVE FOR YOU...? HOW SINCERELY I'VE GIVEN MY HEART TO YOU...? Y-YOU...!
BUT, CLAUDINE.
YOU'RE A GIRL...

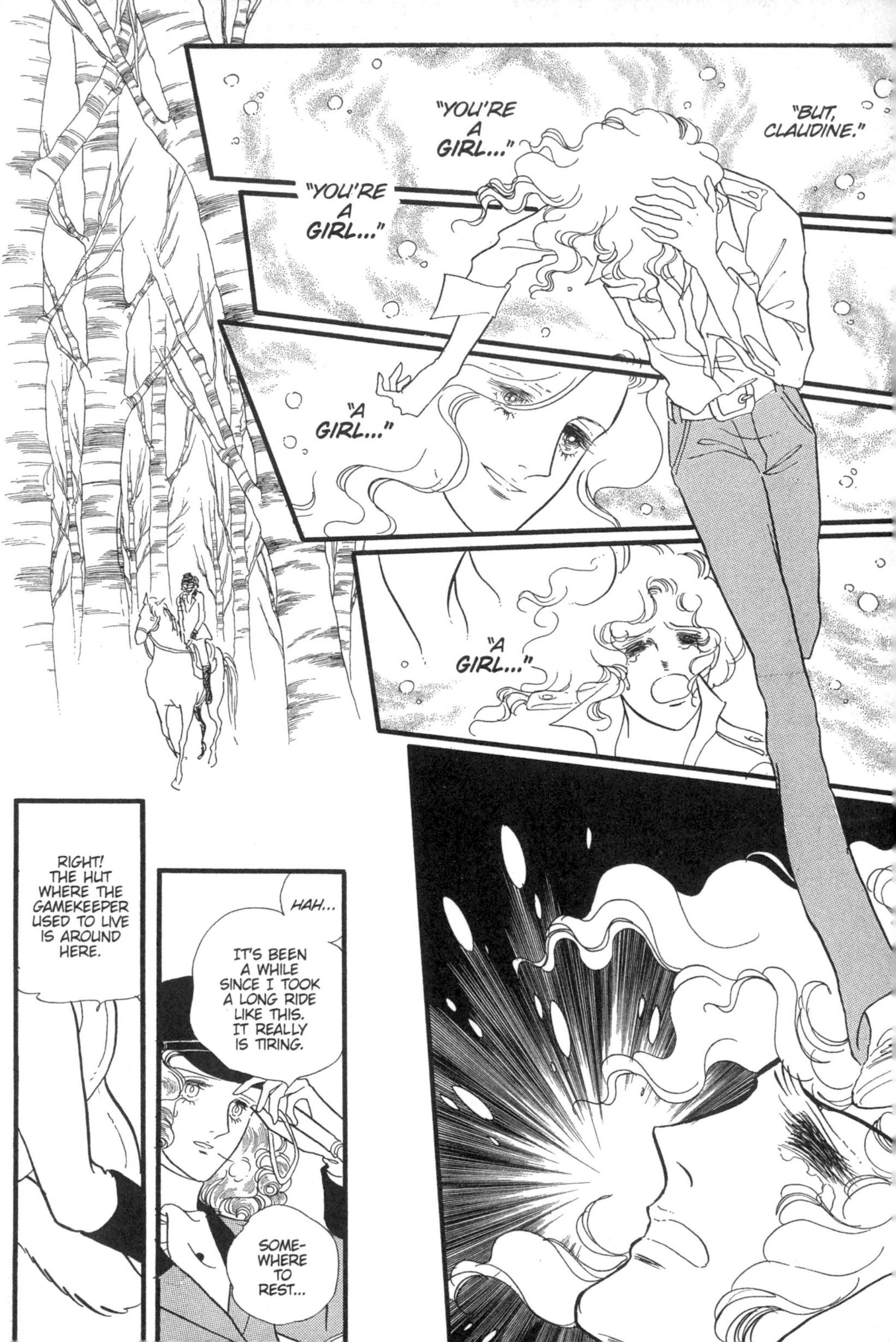
"BUT, CLAUDINE."
"YOU'RE A GIRL..."
"YOU'RE A GIRL..."
"A GIRL..."
"A GIRL..."
HAH...
IT'S BEEN A WHILE SINCE I TOOK A LONG RIDE LIKE THIS. IT REALLY IS TIRING.
SOME-WHERE TO REST...
RIGHT! THE HUT WHERE THE GAMEKEEPER USED TO LIVE IS AROUND HERE.

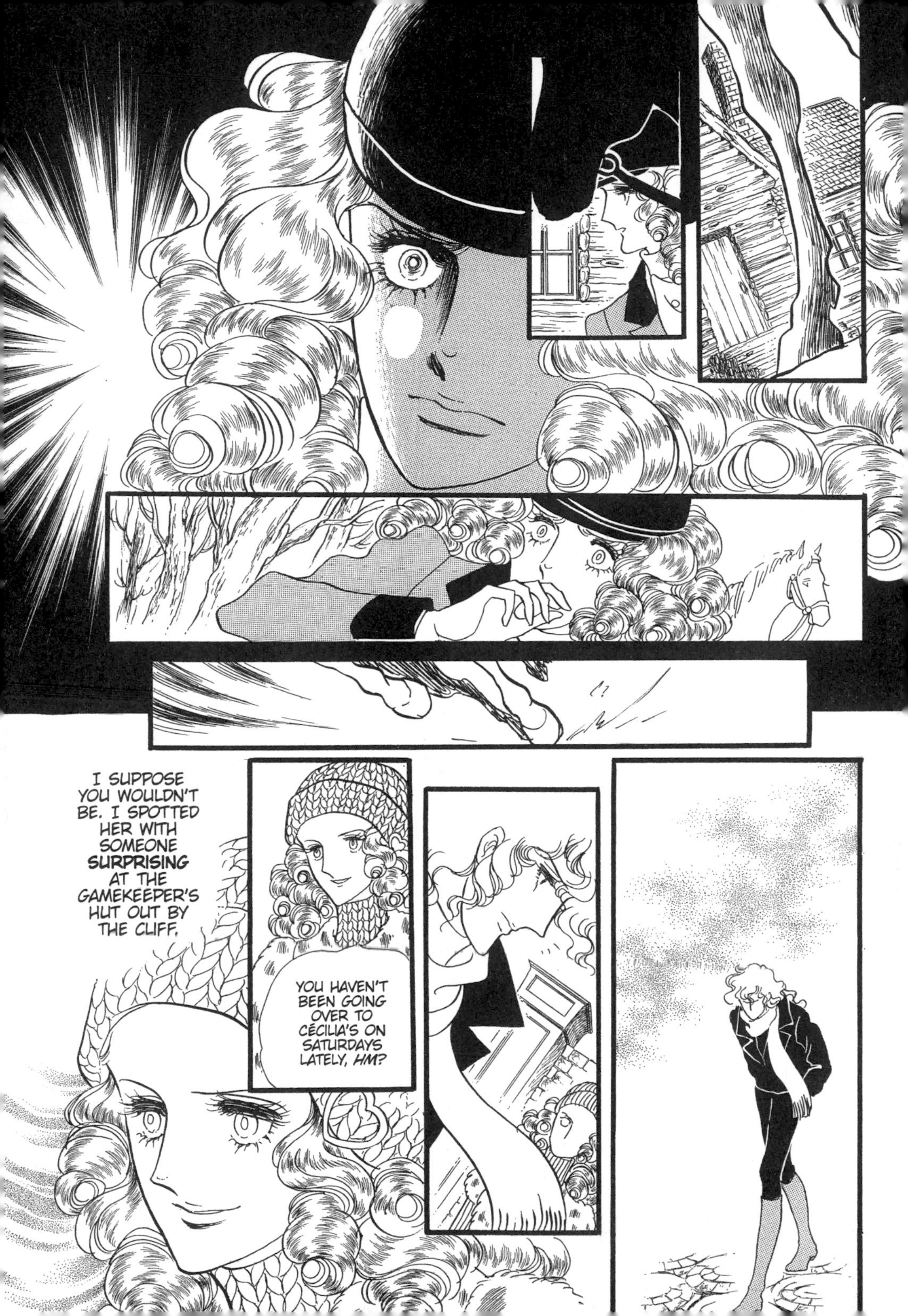
YOU HAVEN'T BEEN GOING OVER TO CÉCILIA'S ON SATURDAYS LATELY, *HM*?
I SUPPOSE YOU WOULDN'T BE. I SPOTTED HER WITH SOMEONE **SURPRISING** AT THE GAMEKEEPER'S HUT OUT BY THE CLIFF.

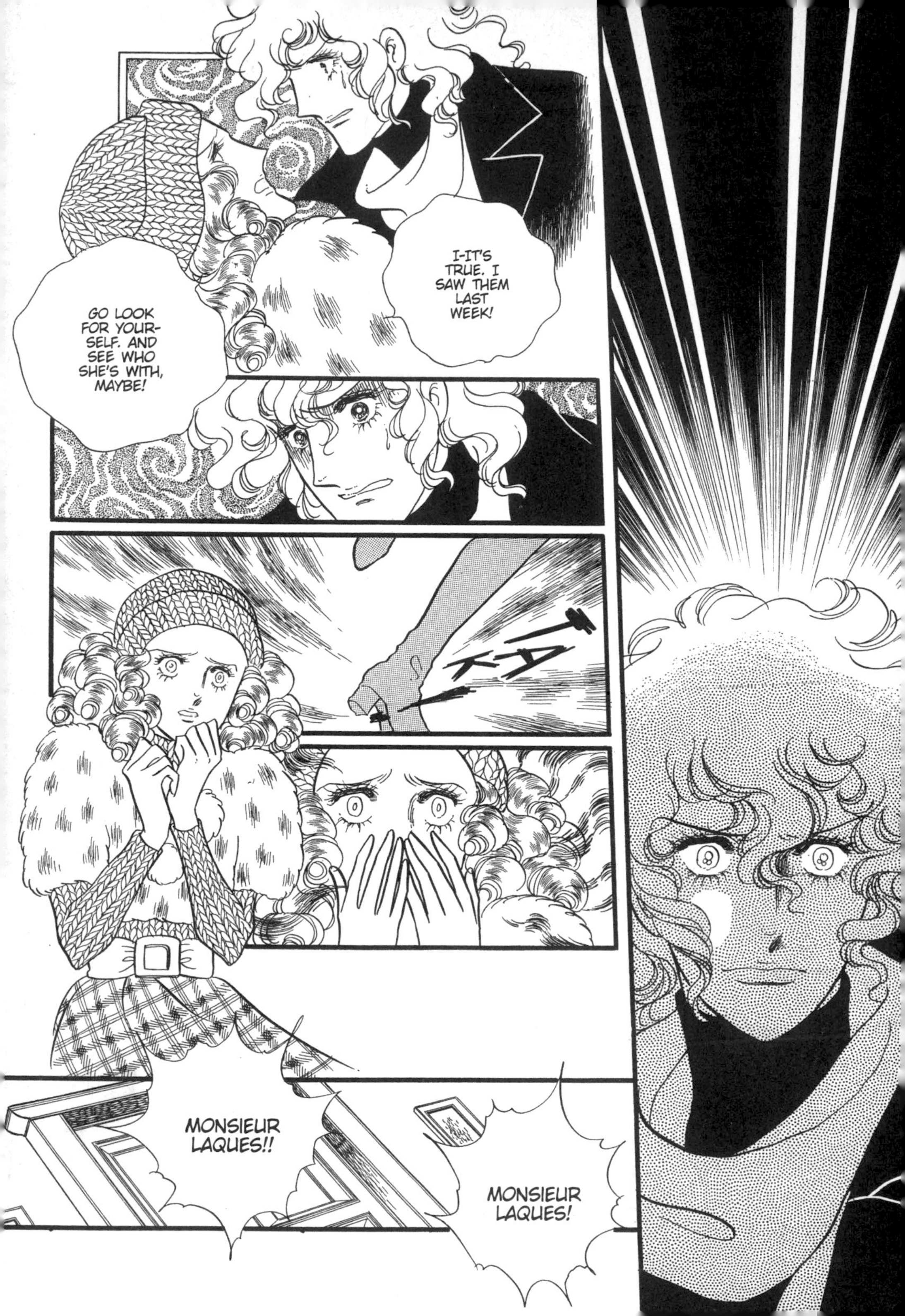
I-IT'S TRUE. I SAW THEM LAST WEEK!
GO LOOK FOR YOUR-SELF. AND SEE WHO SHE'S WITH, MAYBE!
TKA
MONSIEUR LAQUES!
MONSIEUR LAQUES!!

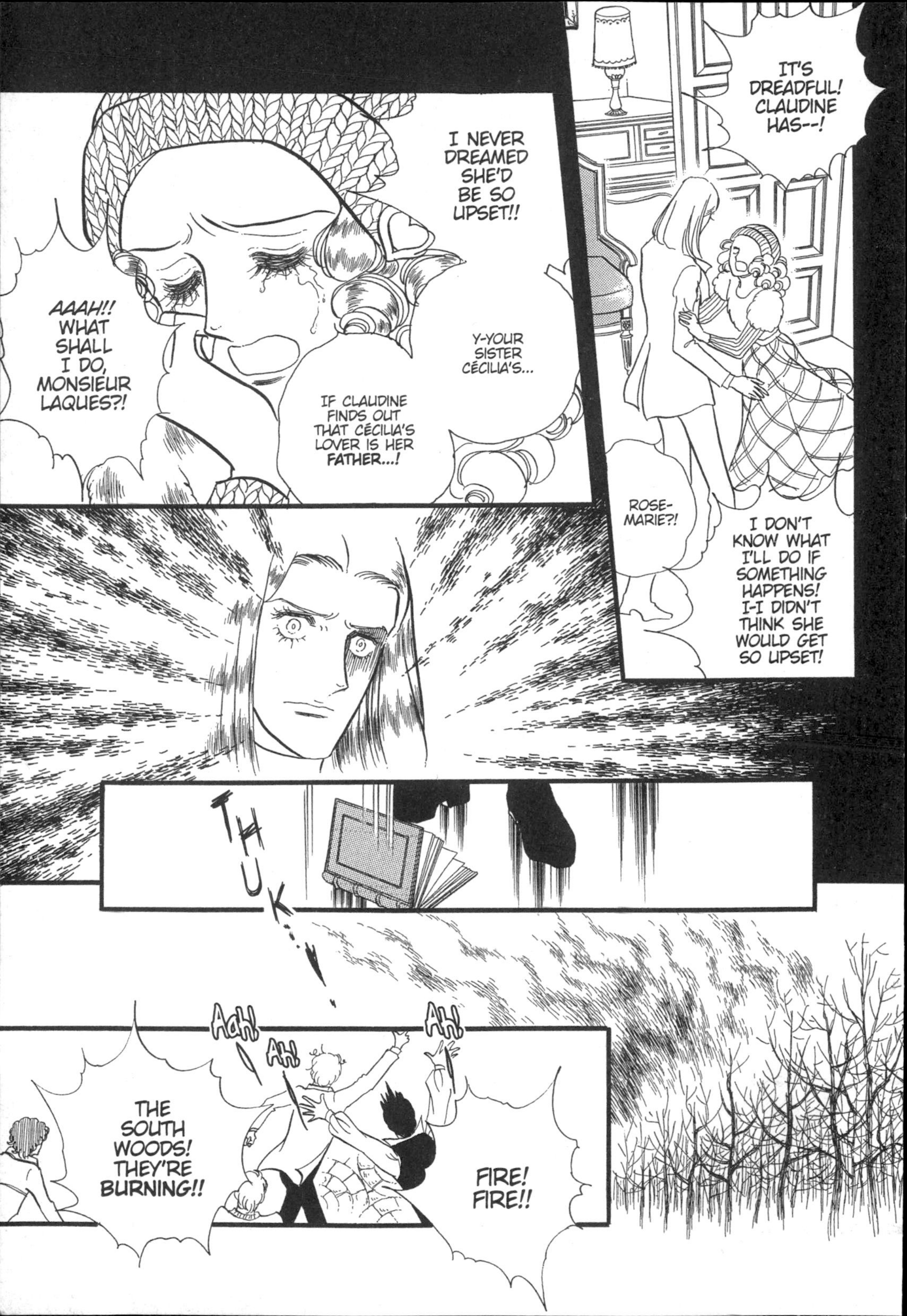
IT'S DREADFUL! CLAUDINE HAS--!
ROSE-MARIE?!
I DON'T KNOW WHAT I'LL DO IF SOMETHING HAPPENS! I-I DIDN'T THINK SHE WOULD GET SO UPSET!
I NEVER DREAMED SHE'D BE SO UPSET!!
Y-YOUR SISTER CÉCILIA'S...
IF CLAUDINE FINDS OUT THAT CÉCILIA'S LOVER IS HER **FATHER**...!
AAAH!! WHAT SHALL I DO, MONSIEUR LAQUES?!
THUK...
FIRE! FIRE!!
Ah!
Ah!
Aah!
THE SOUTH WOODS! THEY'RE BURNING!!

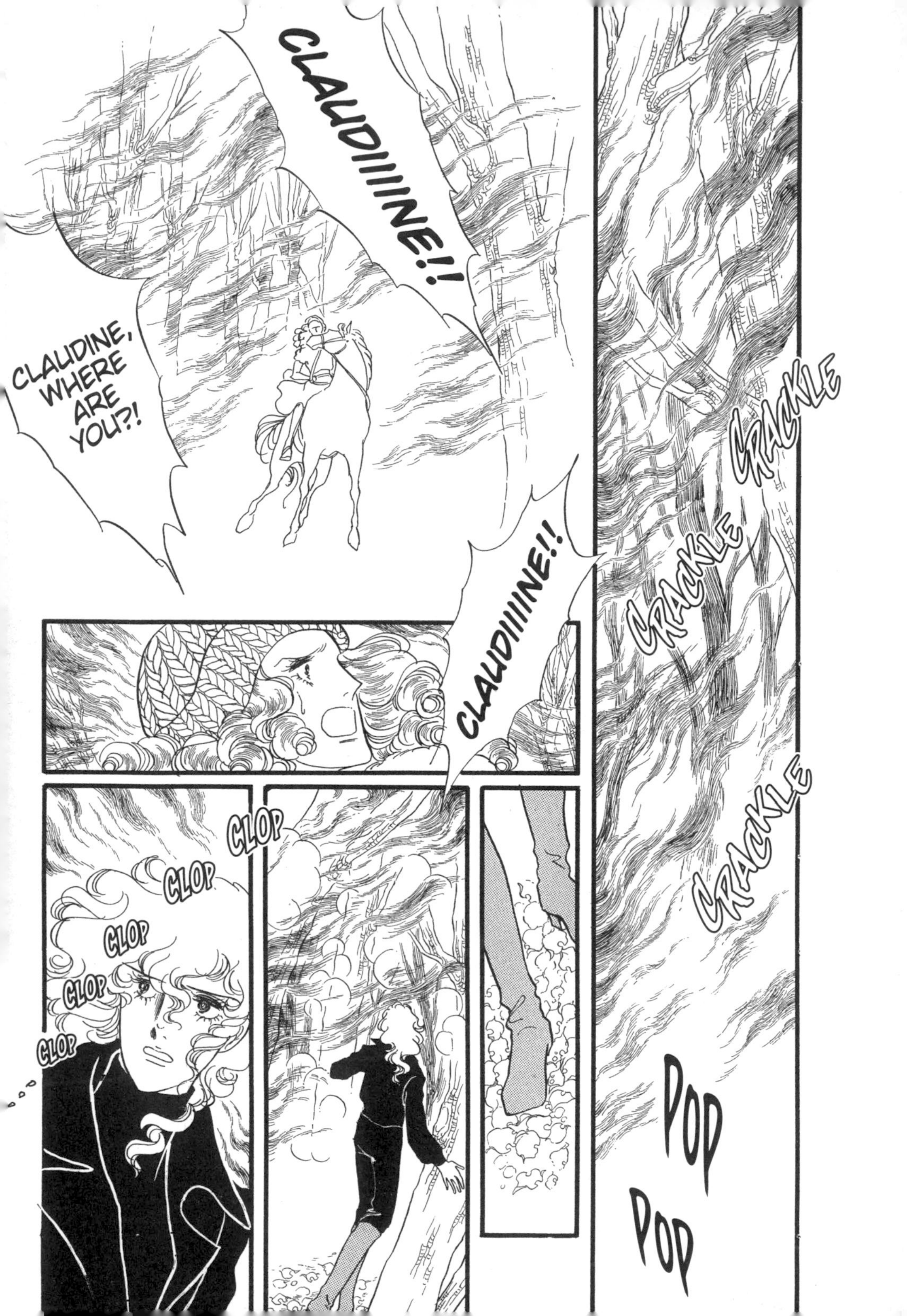
CRACKLE
CRACKLE
CRACKLE
POP
POP
CLAUDIIIIINE!!
CLAUDINE, WHERE ARE YOU?!
CLAUDIIIIINE!!
CLOP
CLOP
CLOP
CLOP
CLOP
...

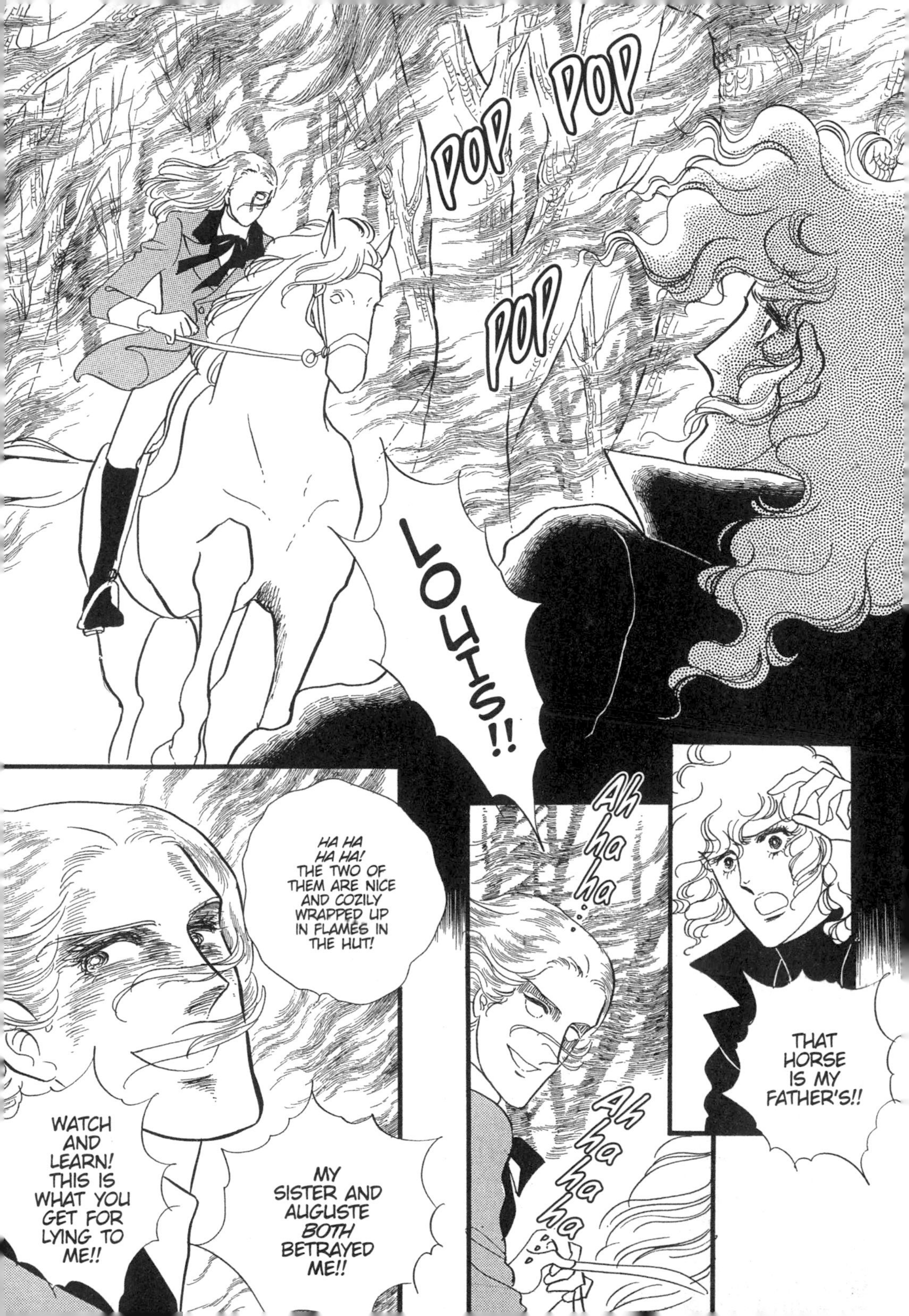
POP POP
POP
LOUIS!!
THAT HORSE IS MY FATHER'S!!
Ah ha ha ha...
Ah ha ha ha ha...
HA HA HA HA! THE TWO OF THEM ARE NICE AND COZILY WRAPPED UP IN FLAMES IN THE HUT!
MY SISTER AND AUGUSTE BOTH BETRAYED ME!!
WATCH AND LEARN! THIS IS WHAT YOU GET FOR LYING TO ME!!

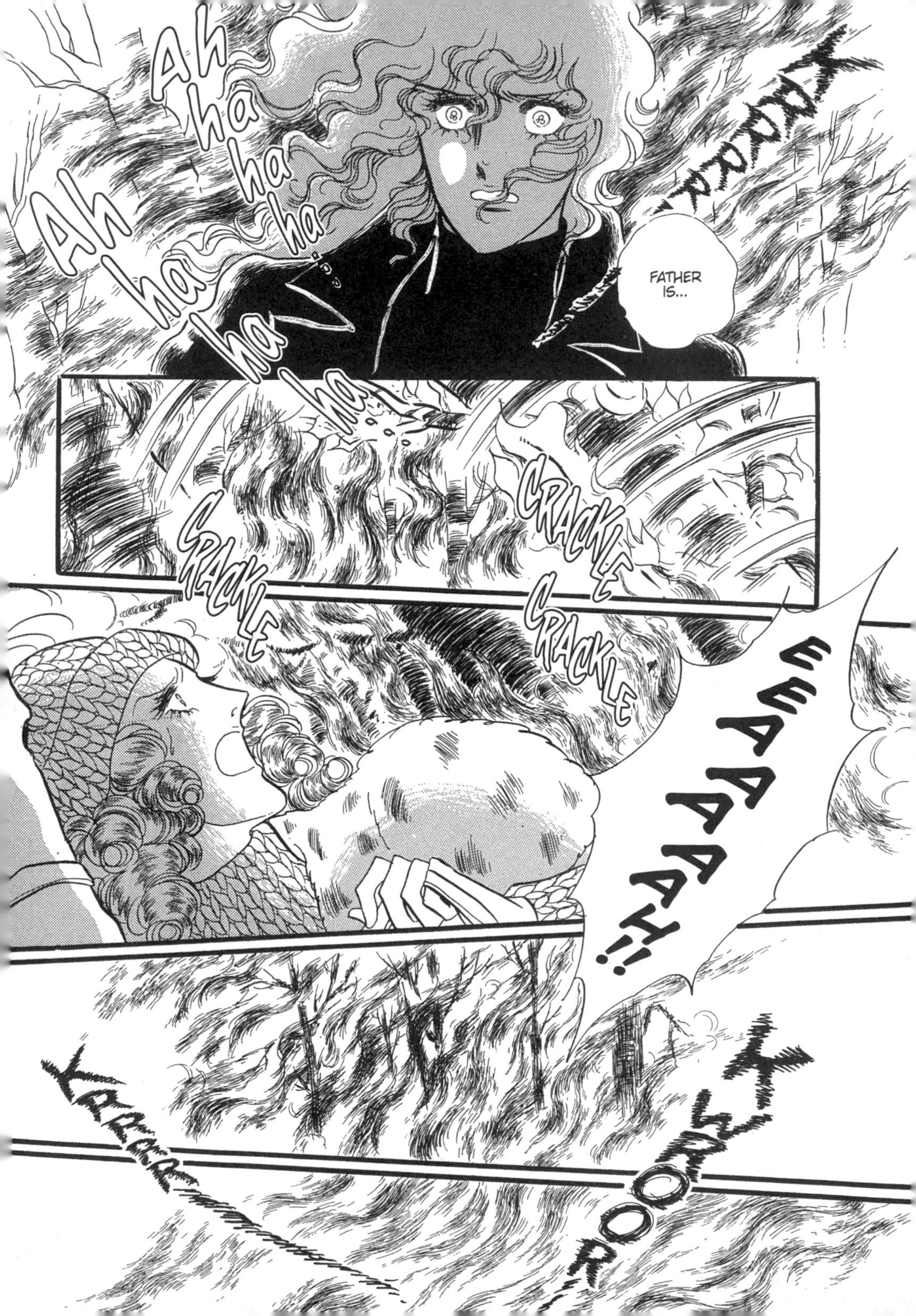
FATHER IS...
Ah ha ha ha ha
Ah ha ha ha ha...
CRACKLE CRACKLE
CRACKLE
EEAAAAAH!!!

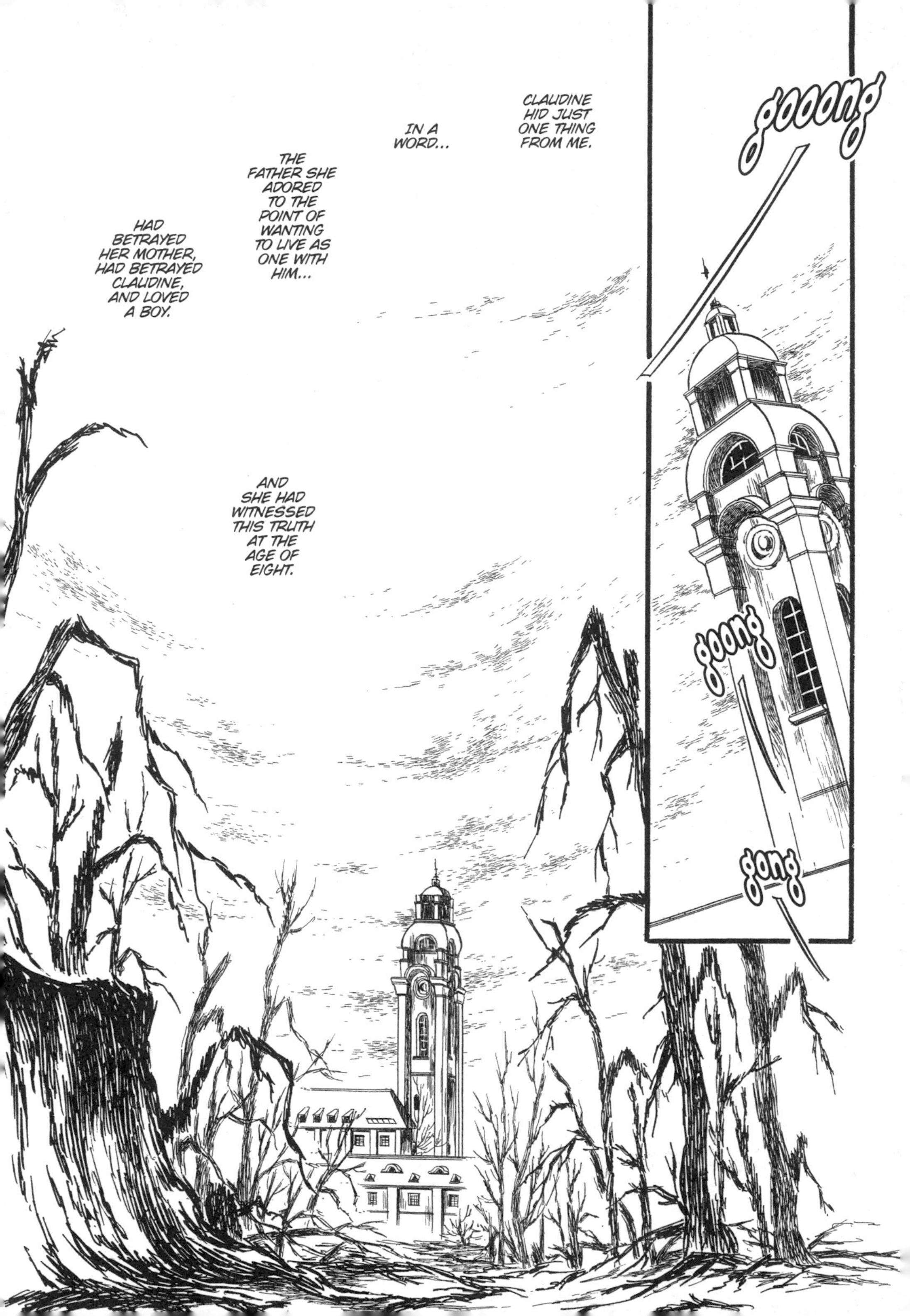
gooong
goong
gong
CLAUDINE HID JUST ONE THING FROM ME.
IN A WORD...
THE FATHER SHE ADORED TO THE POINT OF WANTING TO LIVE AS ONE WITH HIM...
HAD BETRAYED HER MOTHER, HAD BETRAYED CLAUDINE, AND LOVED A BOY.
AND SHE HAD WITNESSED THIS TRUTH AT THE AGE OF EIGHT.

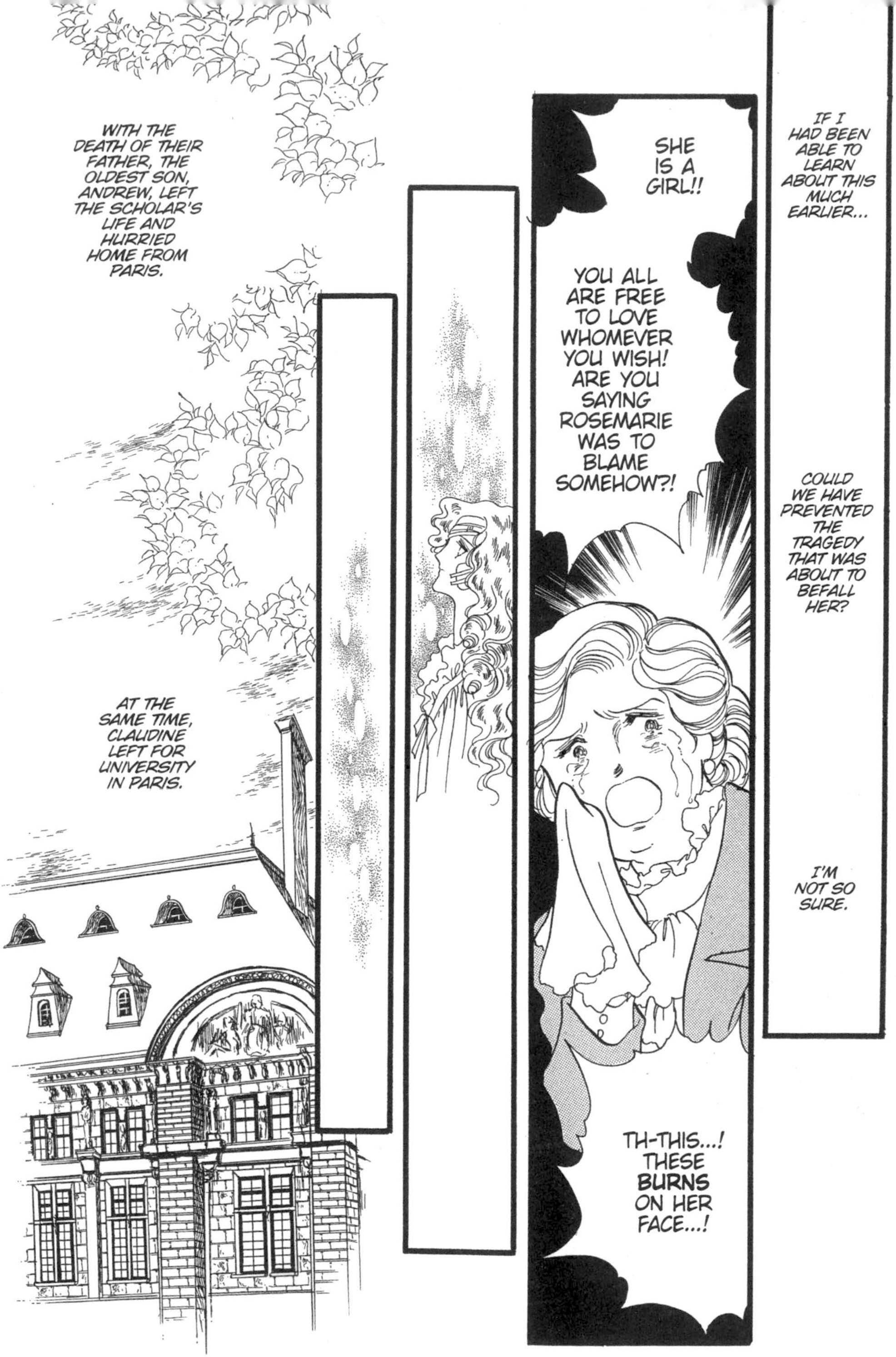
IF I HAD BEEN ABLE TO LEARN ABOUT THIS MUCH EARLIER...
COULD WE HAVE PREVENTED THE TRAGEDY THAT WAS ABOUT TO BEFALL HER?
I'M NOT SO SURE.
SHE IS A GIRL!!
YOU ALL ARE FREE TO LOVE WHOMEVER YOU WISH! ARE YOU SAYING ROSEMARIE WAS TO BLAME SOMEHOW?!
TH-THIS...! THESE **BURNS** ON HER FACE...!
WITH THE DEATH OF THEIR FATHER, THE OLDEST SON, ANDREW, LEFT THE SCHOLAR'S LIFE AND HURRIED HOME FROM PARIS.
AT THE SAME TIME, CLAUDINE LEFT FOR UNIVERSITY IN PARIS.

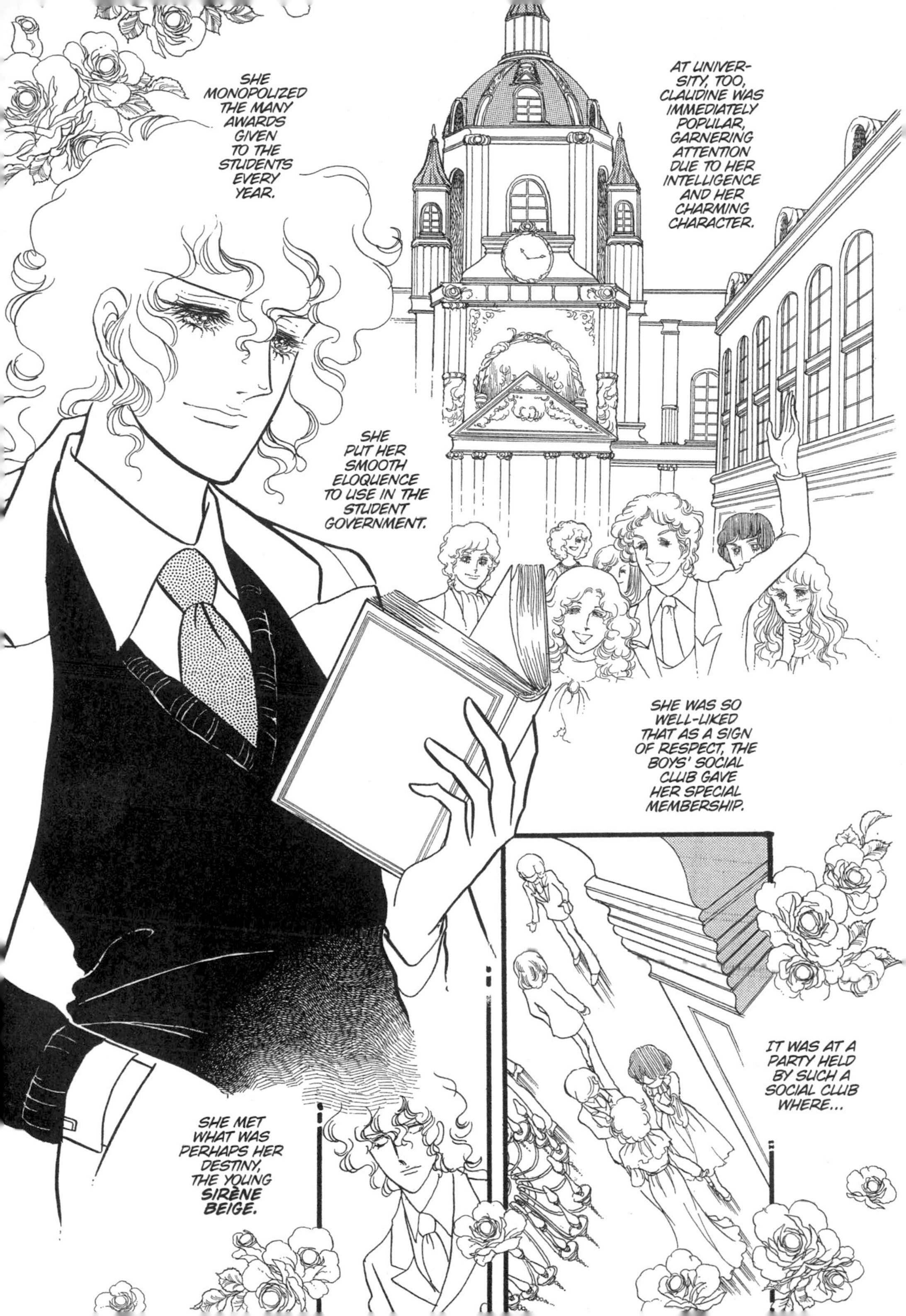
AT UNIVERSITY, TOO, CLAUDINE WAS IMMEDIATELY POPULAR, GARNERING ATTENTION DUE TO HER INTELLIGENCE AND HER CHARMING CHARACTER.
SHE MONOPOLIZED THE MANY AWARDS GIVEN TO THE STUDENTS EVERY YEAR.
SHE PUT HER SMOOTH ELOQUENCE TO USE IN THE STUDENT GOVERNMENT.
SHE WAS SO WELL-LIKED THAT AS A SIGN OF RESPECT, THE BOYS' SOCIAL CLUB GAVE HER SPECIAL MEMBERSHIP.
IT WAS AT A PARTY HELD BY SUCH A SOCIAL CLUB WHERE...
SHE MET WHAT WAS PERHAPS HER DESTINY, THE YOUNG SIRÈNE BEIGE.

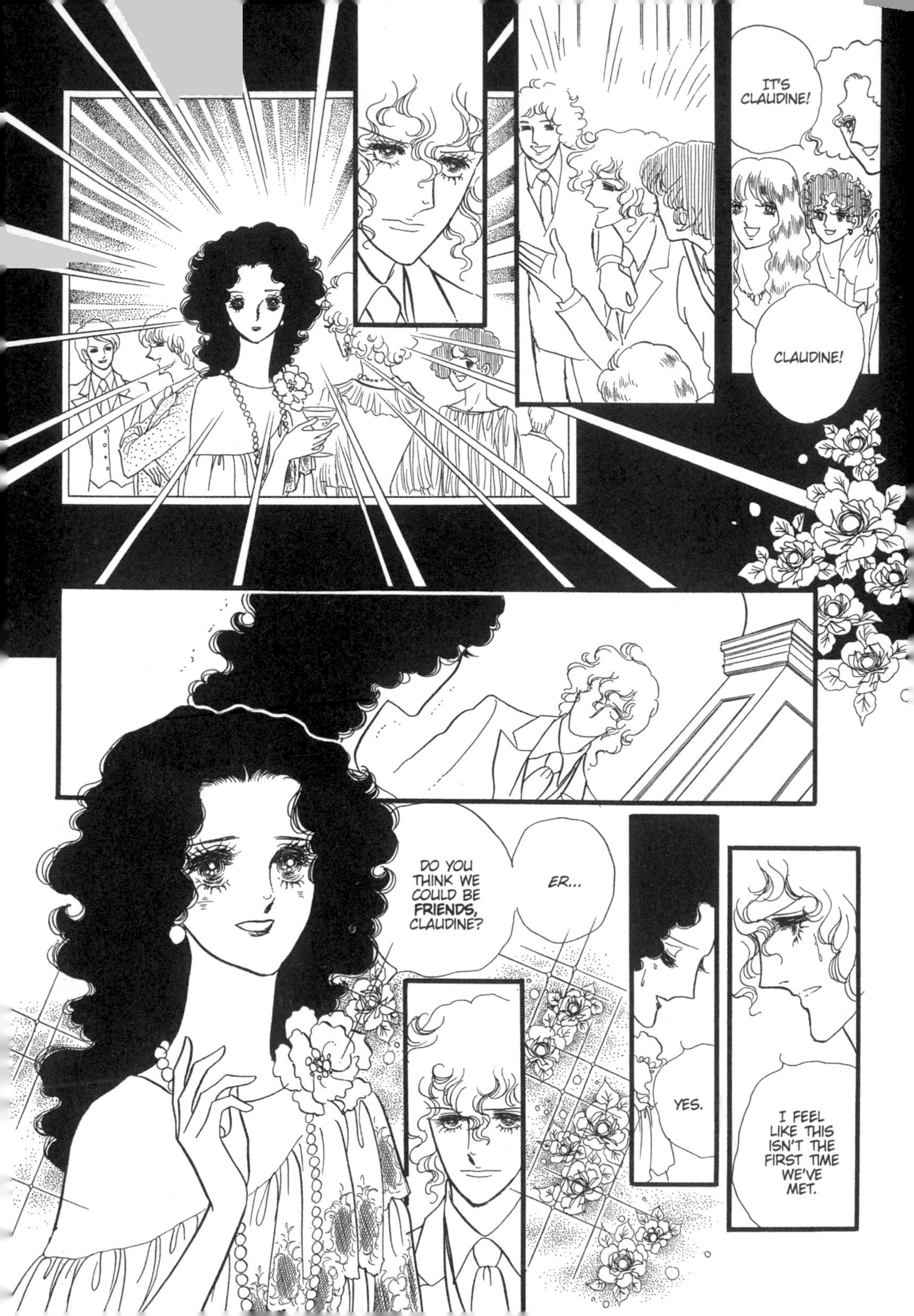
IT'S CLAUDINE!
CLAUDINE!
I FEEL LIKE THIS ISN'T THE FIRST TIME WE'VE MET.
YES.
DO YOU THINK WE COULD BE **FRIENDS**, CLAUDINE?
ER...

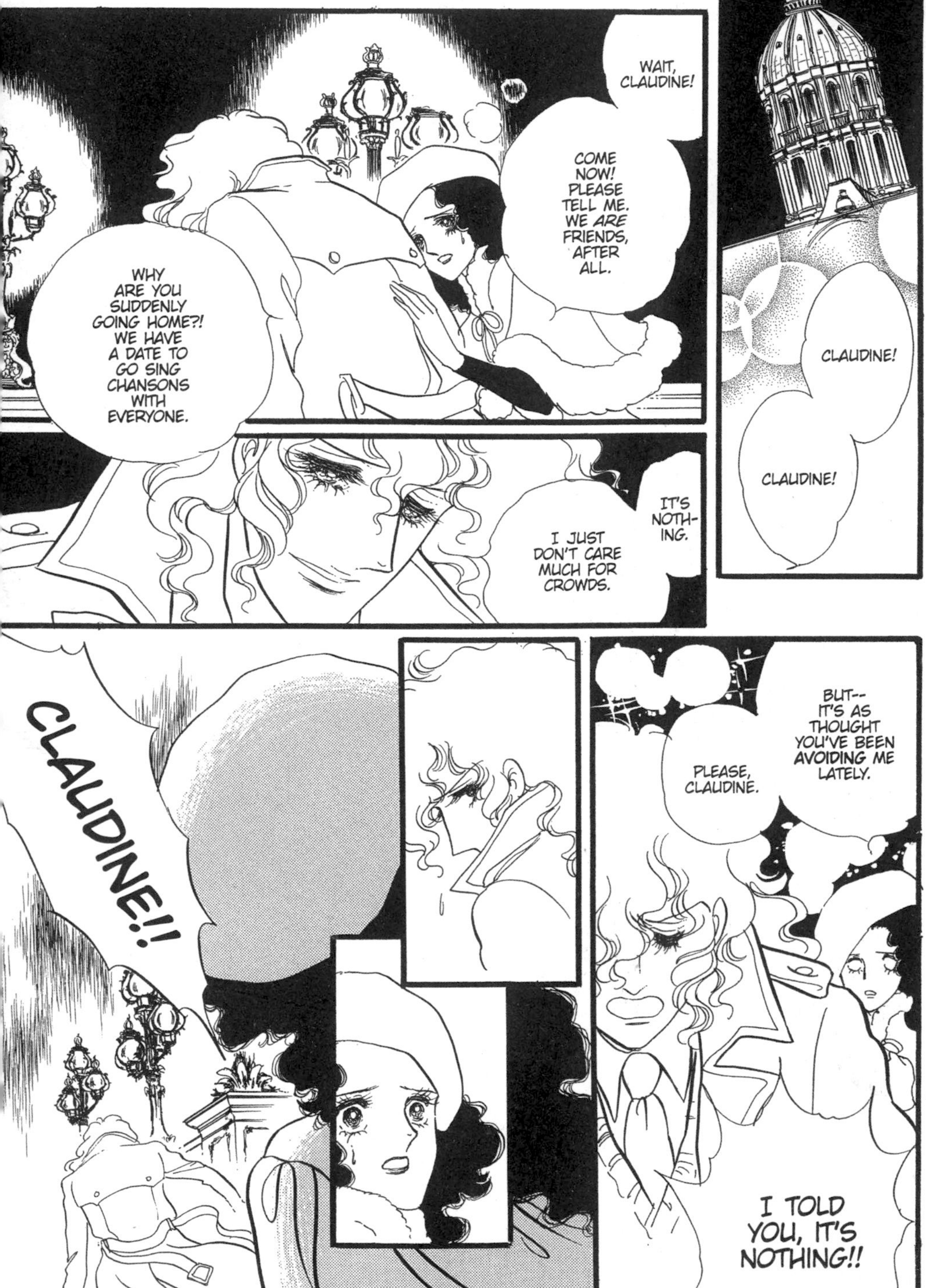
CLAUDINE!
CLAUDINE!
WAIT, CLAUDINE!
COME NOW! PLEASE TELL ME. WE *ARE* FRIENDS, AFTER ALL.
WHY ARE YOU SUDDENLY GOING HOME?! WE HAVE A DATE TO GO SING CHANSONS WITH EVERYONE.
IT'S NOTHING.
I JUST DON'T CARE MUCH FOR CROWDS.
BUT-- IT'S AS THOUGHT YOU'VE BEEN AVOIDING ME LATELY.
PLEASE, CLAUDINE.
I TOLD YOU, IT'S NOTHING!!
CLAUDINE!!

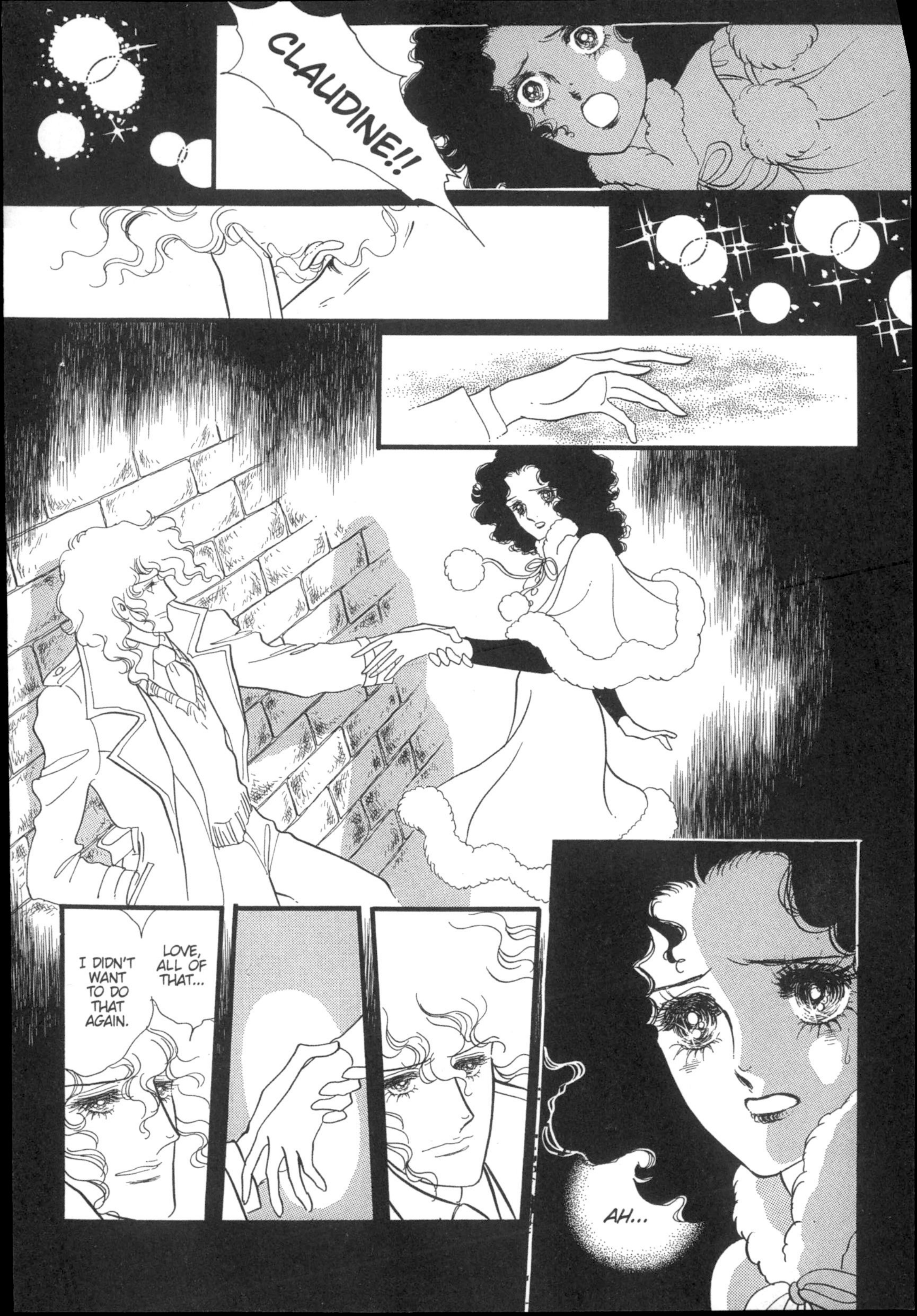
CLAUDINE!!
AH...
LOVE, ALL OF THAT...
I DIDN'T WANT TO DO THAT AGAIN.

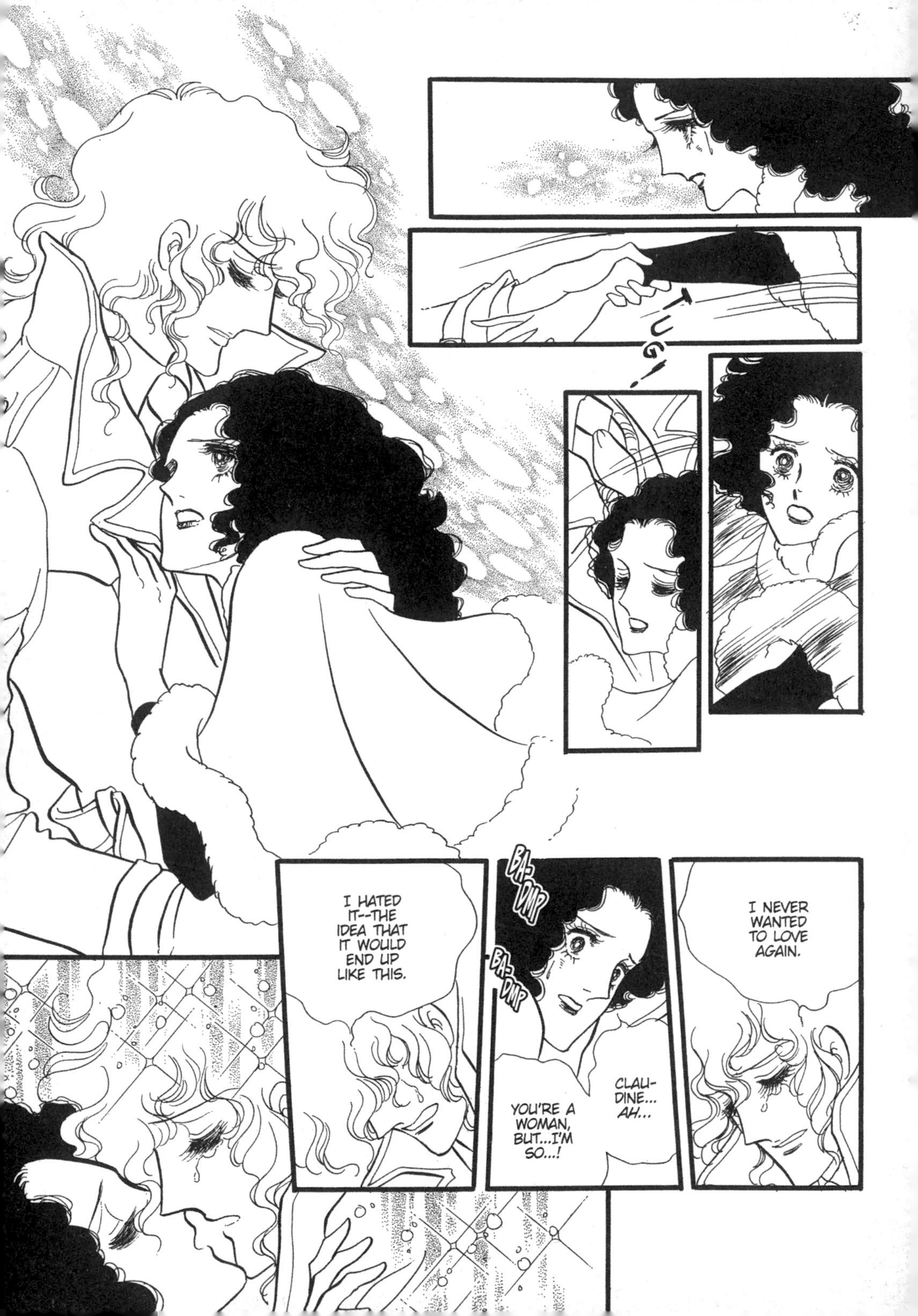
TUG!
I NEVER WANTED TO LOVE AGAIN.
BA-DMP
BA-DMP
CLAU-DINE... AH...
YOU'RE A WOMAN, BUT...I'M SO...!
I HATED IT--THE IDEA THAT IT WOULD END UP LIKE THIS.

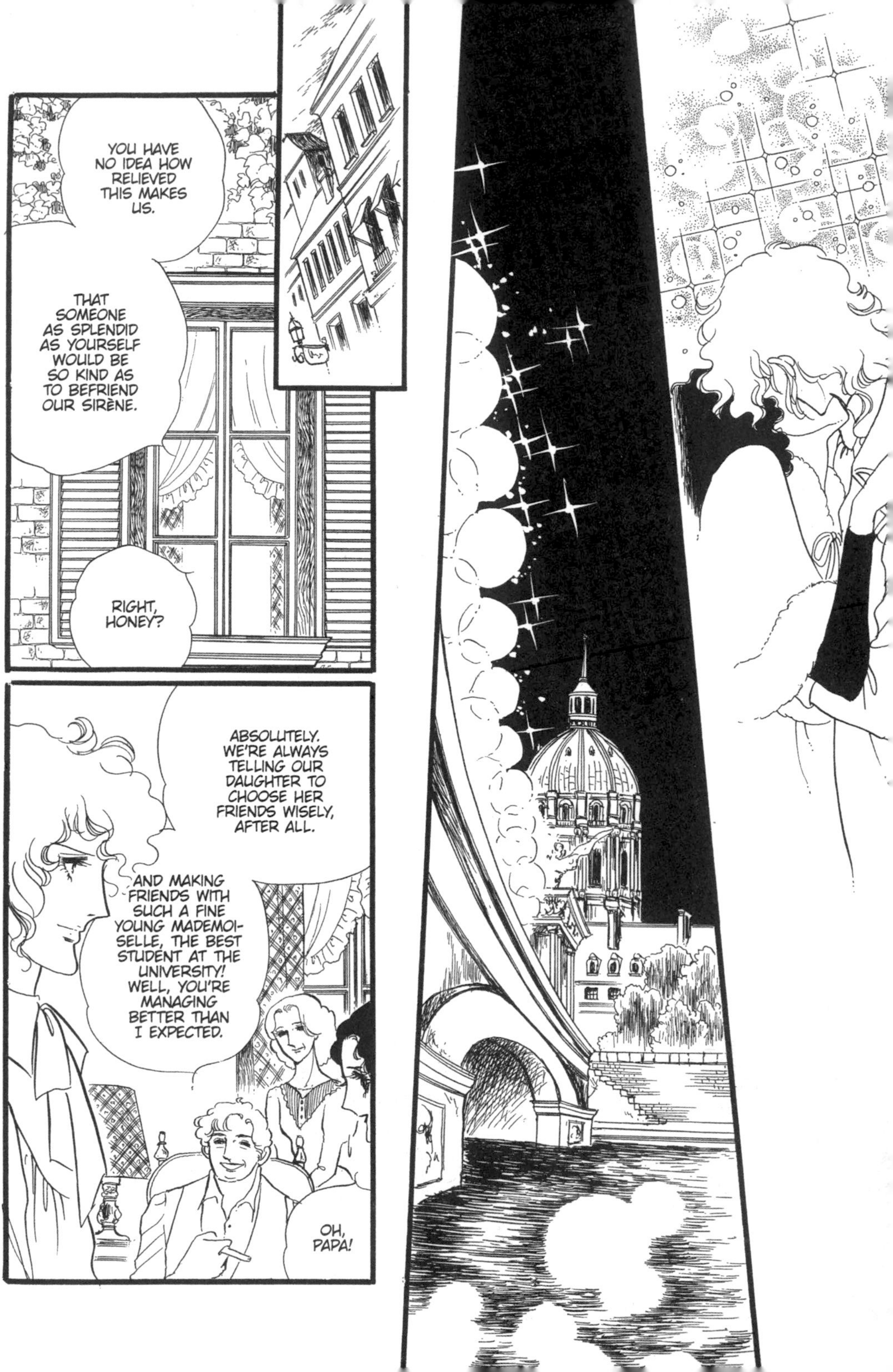
YOU HAVE NO IDEA HOW RELIEVED THIS MAKES US.
THAT SOMEONE AS SPLENDID AS YOURSELF WOULD BE SO KIND AS TO BEFRIEND OUR SIRÈNE.
RIGHT, HONEY?
ABSOLUTELY. WE'RE ALWAYS TELLING OUR DAUGHTER TO CHOOSE HER FRIENDS WISELY, AFTER ALL.
AND MAKING FRIENDS WITH SUCH A FINE YOUNG MADEMOI-SELLE, THE BEST STUDENT AT THE UNIVERSITY! WELL, YOU'RE MANAGING BETTER THAN I EXPECTED.
OH, PAPA!

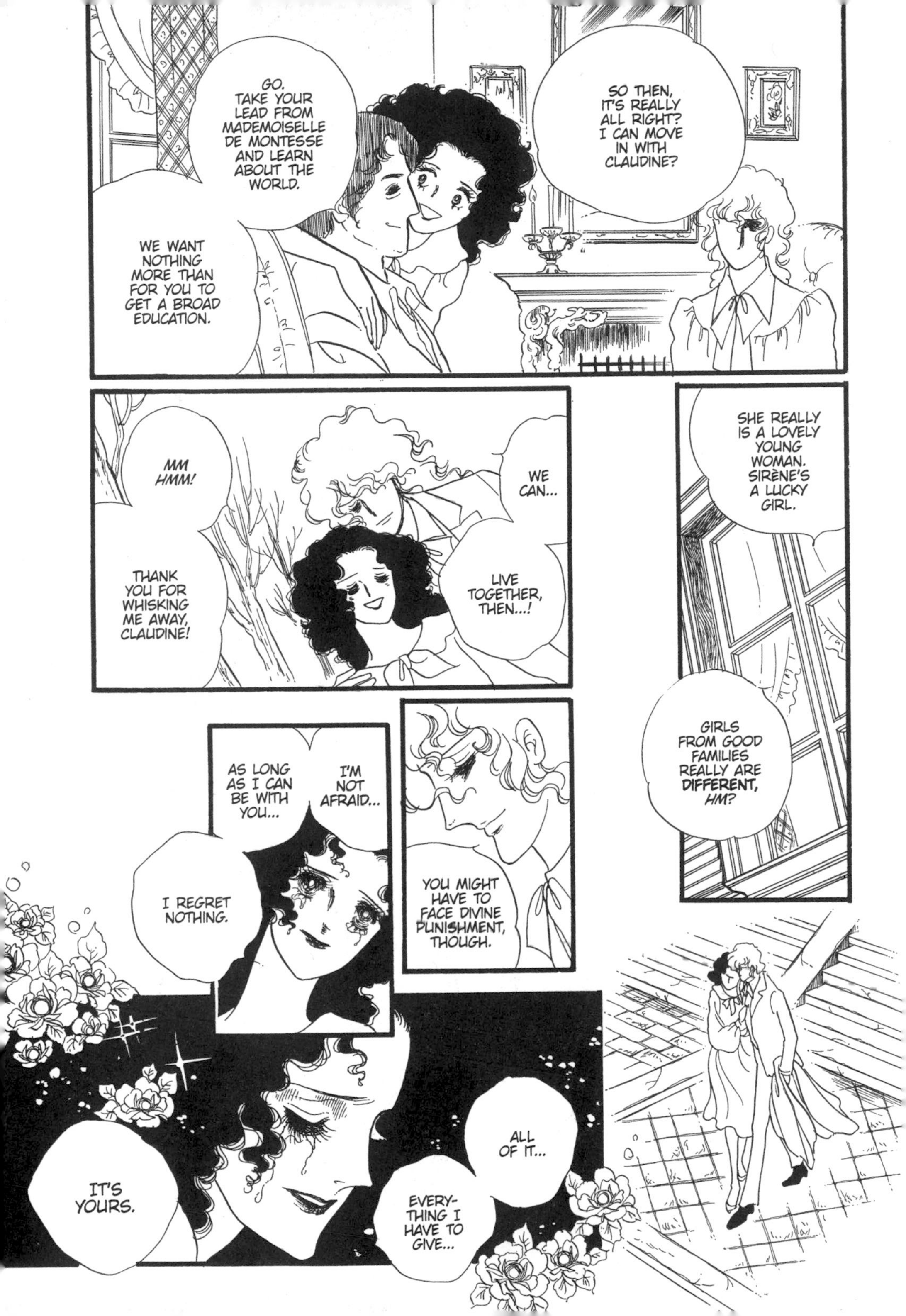
SO THEN, IT'S REALLY ALL RIGHT? I CAN MOVE IN WITH CLAUDINE?
GO. TAKE YOUR LEAD FROM MADEMOISELLE DE MONTESSE AND LEARN ABOUT THE WORLD.
WE WANT NOTHING MORE THAN FOR YOU TO GET A BROAD EDUCATION.
SHE REALLY IS A LOVELY YOUNG WOMAN. SIRÈNE'S A LUCKY GIRL.
GIRLS FROM GOOD FAMILIES REALLY ARE **DIFFERENT**, *HM?*
WE CAN...
LIVE TOGETHER, THEN...!
MM HMM!
THANK YOU FOR WHISKING ME AWAY, CLAUDINE!
YOU MIGHT HAVE TO FACE DIVINE PUNISHMENT, THOUGH.
I'M NOT AFRAID...
AS LONG AS I CAN BE WITH YOU...
I REGRET NOTHING.
ALL OF IT...
EVERY-THING I HAVE TO GIVE...
IT'S YOURS.

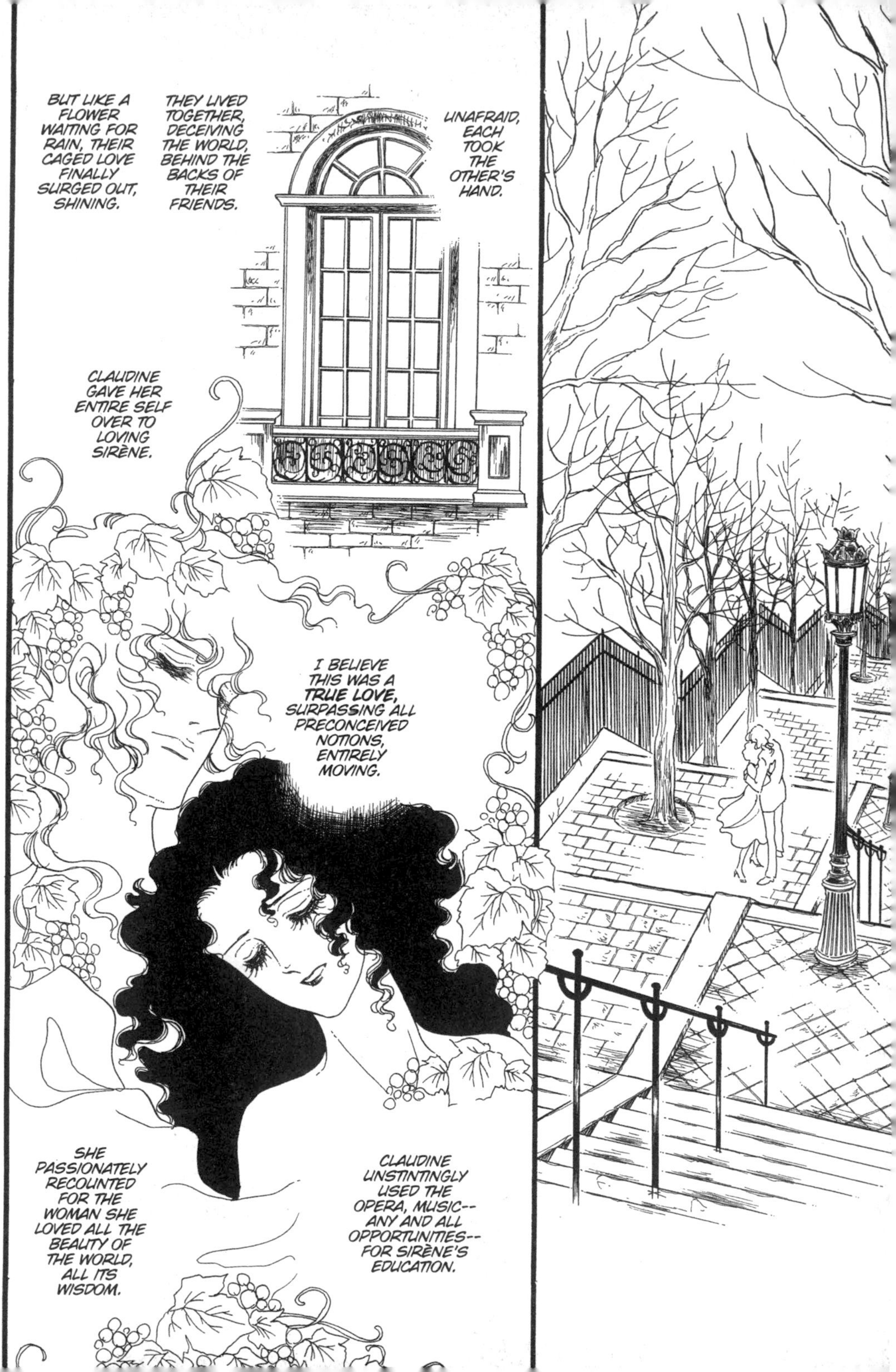
UNAFRAID, EACH TOOK THE OTHER'S HAND.
THEY LIVED TOGETHER, DECEIVING THE WORLD, BEHIND THE BACKS OF THEIR FRIENDS.
BUT LIKE A FLOWER WAITING FOR RAIN, THEIR CAGED LOVE FINALLY SURGED OUT, SHINING.
CLAUDINE GAVE HER ENTIRE SELF OVER TO LOVING SIRÈNE.
I BELIEVE THIS WAS A **TRUE LOVE**, SURPASSING ALL PRECONCEIVED NOTIONS, ENTIRELY MOVING.
CLAUDINE UNSTINTINGLY USED THE OPERA, MUSIC-- ANY AND ALL OPPORTUNITIES-- FOR SIRÈNE'S EDUCATION.
SHE PASSIONATELY RECOUNTED FOR THE WOMAN SHE LOVED ALL THE BEAUTY OF THE WORLD, ALL ITS WISDOM.

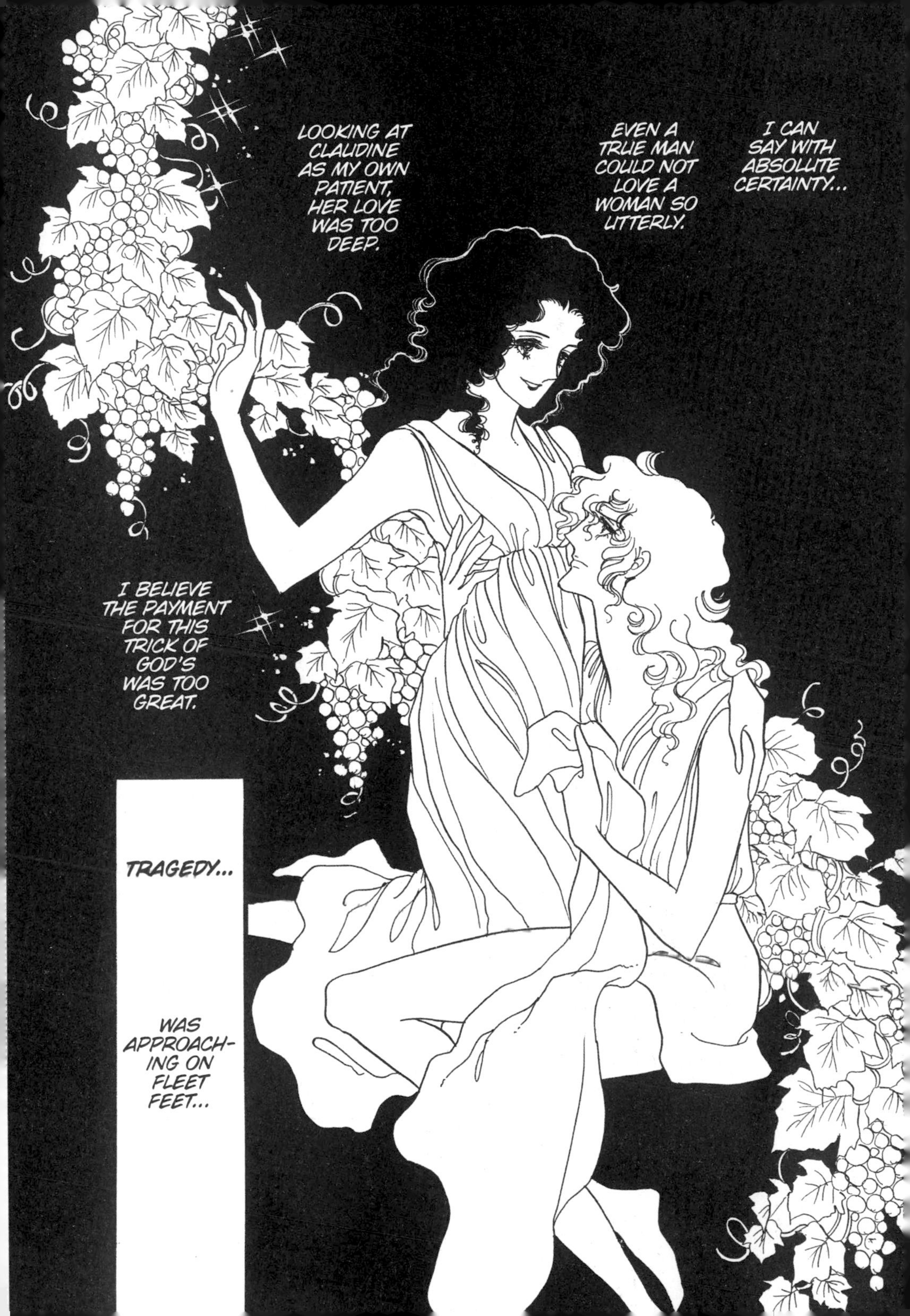
I CAN SAY WITH ABSOLUTE CERTAINTY...
EVEN A TRUE MAN COULD NOT LOVE A WOMAN SO UTTERLY.
LOOKING AT CLAUDINE AS MY OWN PATIENT, HER LOVE WAS TOO DEEP.
I BELIEVE THE PAYMENT FOR THIS TRICK OF GOD'S WAS TOO GREAT.
TRAGEDY...
WAS APPROACH-ING ON FLEET FEET...

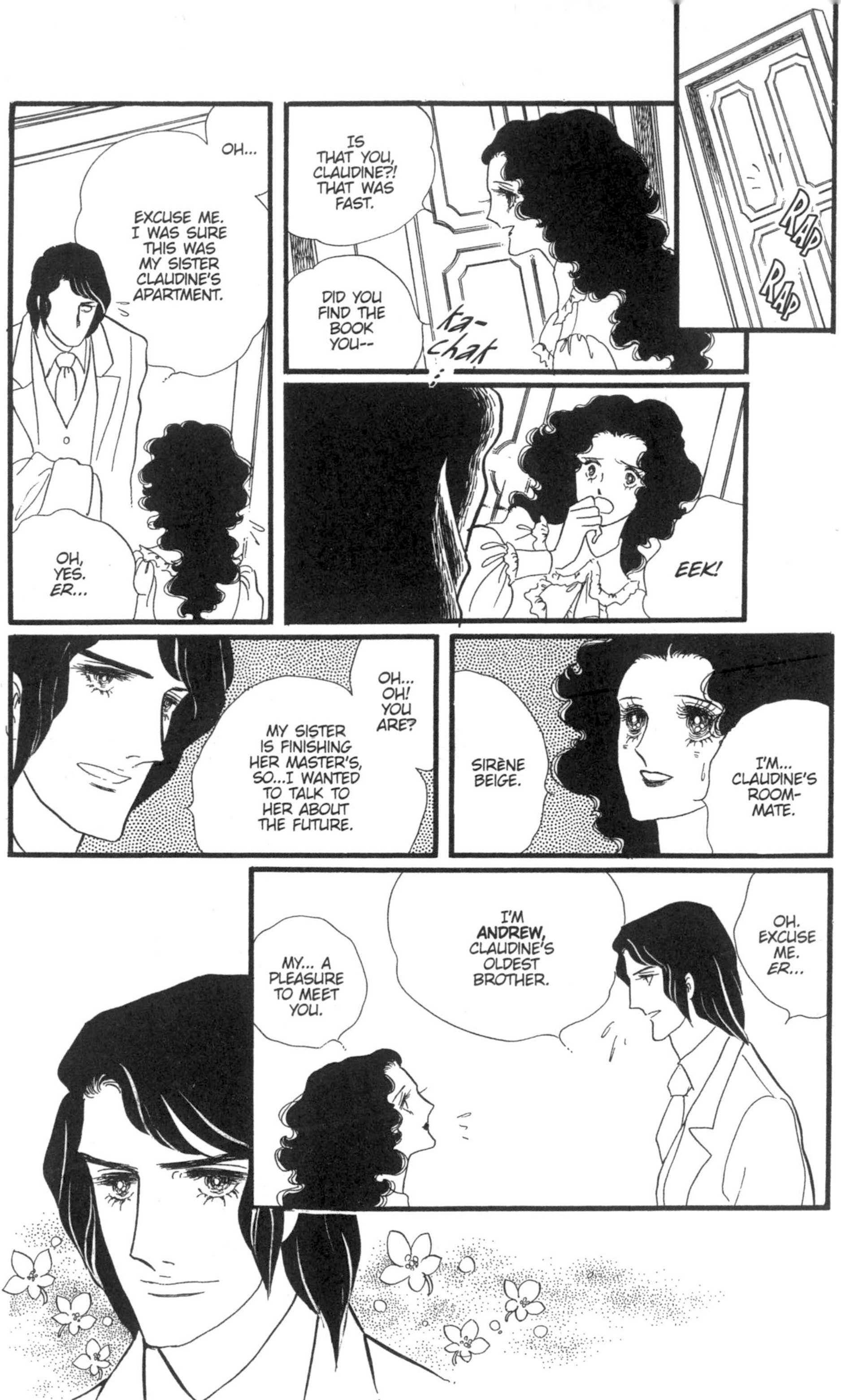
RAP
RAP
IS THAT YOU, CLAUDINE?! THAT WAS FAST.
DID YOU FIND THE BOOK YOU--
ka-chak
EEK!
OH...
EXCUSE ME. I WAS SURE THIS WAS MY SISTER CLAUDINE'S APARTMENT.
OH, YES. ER...
I'M... CLAUDINE'S ROOM-MATE.
SIRÈNE BEIGE.
OH... OH! YOU ARE?
MY SISTER IS FINISHING HER MASTER'S, SO...I WANTED TO TALK TO HER ABOUT THE FUTURE.
OH. EXCUSE ME. ER...
I'M ANDREW, CLAUDINE'S OLDEST BROTHER.
MY... A PLEASURE TO MEET YOU.

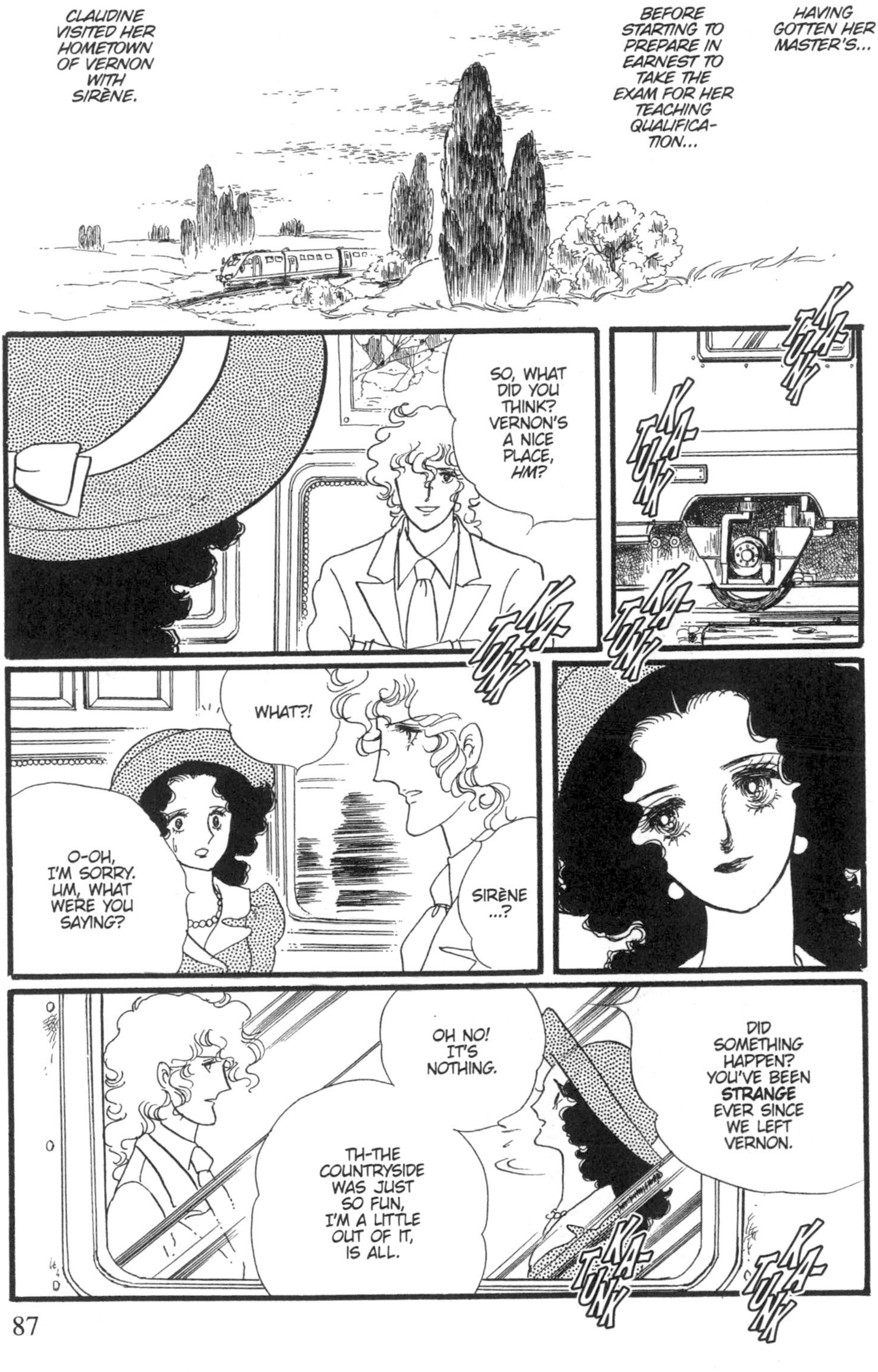

HAVING GOTTEN HER MASTER'S...
BEFORE STARTING TO PREPARE IN EARNEST TO TAKE THE EXAM FOR HER TEACHING QUALIFICA-TION...
CLAUDINE VISITED HER HOMETOWN OF VERNON WITH SIRÈNE.
KA-TUNK
KA-TUNK
KA-TUNK
SO, WHAT DID YOU THINK? VERNON'S A NICE PLACE, HM?
KA-TUNK
SIRÈNE ...?
WHAT?!
O-OH, I'M SORRY. UM, WHAT WERE YOU SAYING?
DID SOMETHING HAPPEN? YOU'VE BEEN **STRANGE** EVER SINCE WE LEFT VERNON.
KA-TUNK
OH NO! IT'S NOTHING.
TH-THE COUNTRYSIDE WAS JUST SO FUN, I'M A LITTLE OUT OF IT, IS ALL.
KA-TUNK

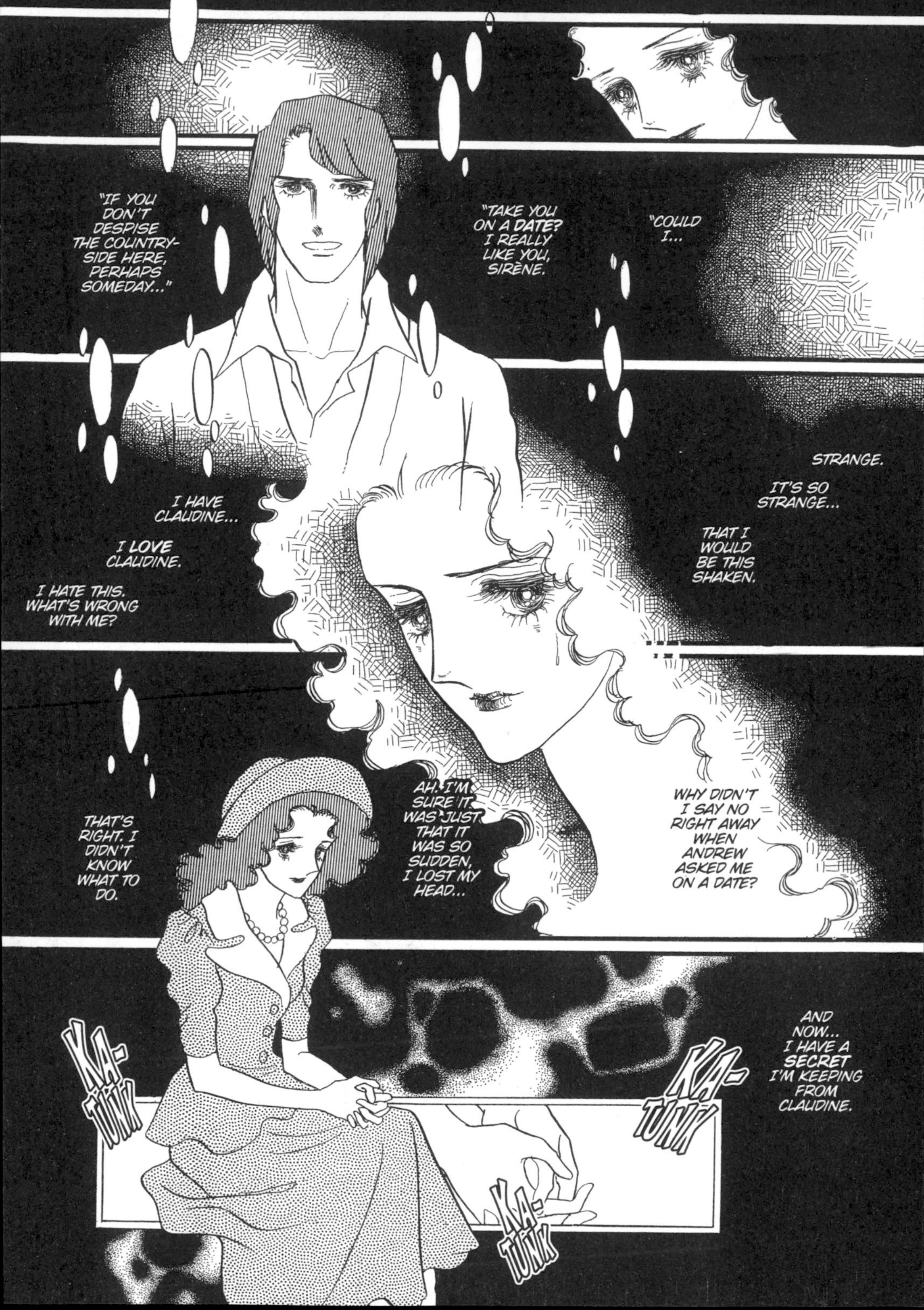

"IF YOU DON'T DESPISE THE COUNTRY-SIDE HERE, PERHAPS SOMEDAY..."
"TAKE YOU ON A DATE? I REALLY LIKE YOU, SIRÈNE.
"COULD I...
STRANGE.
IT'S SO STRANGE...
THAT I WOULD BE THIS SHAKEN.
I HAVE CLAUDINE...
I LOVE CLAUDINE.
I HATE THIS. WHAT'S WRONG WITH ME?
WHY DIDN'T I SAY NO RIGHT AWAY WHEN ANDREW ASKED ME ON A DATE?
AH. I'M SURE IT WAS JUST THAT IT WAS SO SUDDEN, I LOST MY HEAD...
THAT'S RIGHT. I DIDN'T KNOW WHAT TO DO.
AND NOW... I HAVE A SECRET I'M KEEPING FROM CLAUDINE.
KA-TUNK
KA-TUNK
KA-TUNK

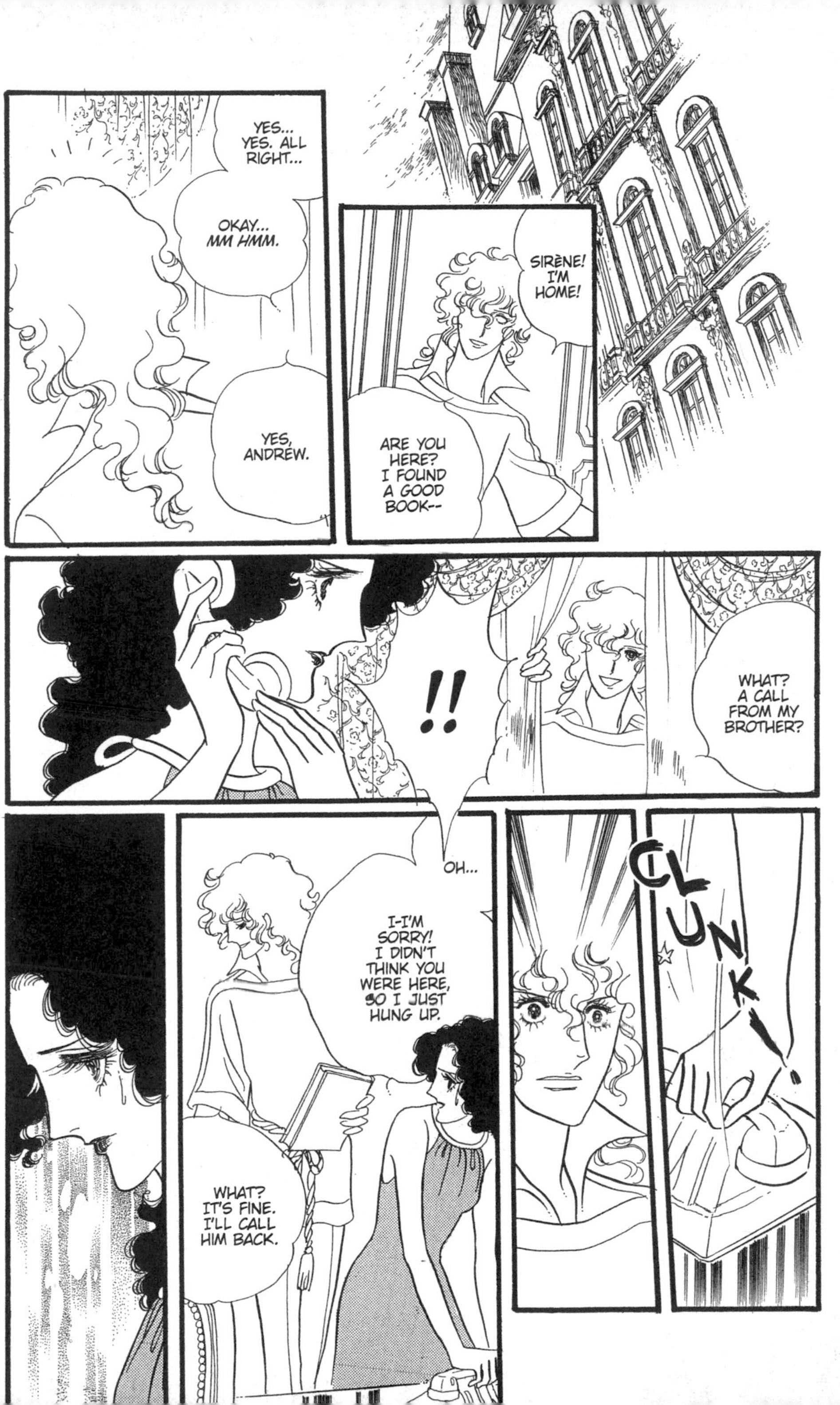
SIRÈNE! I'M HOME!
ARE YOU HERE? I FOUND A GOOD BOOK--
YES... YES. ALL RIGHT...
OKAY... MM HMM.
YES, ANDREW.
WHAT? A CALL FROM MY BROTHER?
!!
CLUNK!
OH...
I-I'M SORRY! I DIDN'T THINK YOU WERE HERE, SO I JUST HUNG UP.
WHAT? IT'S FINE. I'LL CALL HIM BACK.

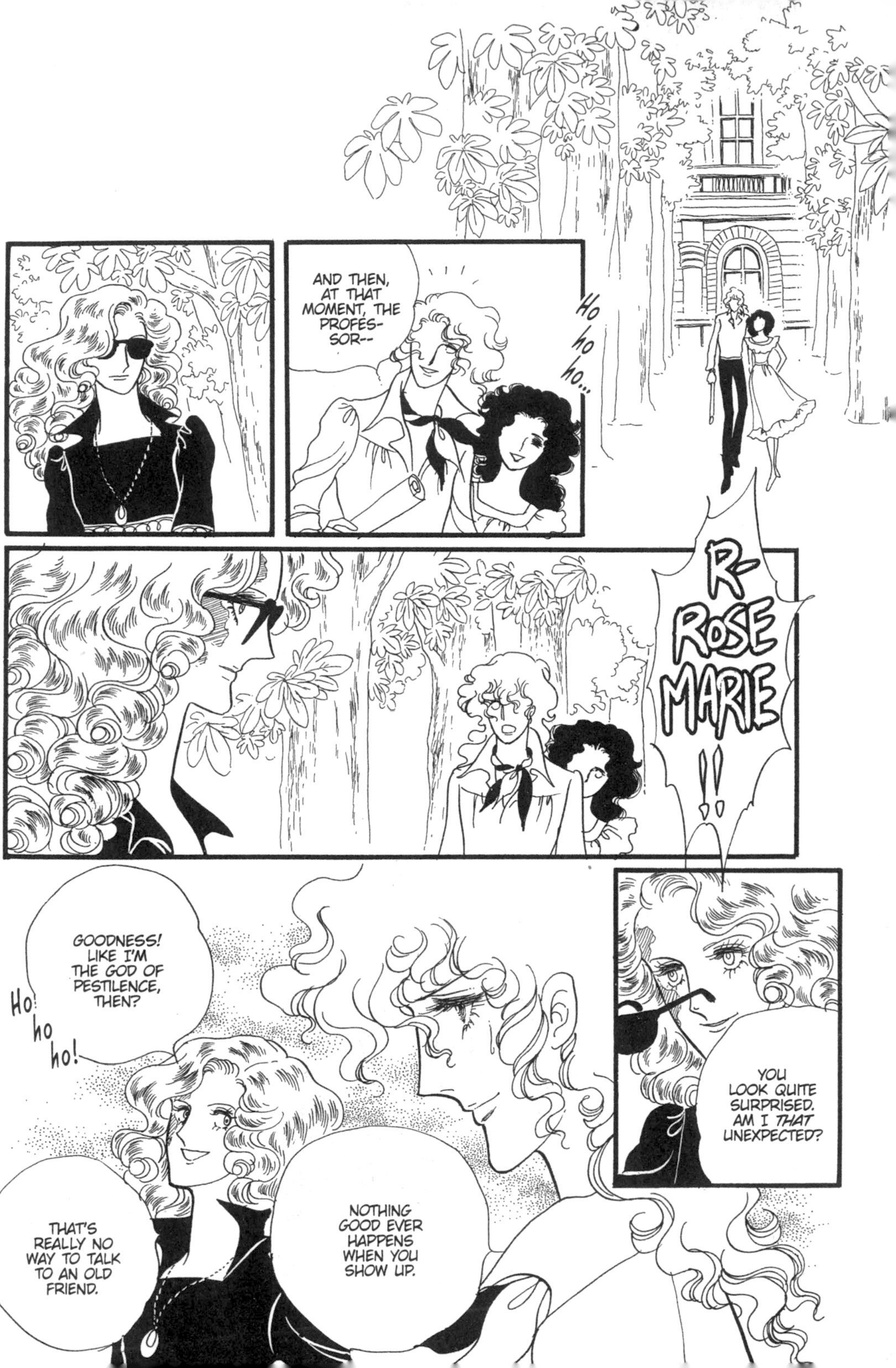
Ho ho ho...
AND THEN, AT THAT MOMENT, THE PROFES-SOR--
R-ROSE MARIE!!
YOU LOOK QUITE SURPRISED. AM I *THAT* UNEXPECTED?
NOTHING GOOD EVER HAPPENS WHEN YOU SHOW UP.
GOODNESS! LIKE I'M THE GOD OF PESTILENCE, THEN?
Ho! ho ho!
THAT'S REALLY NO WAY TO TALK TO AN OLD FRIEND.

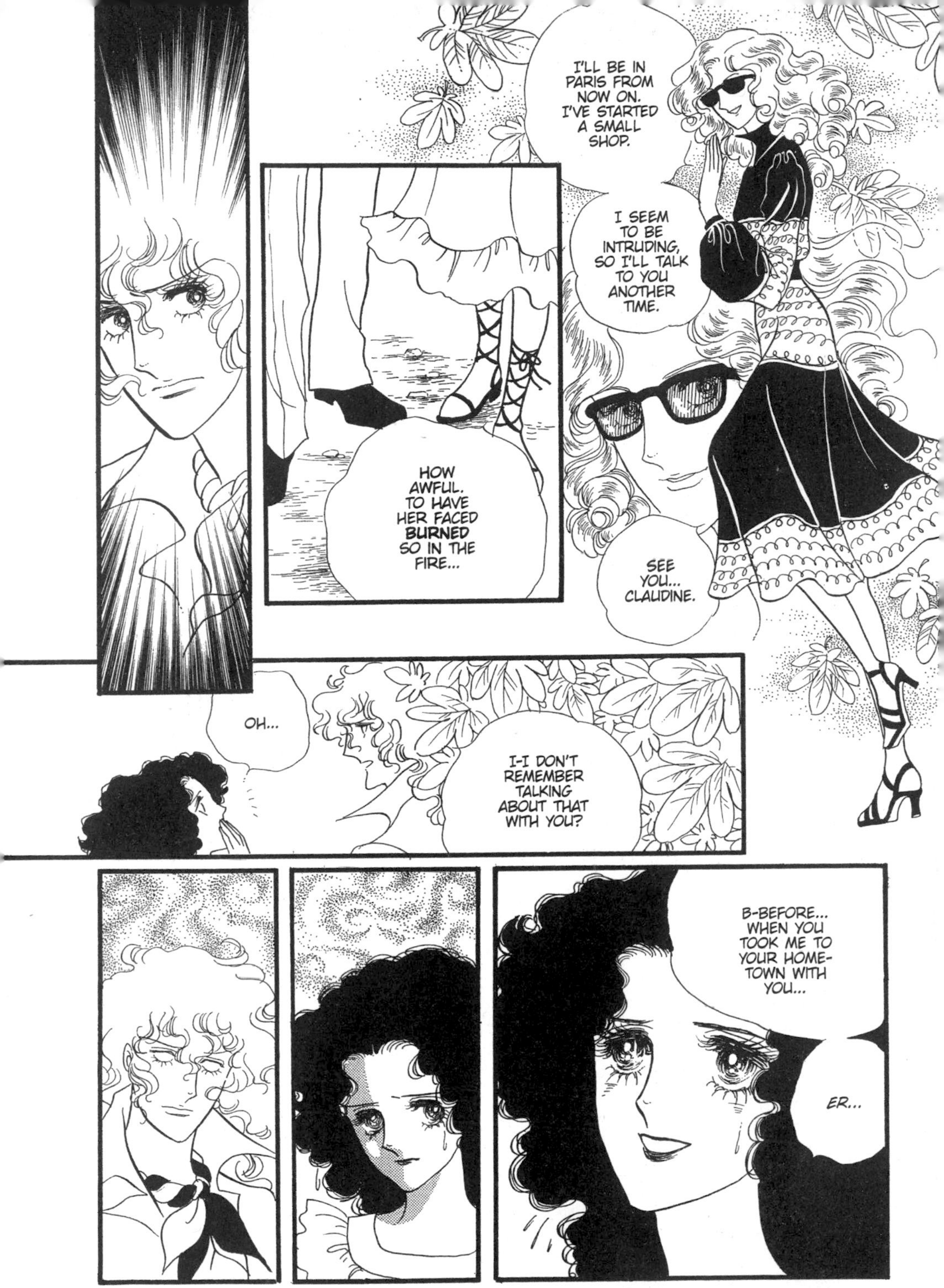
I'LL BE IN PARIS FROM NOW ON. I'VE STARTED A SMALL SHOP.
I SEEM TO BE INTRUDING, SO I'LL TALK TO YOU ANOTHER TIME.
SEE YOU... CLAUDINE.
HOW AWFUL. TO HAVE HER FACED **BURNED** SO IN THE FIRE...
I-I DON'T REMEMBER TALKING ABOUT THAT WITH YOU?
OH...
B-BEFORE... WHEN YOU TOOK ME TO YOUR HOME-TOWN WITH YOU...
ER...

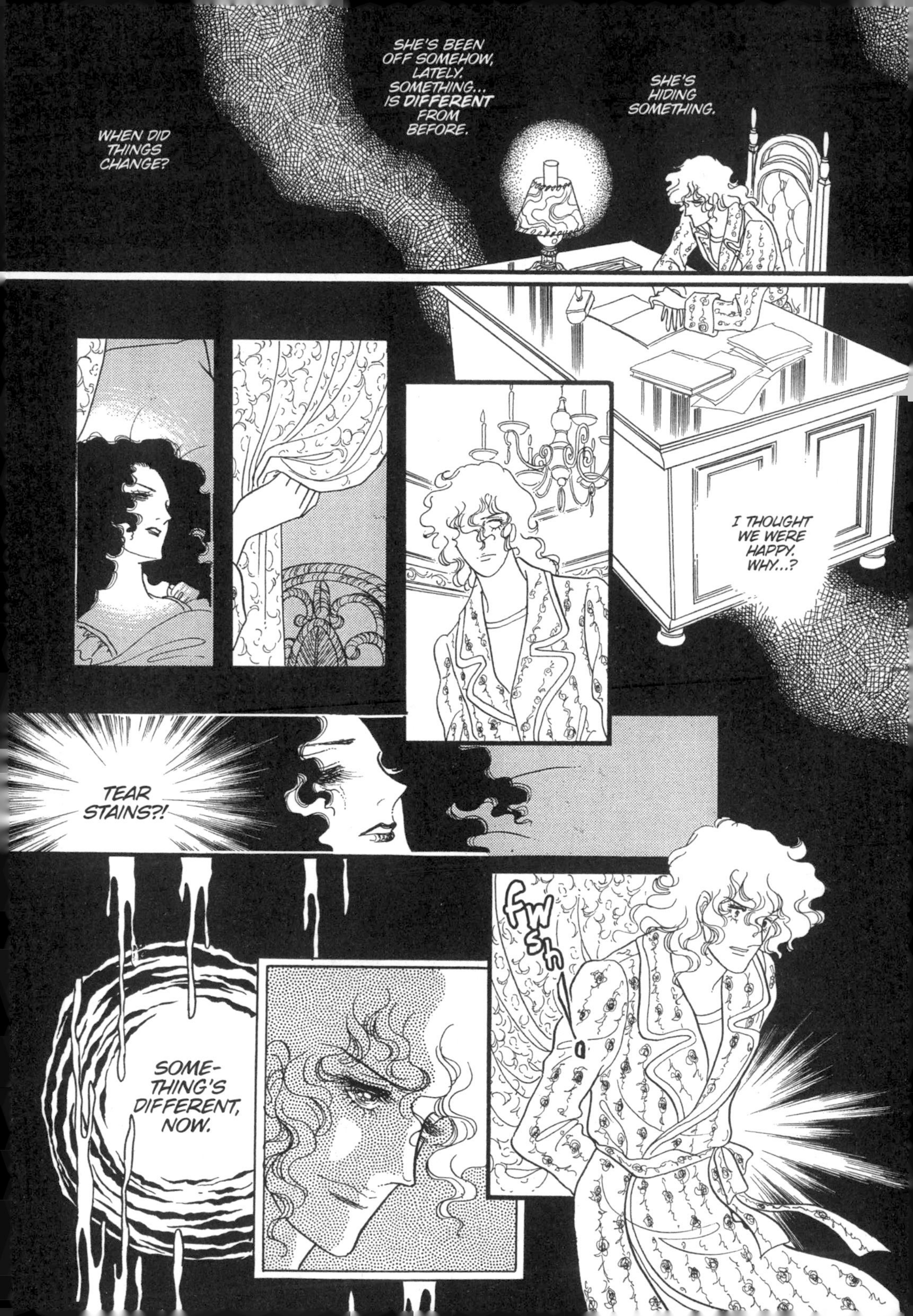
SHE'S BEEN OFF SOMEHOW, LATELY. SOMETHING... IS **DIFFERENT** FROM BEFORE.
SHE'S HIDING SOMETHING.
WHEN DID THINGS CHANGE?
I THOUGHT WE WERE HAPPY. WHY...?
TEAR STAINS?!
fwsh
SOME-THING'S DIFFERENT, NOW.

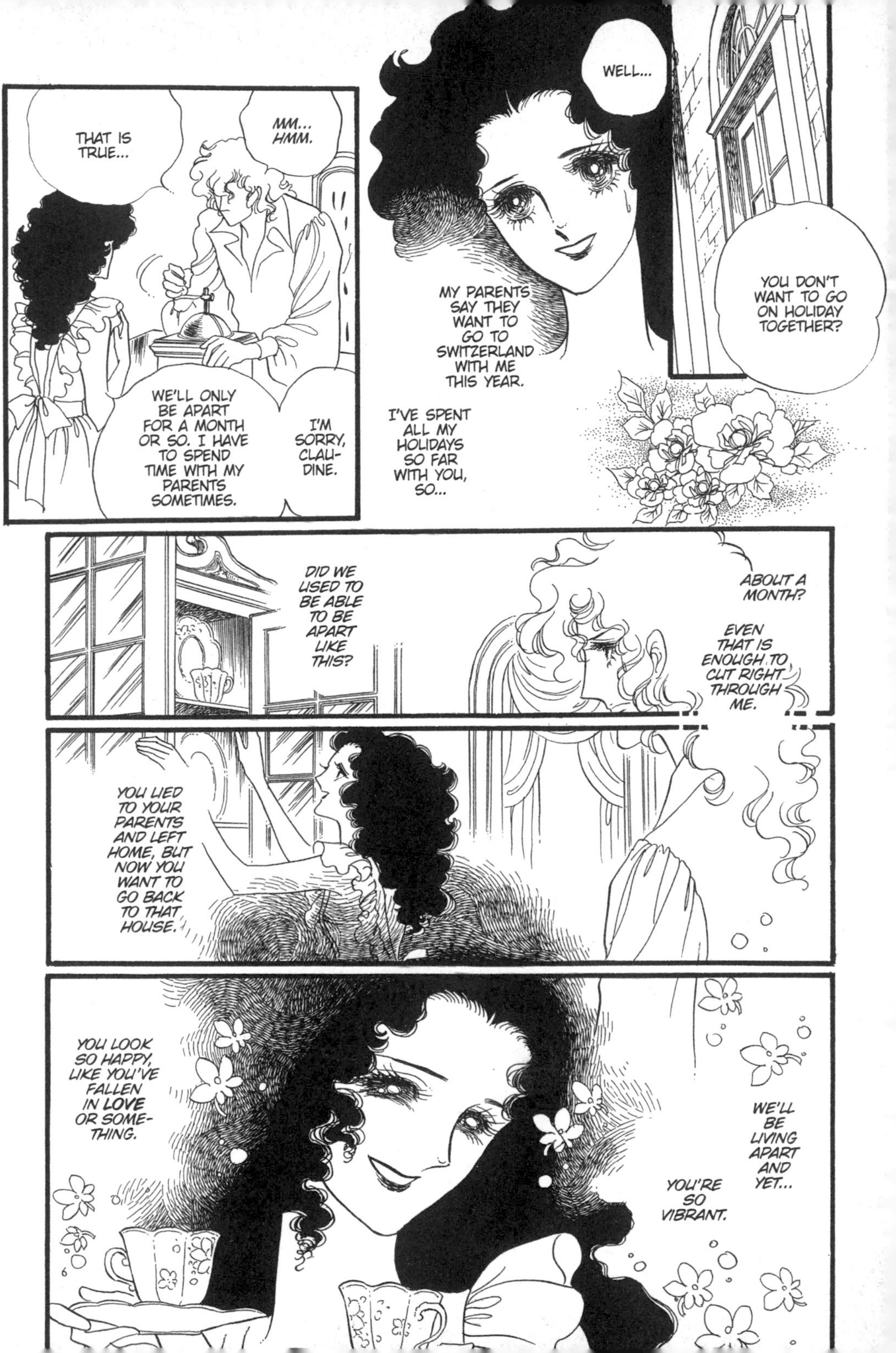
WELL...
YOU DON'T WANT TO GO ON HOLIDAY TOGETHER?
MY PARENTS SAY THEY WANT TO GO TO SWITZERLAND WITH ME THIS YEAR.
I'VE SPENT ALL MY HOLIDAYS SO FAR WITH YOU, SO...
MM... HMM.
THAT IS TRUE...
I'M SORRY, CLAUDINE.
WE'LL ONLY BE APART FOR A MONTH OR SO. I HAVE TO SPEND TIME WITH MY PARENTS SOMETIMES.
ABOUT A MONTH?
EVEN THAT IS ENOUGH TO CUT RIGHT THROUGH ME.
DID WE USED TO BE ABLE TO BE APART LIKE THIS?
YOU LIED TO YOUR PARENTS AND LEFT HOME, BUT NOW YOU WANT TO GO BACK TO THAT HOUSE.
WE'LL BE LIVING APART AND YET...
YOU'RE SO VIBRANT.
YOU LOOK SO HAPPY, LIKE YOU'VE FALLEN IN **LOVE** OR SOMETHING.

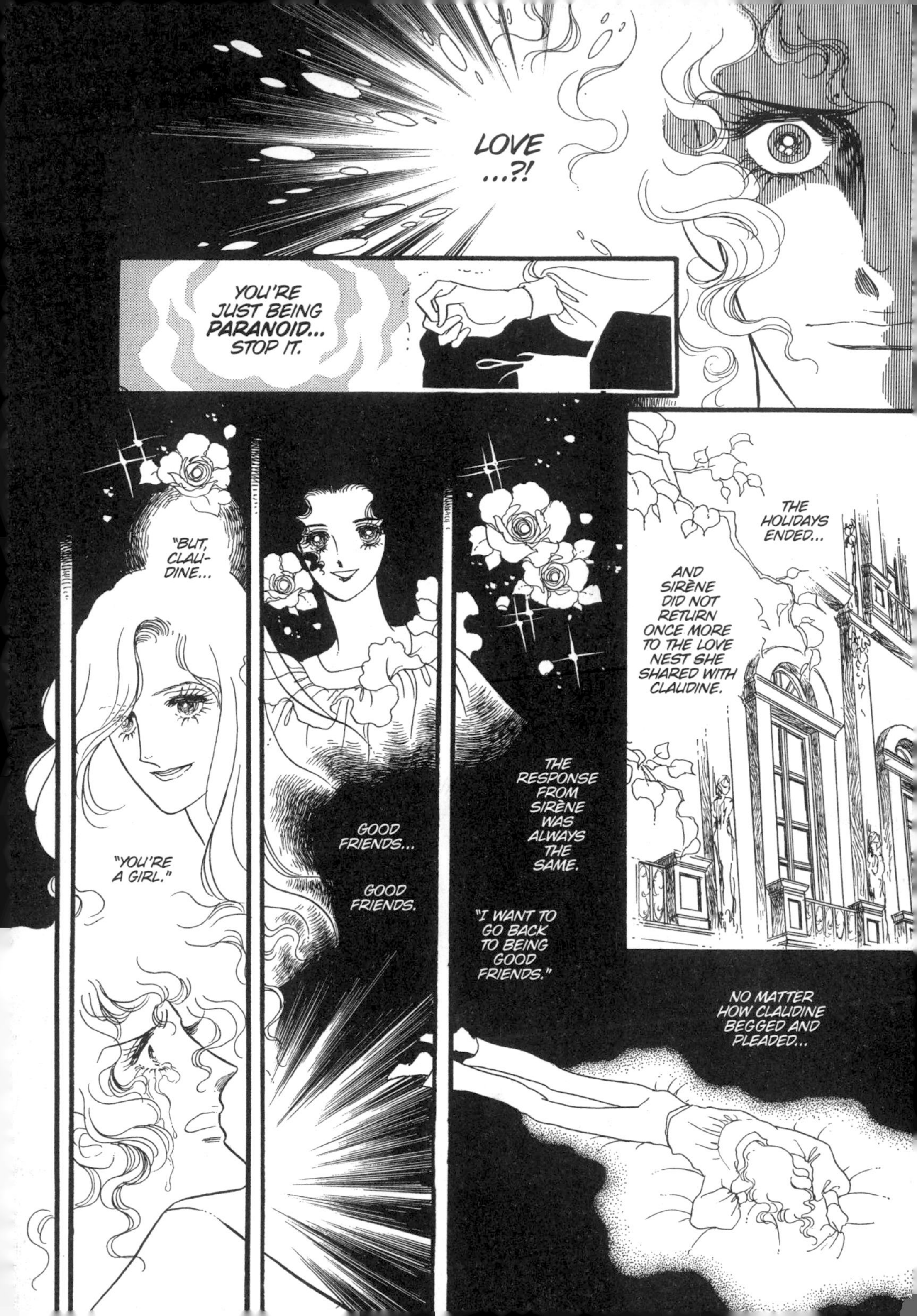
LOVE ...?!
YOU'RE JUST BEING PARANOID... STOP IT.
THE HOLIDAYS ENDED...
AND SIRÈNE DID NOT RETURN ONCE MORE TO THE LOVE NEST SHE SHARED WITH CLAUDINE.
THE RESPONSE FROM SIRÈNE WAS ALWAYS THE SAME.
"I WANT TO GO BACK TO BEING GOOD FRIENDS."
GOOD FRIENDS...
GOOD FRIENDS.
"BUT, CLAU-DINE...
"YOU'RE A GIRL."
NO MATTER HOW CLAUDINE BEGGED AND PLEADED...

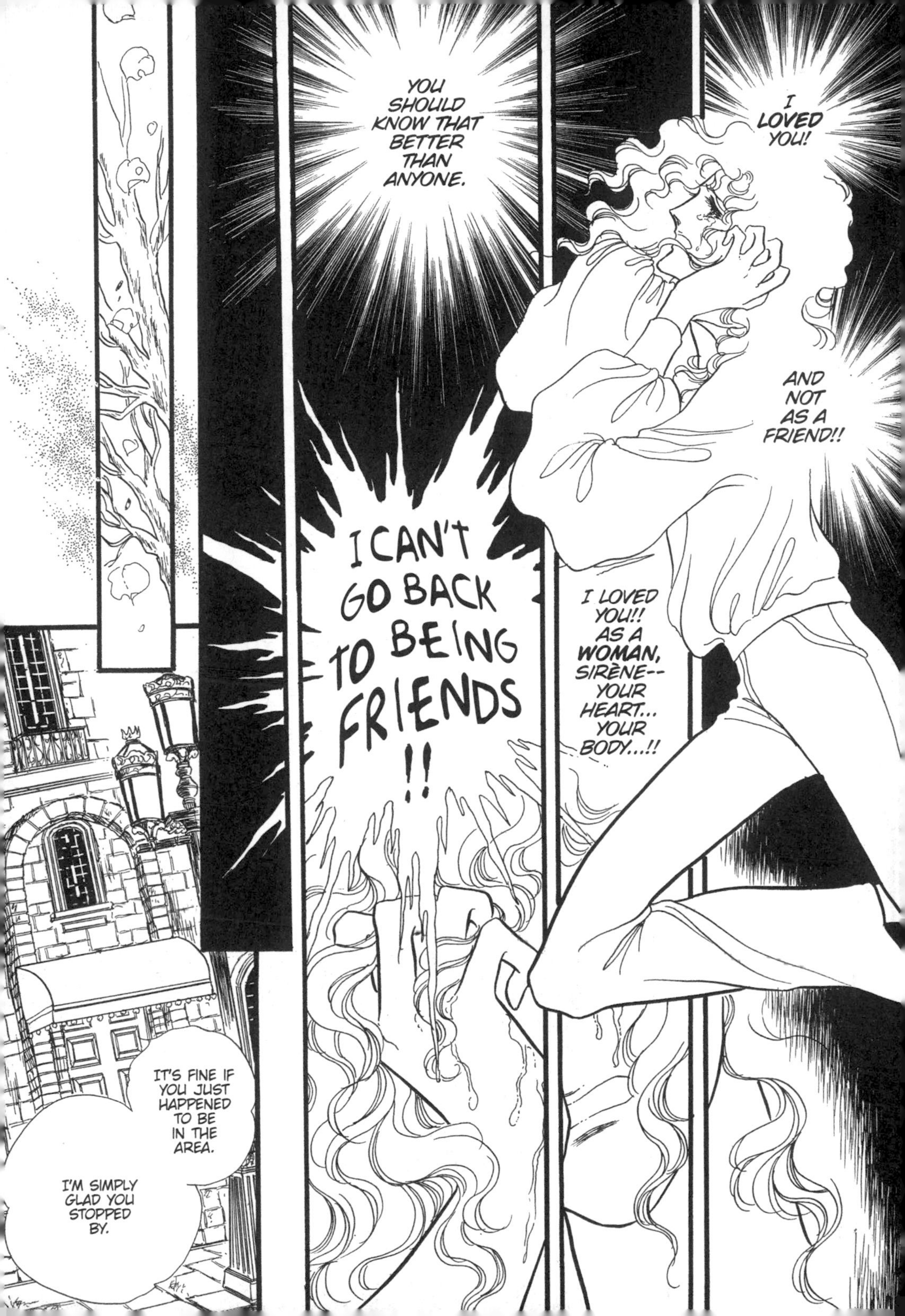
I LOVED YOU!
AND NOT AS A FRIEND!!
I LOVED YOU!! AS A WOMAN, SIRÈNE-- YOUR HEART... YOUR BODY...!!
YOU SHOULD KNOW THAT BETTER THAN ANYONE.
I CAN'T GO BACK TO BEING FRIENDS!!
IT'S FINE IF YOU JUST HAPPENED TO BE IN THE AREA.
I'M SIMPLY GLAD YOU STOPPED BY.

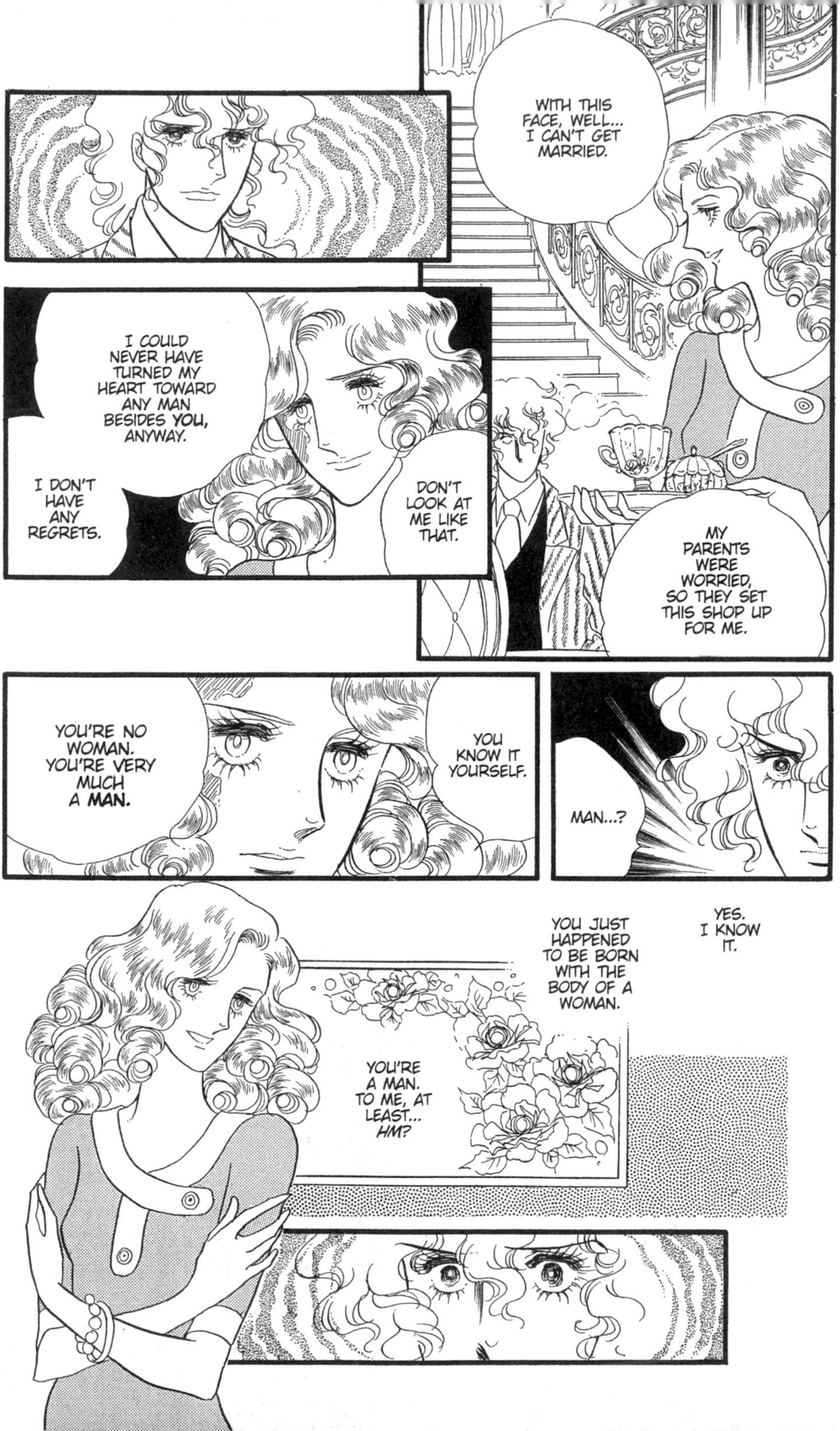
WITH THIS FACE, WELL... I CAN'T GET MARRIED.
MY PARENTS WERE WORRIED, SO THEY SET THIS SHOP UP FOR ME.
DON'T LOOK AT ME LIKE THAT.
I COULD NEVER HAVE TURNED MY HEART TOWARD ANY MAN BESIDES YOU, ANYWAY.
I DON'T HAVE ANY REGRETS.
MAN...?
YOU KNOW IT YOURSELF.
YOU'RE NO WOMAN. YOU'RE VERY MUCH A MAN.
YES. I KNOW IT.
YOU JUST HAPPENED TO BE BORN WITH THE BODY OF A WOMAN.
YOU'RE A MAN. TO ME, AT LEAST... HM?

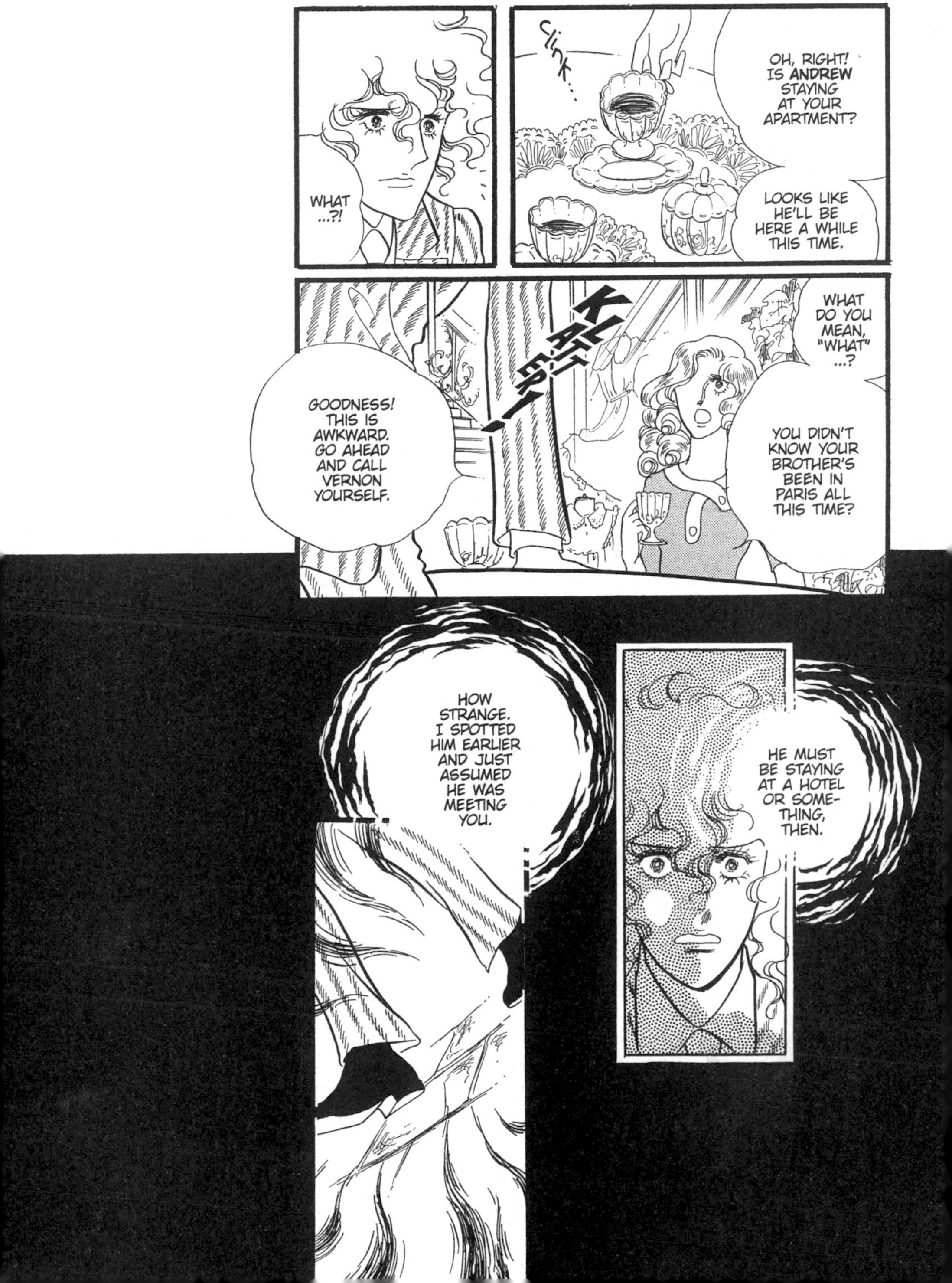
clink...
OH, RIGHT! IS ANDREW STAYING AT YOUR APARTMENT?
LOOKS LIKE HE'LL BE HERE A WHILE THIS TIME.
WHAT ...?!
WHAT DO YOU MEAN, "WHAT" ...?
YOU DIDN'T KNOW YOUR BROTHER'S BEEN IN PARIS ALL THIS TIME?
KLATTER!!
GOODNESS! THIS IS AWKWARD. GO AHEAD AND CALL VERNON YOURSELF.
HE MUST BE STAYING AT A HOTEL OR SOME-THING, THEN.
HOW STRANGE. I SPOTTED HIM EARLIER AND JUST ASSUMED HE WAS MEETING YOU.

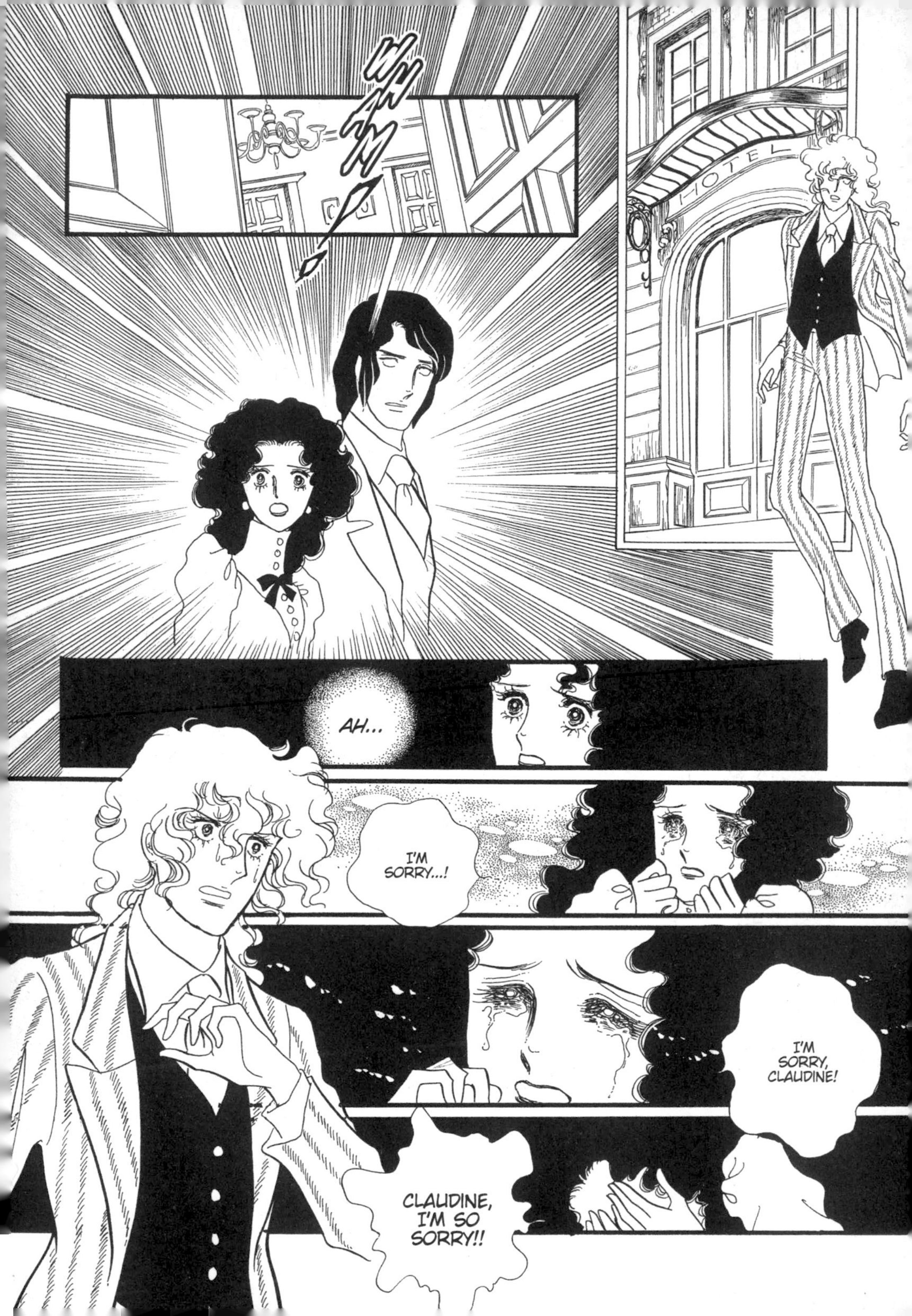
HOTEL
WHAM
AH...
I'M SORRY...!
I'M SORRY, CLAUDINE!
CLAUDINE, I'M SO SORRY!!

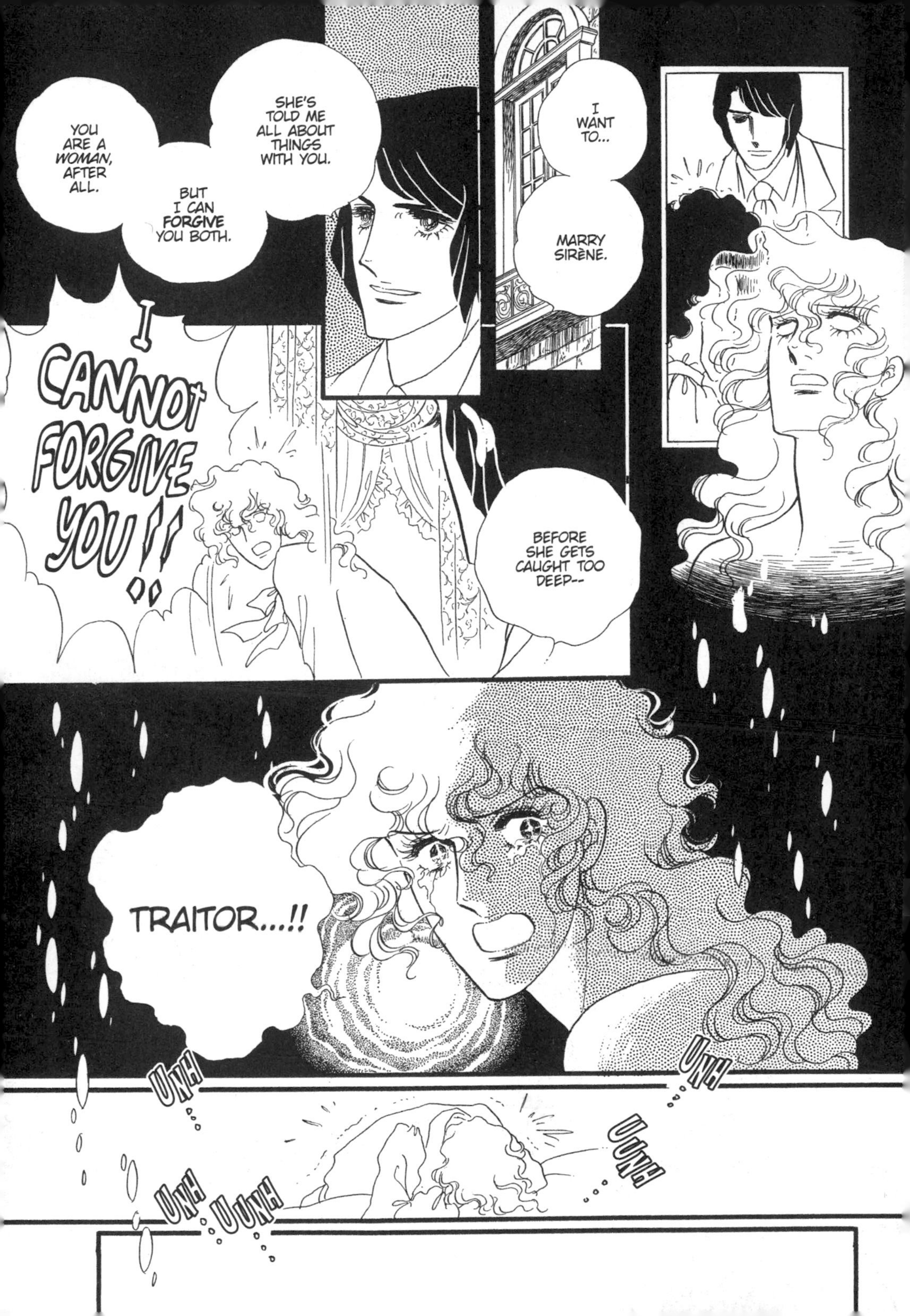
I WANT TO...
MARRY SIRÈNE.
BEFORE SHE GETS CAUGHT TOO DEEP--
SHE'S TOLD ME ALL ABOUT THINGS WITH YOU.
YOU ARE A *WOMAN*, AFTER ALL.
BUT I CAN **FORGIVE** YOU BOTH.
I CANNOT FORGIVE YOU!!
TRAITOR...!!
UNH...
UUNH...
UNH...
UNH
UUNH...

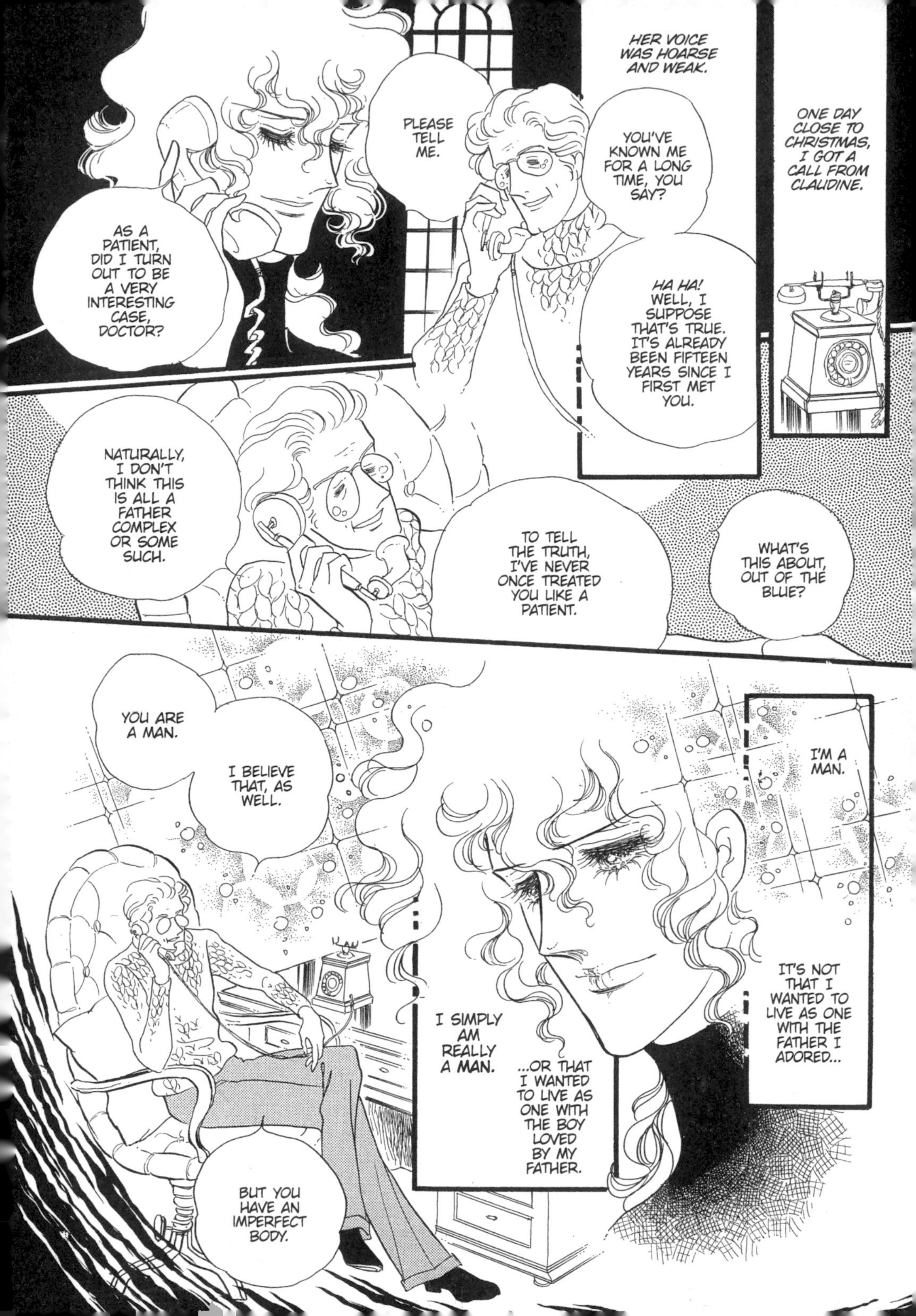
ONE DAY CLOSE TO CHRISTMAS, I GOT A CALL FROM CLAUDINE.
HER VOICE WAS HOARSE AND WEAK.
YOU'VE KNOWN ME FOR A LONG TIME, YOU SAY?
PLEASE TELL ME.
HA HA! WELL, I SUPPOSE THAT'S TRUE. IT'S ALREADY BEEN FIFTEEN YEARS SINCE I FIRST MET YOU.
AS A PATIENT, DID I TURN OUT TO BE A VERY INTERESTING CASE, DOCTOR?
WHAT'S THIS ABOUT, OUT OF THE BLUE?
TO TELL THE TRUTH, I'VE NEVER ONCE TREATED YOU LIKE A PATIENT.
NATURALLY, I DON'T THINK THIS IS ALL A FATHER COMPLEX OR SOME SUCH.
I'M A MAN.
IT'S NOT THAT I WANTED TO LIVE AS ONE WITH THE FATHER I ADORED...
...OR THAT I WANTED TO LIVE AS ONE WITH THE BOY LOVED BY MY FATHER.
I SIMPLY AM REALLY A MAN.
YOU ARE A MAN.
I BELIEVE THAT, AS WELL.
BUT YOU HAVE AN IMPERFECT BODY.

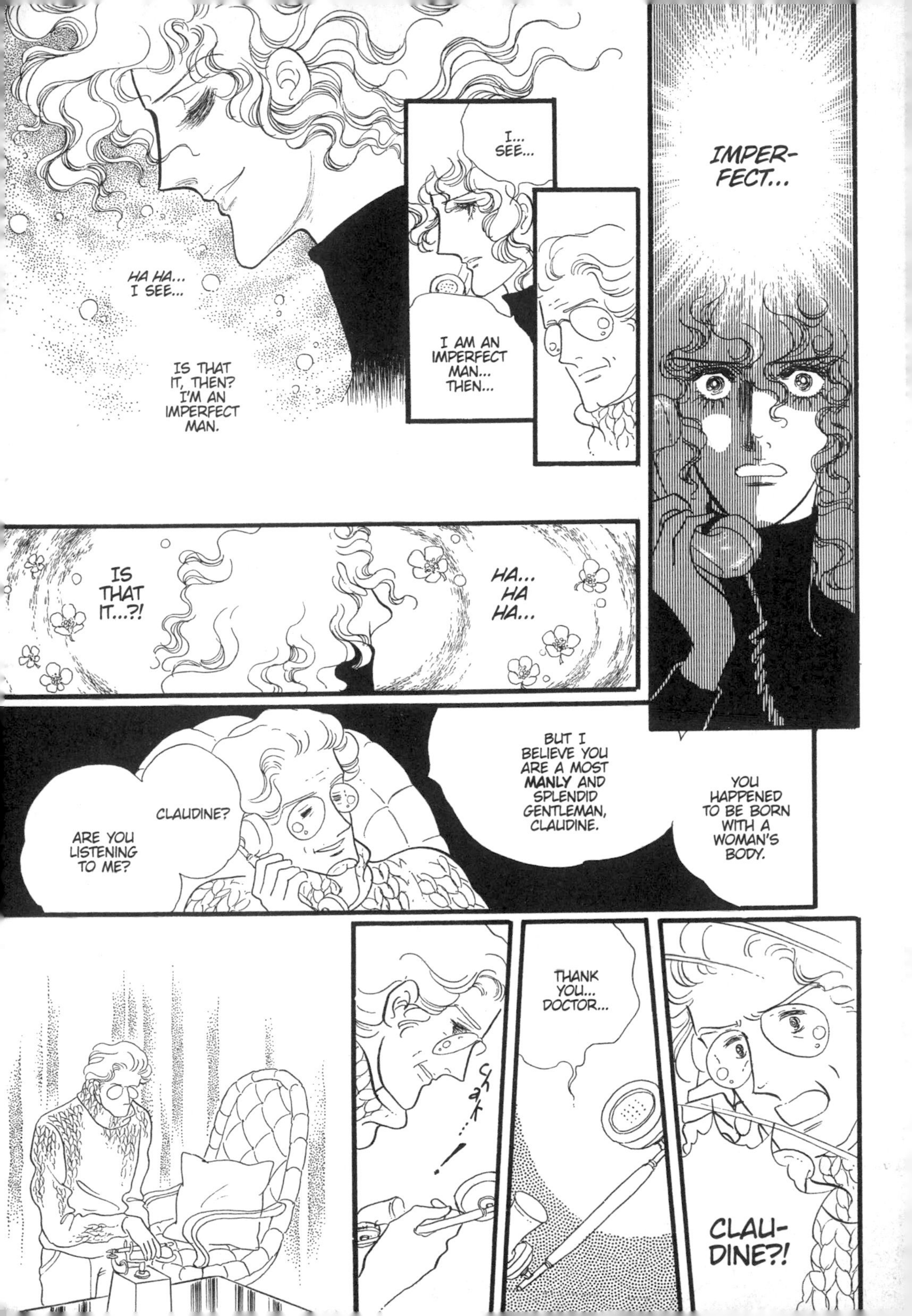
IMPERFECT...
I... SEE...
I AM AN IMPERFECT MAN... THEN...
HA HA... I SEE...
IS THAT IT, THEN? I'M AN IMPERFECT MAN.
HA... HA HA...
IS THAT IT...?!
YOU HAPPENED TO BE BORN WITH A WOMAN'S BODY.
BUT I BELIEVE YOU ARE A MOST MANLY AND SPLENDID GENTLEMAN, CLAUDINE.
CLAUDINE?
ARE YOU LISTENING TO ME?
CLAUDINE?!
THANK YOU... DOCTOR...

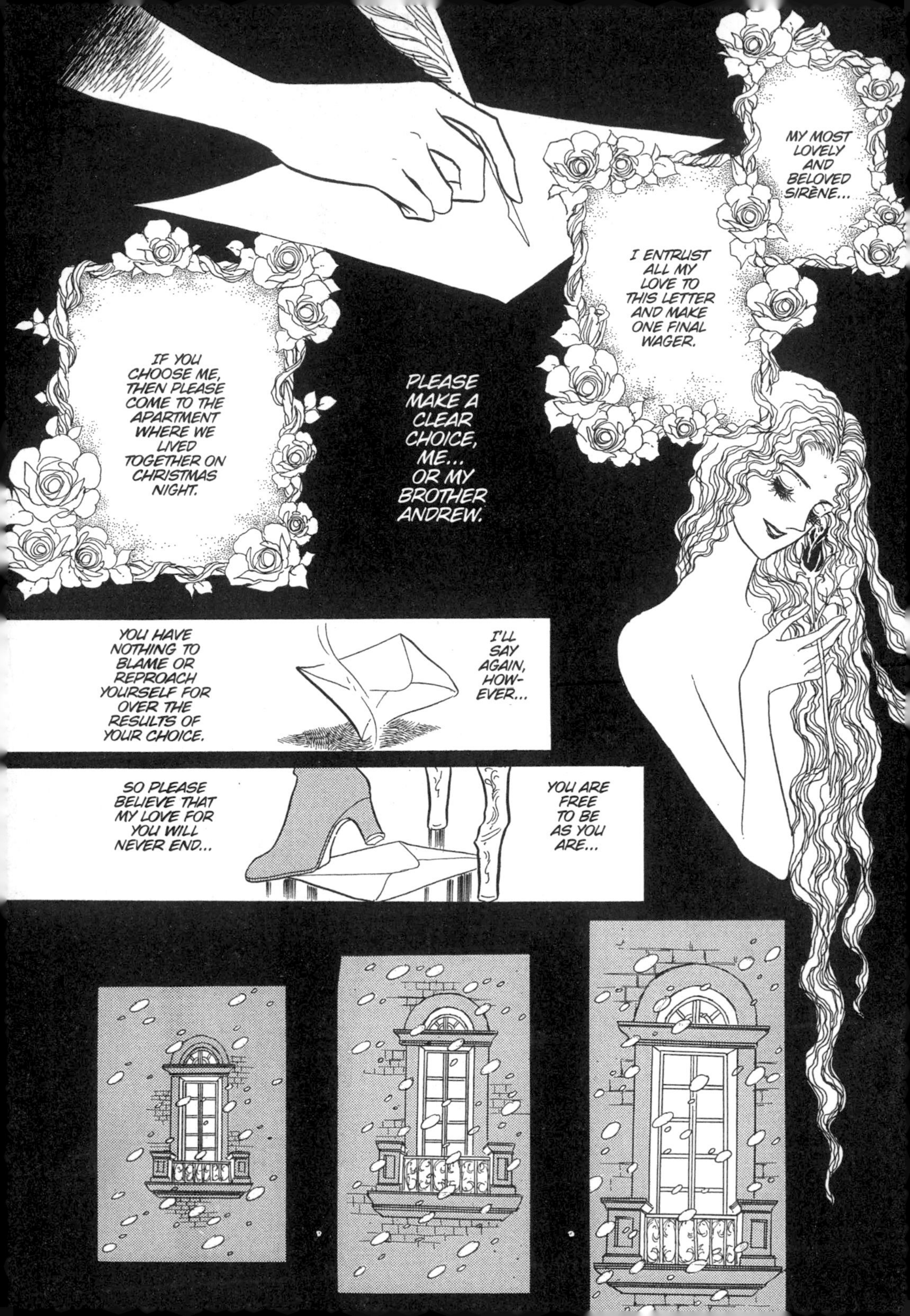
MY MOST LOVELY AND BELOVED SIRÈNE...
I ENTRUST ALL MY LOVE TO THIS LETTER AND MAKE ONE FINAL WAGER.
PLEASE MAKE A CLEAR CHOICE, ME... OR MY BROTHER ANDREW.
IF YOU CHOOSE ME, THEN PLEASE COME TO THE APARTMENT WHERE WE LIVED TOGETHER ON CHRISTMAS NIGHT.
I'LL SAY AGAIN, HOW-EVER...
YOU HAVE NOTHING TO BLAME OR REPROACH YOURSELF FOR OVER THE RESULTS OF YOUR CHOICE.
YOU ARE FREE TO BE AS YOU ARE...
SO PLEASE BELIEVE THAT MY LOVE FOR YOU WILL NEVER END...

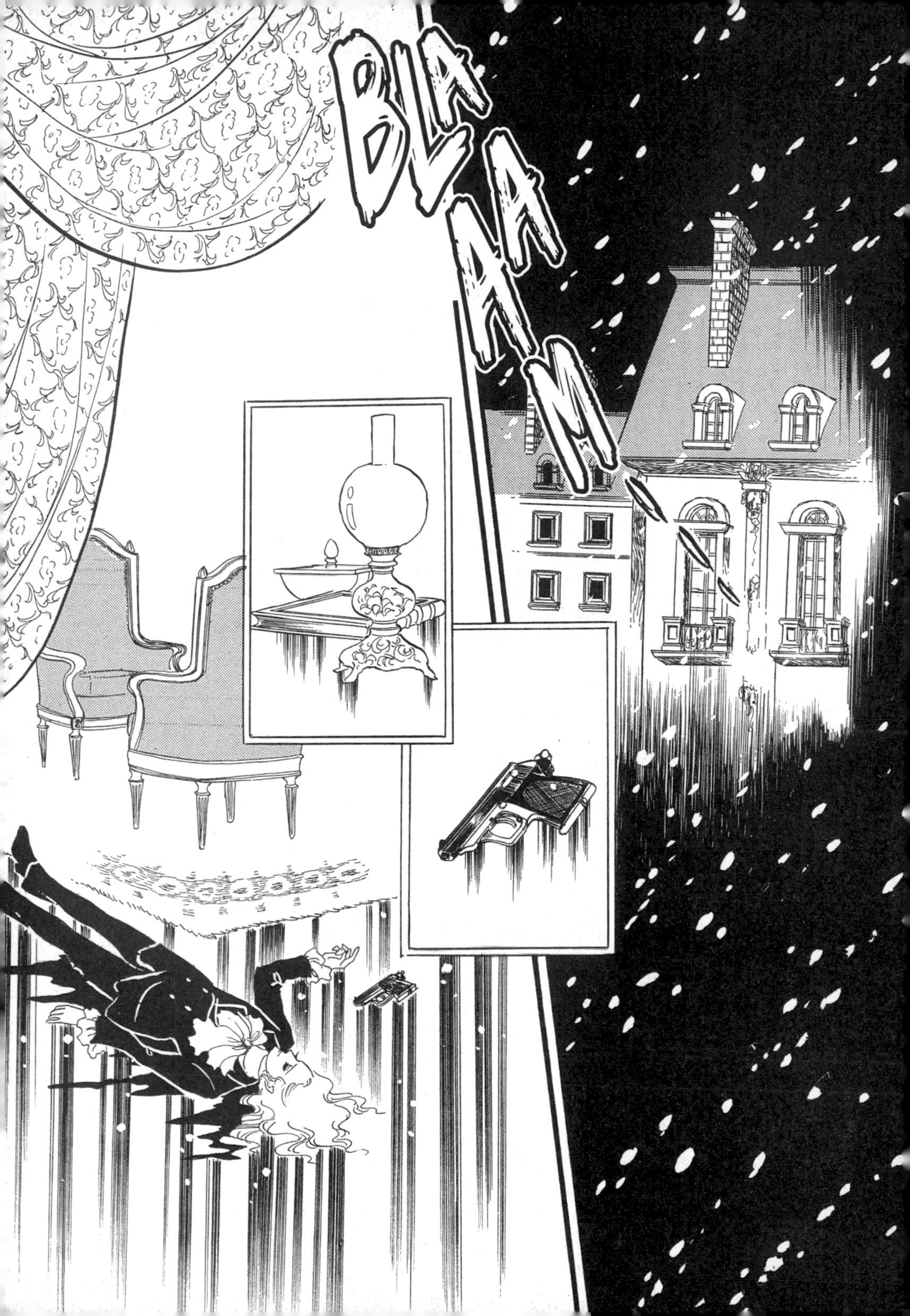
BLAAAM

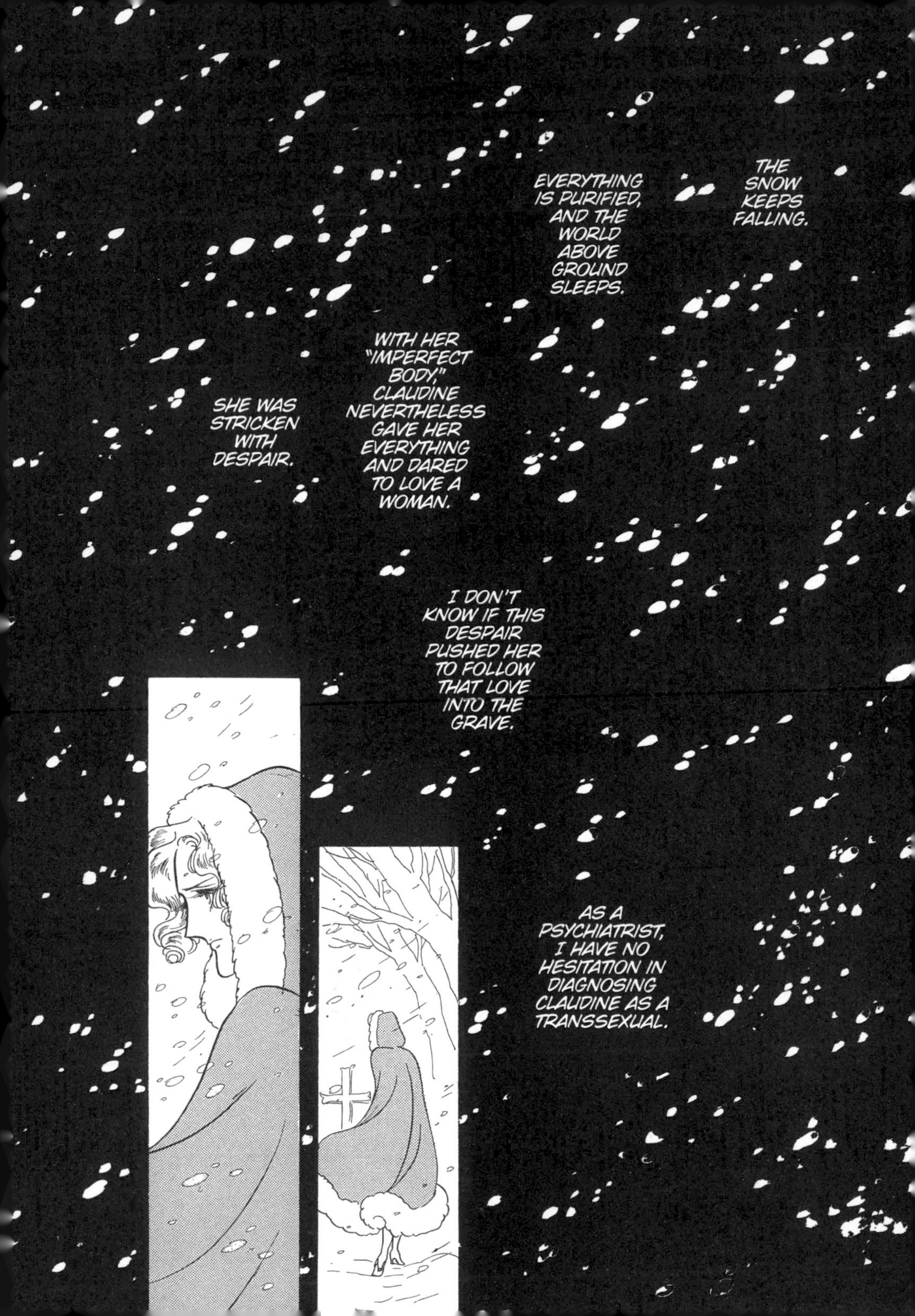
THE SNOW KEEPS FALLING.
EVERYTHING IS PURIFIED, AND THE WORLD ABOVE GROUND SLEEPS.
WITH HER "IMPERFECT BODY," CLAUDINE NEVERTHELESS GAVE HER EVERYTHING AND DARED TO LOVE A WOMAN.
SHE WAS STRICKEN WITH DESPAIR.
I DON'T KNOW IF THIS DESPAIR PUSHED HER TO FOLLOW THAT LOVE INTO THE GRAVE.
AS A PSYCHIATRIST, I HAVE NO HESITATION IN DIAGNOSING CLAUDINE AS A TRANSSEXUAL.

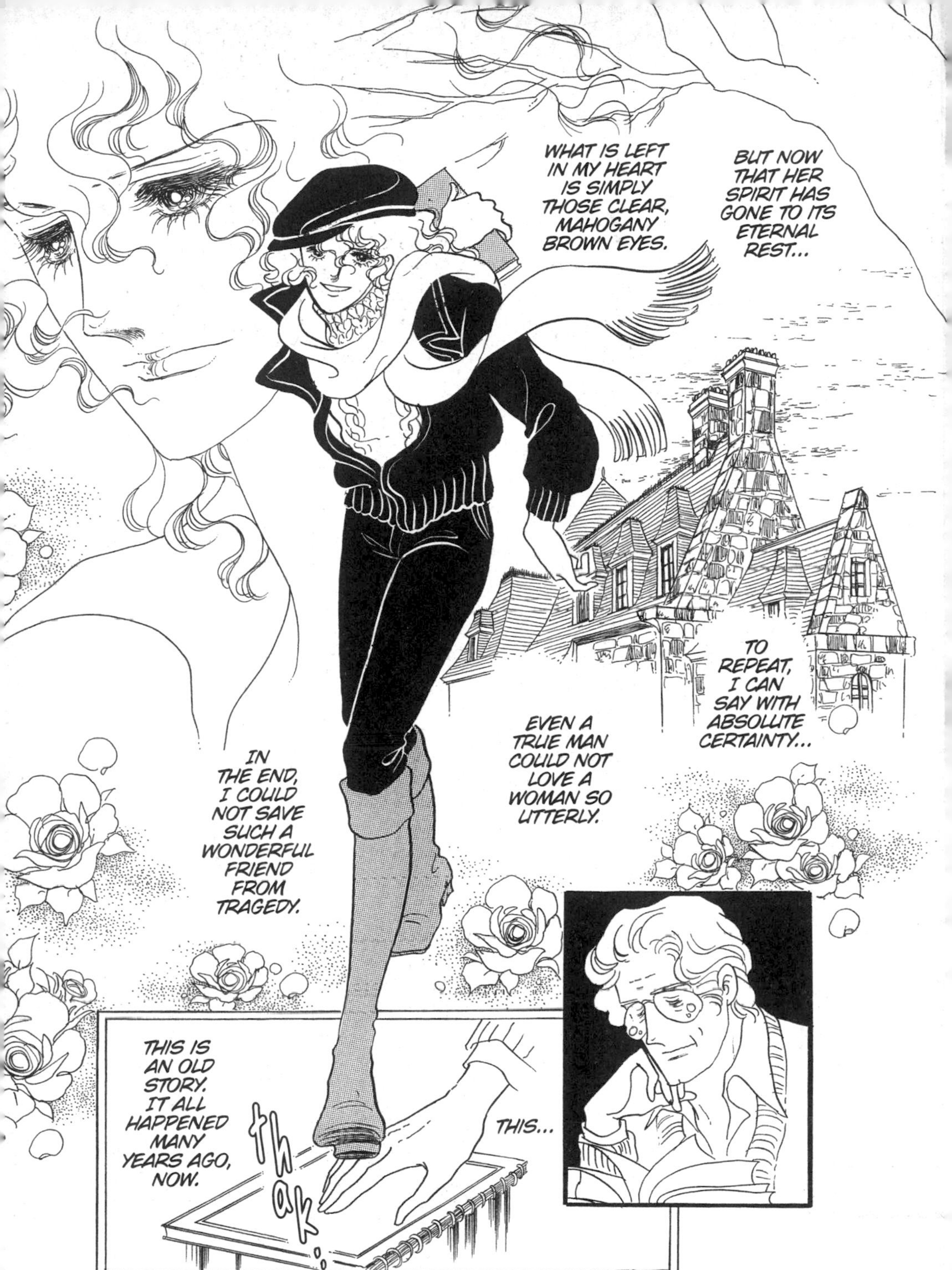
BUT NOW THAT HER SPIRIT HAS GONE TO ITS ETERNAL REST...
WHAT IS LEFT IN MY HEART IS SIMPLY THOSE CLEAR, MAHOGANY BROWN EYES.
TO REPEAT, I CAN SAY WITH ABSOLUTE CERTAINTY...
EVEN A TRUE MAN COULD NOT LOVE A WOMAN SO UTTERLY.
IN THE END, I COULD NOT SAVE SUCH A WONDERFUL FRIEND FROM TRAGEDY.
THIS...
thak
THIS IS AN OLD STORY. IT ALL HAPPENED MANY YEARS AGO, NOW.

Fin

SEVEN SEAS ENTERTAINMENT PRESENTS

Claudine

story & art by RIYOKO IKEDA

RECEIVED AUG - - 2018 BY:

TRANSLATION
Jocelyne Allen

LETTERING AND RETOUCH
CK Russell

COVER DESIGN
Karis Page

PROOFREADER
Shanti Whitesides
Danielle King

EDITOR
Jenn Grunigen

PRODUCTION MANAGER
Lissa Pattillo

EDITOR-IN-CHIEF
Adam Arnold

PUBLISHER
Jason DeAngelis

CLAUDINE...!
© Ikeda Riyoko Production 1978
All rights reserved.
English translation rights arranged with FAIRBELL CO., LTD., Tokyo,
through TOHAN CORPORATION, Tokyo.

Seven Seas books may be purchased in bulk for educational, business, or
promotional use. For information on bulk purchases, please contact Macmillan
Corporate & Premium Sales Department at 1-800-221-7945 (ext 5442)
or write specialmarkets@macmillan.com.

Seven Seas and the Seven Seas logo are trademarks of
Seven Seas Entertainment, LLC. All rights reserved.

ISBN: 978-1-626928-91-6

Printed in Canada

First Printing: June 2018

10 9 8 7 6 5 4 3 2 1

FOLLOW US ONLINE: www.sevenseasentertainment.com

READING DIRECTIONS

This book reads from *right to left*, Japanese style. If
this is your first time reading manga, you start
reading from the top right panel on each page and
take it from there. If you get lost, just follow the
numbered diagram here. It may seem backwards at
first, but you'll get the hang of it! Have fun!!

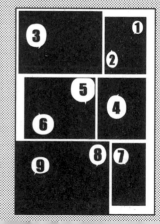